Law and Emerging Issues

First published 2024
by Routledge
4 Park Square, Milton Park, Abingdon, Oxon OX14 4RN

and by Routledge
605 Third Avenue, New York, NY 10158

Routledge is an imprint of the Taylor & Francis Group, an informa business

British Library Cataloguing-in-Publication Data
A catalogue record for this book is available from the British Library

ISBN: 9781032549446 (pbk)
ISBN: 9781003428213 (ebk)

DOI: 10.4324/9781003428213

Typeset in Sabon LT Std
by Ozone Publishing Services

Law and Emerging Issues

Editors

Dr. Shilpi Sharma
Associate Professor and Head of the Department
School of Law
AURO University, Surat

Baidya nath Mukherjee
Assistant Professor
School of Law
AURO University, Surat

Routledge
Taylor & Francis Group

Contents

List of Figures

List of Table

Chapter: 3

Chapter: 7

Chapter: 9

Chapter:10

Chapter:18

Preface

In the ever-evolving landscape of law and governance, adaptation and innovation are key to addressing the challenges of our times. This edited volume is a testament to the ever-evolving nature of the legal field and the ongoing efforts of legal scholars and academicians to dissect, analyze, and grapple with the challenges and opportunities presented by these changes.

The topics covered in this book span a wide spectrum of legal domains, reflecting the complex and rapidly changing nature of our contemporary world. From corporate governance structures to emerging challenges in the digital space, from analyzing the implications of the Social Security Code 2020 in India to understanding the legal developments surrounding unorganized migrant workers during the COVID-19 pandemic, the breadth of subjects addressed here is both impressive and vital.

The chapters in this volume have been penned by eminent academicians and scholars who have dedicated their careers to the pursuit of knowledge and the understanding of the intricate mechanisms that govern our society. Their expertise is reflected in their in-depth explorations of topics such as international environmental norms in domestic laws, human rights jurisprudence, gender dynamics in media and society, and the impact of emerging technologies on the legal landscape.

The juxtaposition of traditional legal principles with the rapidly evolving world of technology, communication, and global interconnectedness is an overarching theme throughout this book. These authors navigate the uncharted waters of the law's response to the digital age, the ethical and legal considerations of artificial intelligence, and the critical role of the Supreme Court in imparting environmental justice while implementing the Polluter Pays Principle.

The complexities of our time are not solely confined to corporate boardrooms or courtrooms but also extend to the portrayal of women in Bollywood films, crimes of stalking and sexual harassment, and the fundamental questions surrounding the rights and dignity of women, particularly in the context of menstrual health management and domestic violence.

Furthermore, the book explores the intersection of technology and gender dynamics, examining cyber feminism's role in combating revenge porn and the challenges and implications of facial recognition in the context of criminal justice in India.

In a world that seems to be constantly in flux, the legal scholars and academicians contributing to this volume have offered their invaluable insights into the transformative forces shaping the legal landscape. As we delve into these diverse topics, it is our hope that readers will gain a deeper understanding of the multifaceted nature of emerging legal issues and the vital role of the law in addressing the challenges of our ever-changing world.

It is our sincere hope that the insights contained within these pages will be instrumental in shaping the discourse and direction of the law in the years to come.

Editor 1:
Dr. Shilpi Sharma
Associate Professor and Head of the Department
School of Law
AURO University, Surat

Editor 2:
Baidya nath Mukherjee
Assistant Professor
School of Law
AURO University, Surat

Foreword

It brings me immense joy to introduce the scholarly work "Law and Emerging Issues" presented by the School of Law at AURO University. Upon delving into the concept note of this remarkable endeavor, it becomes evident that this publication will serve as a gateway for our younger generations to unearth and explore the invaluable facets of contemporary legal jurisprudence.

This book stands as a remarkable testament to the collective contributions of distinguished academicians, each possessing expertise in various fields of law and justice. Their collaboration has culminated in a comprehensive discourse that navigates the forefronts of today's legal landscape.

The insights offered by these scholars have been meticulously curated, offering a panoramic view of the multifaceted dimensions of law tailored for our vibrant and dynamic society. This compilation traverses through a diverse array of subjects, dissecting their legal intricacies with remarkable finesse and depth.

In a world rapidly propelled by technological advancements and societal shifts, the legal domain encounters new challenges and ethical dilemmas. The contents of this work not only shed light on the current landscape but also serve as a guiding beacon for the future.

This publication stands as a beacon for legal practitioners, policymakers, researchers, and academics, inviting them to engage and explore the intricate interplay between law and the pressing contemporary issues we face today.

I am confident that this work will significantly contribute to our journey toward a more just and equitable society.

Viney Kapoor

Professor Viney Kapoor

Conference blurb

Dive into the illuminating discourse unveiled at the prestigious International Conference on Law and Emerging Issues, hosted by the esteemed School of Law, AURO University in August 2023. 'Law and Emerging Issues' captures the essence of pioneering research and profound discussions presented by eminent academicians and research scholars from around the world.

This edited volume offers a panoramic view of the evolving landscape of law, reflecting the diverse perspectives of over 250 participants hailing from Bangladesh, the United Kingdom, France, Germany, and various states of India. Within these pages, the confluence of intellects dissects cutting-edge legal paradigms, navigating through the intricate tapestry of contemporary challenges and opportunities.

From the intricacies of international jurisprudence to the nuanced implications of technological advancements, this compilation delves into the crux of emerging issues that shape the legal sphere. Deliberating on the intersections of law with globalization, technology, human rights, and beyond, this anthology serves as a compass guiding readers through the uncharted territories of legal discourse.

Join this scholarly expedition, as 'Law and Emerging Issues' becomes your gateway to comprehending, navigating, and envisaging the evolving contours of law in a rapidly changing world.

1. Interdisciplinary Approach to Corporate Governance Structure

Kostruba Anatoliy, Contractual Researcher
Paris 1 Panthéon - Sorbonne University
Paris, France
E-mail: anatoliy.kostruba@univ-paris1.fr

ABSTRACT: The scientific publication analyses the interdisciplinary concept of corporate governance, thereby illuminating different aspects of this phenomenon. Three interconnected aspects are observed: corporate governance as a management category, its social context and its legal implications. Examining each component in isolation from the others serves to limit the corporation's functionality to its applied value in the social arena. An assessment of corporate governance as behavioural models, considering representation, efficiency, growth, financial structure and attitude toward stakeholders, enables the depersonalisation of organisational unity, a defining characteristic of any legal entity. Through an interdisciplinary approach, we demonstrate how corporate management functions to organise a corporation's activities by influencing the subjects of management in microeconomic processes and their interaction with one another, ultimately ensuring optimal socioeconomic viability of the corporation within the macroeconomic environment.

KEYWORDS: Corporation, corporate governance, board of directors, shareholders, legal entities, ownership, company management

1. INTRODUCTION

Law is a multifaceted socio-legal concept, primarily aimed at regulating critical social domains and ensuring their proper functionality. This objective is accomplished through legal frameworks that govern social relations, which are the most effective means of ensuring their harmonisation. The incorporation of the principle of complementarity into the field of legal science, as suggested by N. Bohr in 1927, enables a thorough comprehension of the legal regulation of social relations and its elements through analysis within mutually exclusive systems. The utilisation of this principle facilitates an objective and concise examination of the subject matter. Additionally, it allows for the avoidance of biased and ornamental language, ensuring the accuracy and neutrality of the analysis. Corporate governance is an element of legal regulations that

Chapter 1 DOI- 10.4324/9781003428213-1

govern social relations. This research focuses on the nature and meaning of corporate governance as a tool for maintaining private law corporations. An interdisciplinary examination of corporate governance reveals various aspects of this phenomenon. It is worth noting that there is insufficient scientific research on this topic. The existing research in this area has a narrow focus on economics or management, which limits its potential and obstructs a multi-perspective analysis. There is a complete absence of legal research in this field, emphasising the urgent need for investigation.

2. LITERATURE REVIEW

The initial proof of the establishment of the corporate governance structure and the following scientific examination links with the research conducted by Adolph Burleigh and Gardiner Means in 'The Modern Corporation and Private Property'. They regarded this classification as a crucial component of market restraint, reinforcing the demands of financiers and other financial market players to guarantee effective operating mechanisms for the corporation. Scholarly works on sectoral and geographical divisions have revealed the research of scientists in the field of corporate governance (*Guo et al., 2013, Khal, 2011*). As corporate governance extends beyond economics, our research analyses the legal aspects of it. The source materials come from legal scholars' scientific works (Kostruba, 2021) revealing the legal context of corporate governance. Our source materials include not only economic research but also sociology and law (Beslikoeva, 2005), emphasising the study's interdisciplinary nature.

3. METHODOLOGY AND MODEL SPECIFICATIONS

The research is founded on a framework of interdisciplinary connections, which carefully examines economic concepts from a legal standpoint. Comprehensive analysis of legal material also encompasses sociological inquiries. Using this approach, we were able to provide a multifaceted view of scientific categories, from various subject perspectives, thereby enhancing our understanding of the subject matter. The comparative research method was crucial in establishing common features and cultural differences within the studied issue. Relevant patterns could be identified as a result. In consideration of the economic and sociological context, statistical analysis was clearly necessary.

4. EMPIRICAL RESULTS

4.1. Corporate Governance – Management Category

Governance typically involves exerting influence over an object, system, or process to maintain its sustainable development or transition it to a new state in alignment with a predetermined goal. The concept of corporate governance has gained significant attention on a global scale, particularly in the aftermath of economic crises in some countries. These crises highlighted the correlation between their severity and the current financial and economic state of the corporation (Vargas-Hernández and Teodoro Cruz, 2018, pp. 59–69). Investors in a corporation can ensure a return on their investment by considering certain mechanisms. Finally, they need to monitor the activities of the corporation. Secondly, they should evaluate how to safeguard their investment capital from potentially unfavorable management actions. Firstly, they need to determine how to obtain their share of the profits. Note that this term has nuanced meanings. The varying cultural, legal and historical differences around the globe pose a challenge in formulating a unified definition of corporate governance. One of these definitions is its interpretation as a management and control system. This description outlines the processes, policies, institutions and laws that a corporation employs to operate.

Corporate governance is generally established as a system of internal and external checks and balances that ensure social responsibility throughout all aspects of a corporation's business activities (Solomon, 2007). In essence, corporate governance primarily falls within the realm of management. An important definition of the term 'corporate governance' is that it denotes the system employed to manage and regulate a corporation. The distribution of rights and responsibilities among company members, including the board of directors, managers, shareholders and others with a vested interest in the company, is determined by the corporate governance structure (OECD, 2015). Corporate governance involves organising a corporation's activities by governance entities that impact microeconomic processes, interacting with each other to ensure the optimal socio-economic existence of the corporation in the macroeconomic environment. The optimal reflection of social, economic and legal aspects indicates that the corporation has achieved its goals and mission statement.

4.2. Sociological Context of Corporate Governance

Given that a corporation is an organised structure within society, corporate governance can be regarded as a form of social governance. Numerous sociological studies suggest that the core of corporate governance lies in the social interactions among several main interest groups, namely shareholders, directors and other stakeholders. It is widely held that the primary objective of corporate governance is to preserve a semblance of sociable responsibility among these interest groups.

The correlation between a legal entity and its founder is evident that corporate law in the 21st century deduces corporation activities based on its members' behavior. The independent legal status of an entity entails an organised framework with governing bodies. The formation of legal entities is tied to the active engagement of the corporation's shareholders, who seek to exercise their corporate rights in management. The activities of any legal entity are inexorably linked to the actions of the individuals who hide behind its corporate veil. This activity is demonstrated not only by the incorporation and development of a corporation's organisational structure by its members (founders) but also by their membership in the respective governing body. The legal capacity of a legal entity, i.e. its ability to acquire civil rights and obligations, is established by a governing body that exerts organisational control over a corporation's activities. Despite the involvement of numerous individuals in its operations and governance, the governing entity is the individual whose actions have a direct impact on the organisation's planning, organisation, motivation and control processes.

4.3. Legal Aspects of Corporate Governance

The term 'corporate governance' refers specifically to the organisational integrity of a legal entity. This involves the internal arrangement of different parts in such a way that the corporation functions as a fully-integrated participant in civil relations.

Organisational integrity involves the process of establishing the pertinent bodies of a corporation, administering their interrelation by distributing responsibilities and devising and carrying out the agreed purpose of the applicable legal entity. Within the legal framework, corporate governance is deemed instrumental in realising the legal capacity of a corporation. In light of the above, it is important to emphasise that the integrity of an organisation, in some form, encompasses the structural and procedural attributes of corporate governance. The structural characteristics of corporate governance disclose the ownership structure (whether ownership is concentrated or dispersed) and the composition of the board (number of members, composition and representation). Procedural features of corporate governance pertain to the regulatory interplay between governance entities grounded in fitting governance arrangements (Guo *et al.*, pp. 257–272), necessitating regulatory recognition.

The concept of a legal entity as a participant in social relations presupposes that it is personified in the actions of real individuals. The legal capacity of a corporation is actualised by the activities of specific individuals who are linked to the corporation by a certain type of legal bond. Because of the differentiated character of corporate governance and the multifaceted nature of legal capacity, the extent of corporate governance abilities cannot be centred on the activities of a single entity. Corporate governance activities have a dynamic aspect and a competency element, which depends on the differentiation of the corporate governance entity's powers. Essentially, managing a corporation involves multiple levels of collaboration among relevant bodies, each with distinct scopes of authority enabled in relation to one another. The relevant entity responsible for managing a corporation's activities within its corporate scope executes its legally divided capacity. In turn, the corporate structure's organisational integrity ensures the legal capacity's integrity of such a legal entity. Differential combinations of the organisational structures of a corporation and the competencies of its constituent elements (governing bodies) lead to suitable models for managing a legal entity.

These models of corporate governance are then given specific economic (for commercial corporations) or social (for non-profit corporations) orientations.

4.4. A Variety of Corporate Governance Models in the Context of Interdisciplinarity

Western European economic scholars have identified a strong correlation between a corporation's representation and its performance. Corporate governance systems are deemed to play an important role in economic activity since they offer mechanisms that affect the outcome of external investment attraction (Edwards and Nibler, 2000, pp. 237–267). Representatives of management science express a similar opinion, emphasising that such socio-economic conditions as the composition of the corporation's members (founders), mechanism of interaction, capital structure and information disclosure requirements extrapolate heterogeneous governance models (Beslikoeva, 2005, p. 80). It is imperative to maintain a logical flow of information and causal connections between statements, while avoiding biased or subjective evaluations. The aforementioned conditions influence the composition of a corporation's capital, its structure and the way its shareholders exercise control over its actions.

In centralised structures, ownership or control is vested in a limited group of individuals, families, managers, directors, holding companies, banks, or other non-financial corporations. As these individuals or groups hold or exercise a significant impact on corporate governance, this model is referred to as 'internal'. Small shareholdings in a corporation's capital do not increase the motivation to control and often prevent shareholders from participating in management. This type of dispersed capital structure is referred to as 'external'. It is commonly used in countries with common law systems (such as the United Kingdom, the United States and some European Community countries, including Cyprus, Belgium, Greece, Luxembourg, Malta, Spain, Lithuania, among others). Under these circumstances, two models of corporate governance can be identified from the perspective of sociological and management sciences. These models have been legally established and rely on the prevalent international economic approach and corresponding normative consolidation within the legal system.

4.4.1. Unitary Model of Corporate Governance

In the external corporate governance system that prevails in the United States and United Kingdom, the efficiency of corporate governance is influenced by exogenous economic factors such as macroeconomic markets. In the external corporate governance system that prevails in the United States and United Kingdom, the efficiency of corporate governance is influenced by exogenous economic factors such as macroeconomic markets. The level of a corporation's capitalisation in the stock market serves as an indicator of its governance efficiency. The corporation's shareholders have a comparatively low level of concentration in the share capital, while the turnover of such capital depends heavily on the stock index and the current relevant financial asset's quotation. Positive dynamics in the respective financial asset's quotation are attributed to the economic efficiency and correctness of corporate governance, whereas poor governance results in a decrease in the asset's value. The stock market serves as a dependable and self-regulating means of evaluating the performance of a legal entity's governing bodies. This influences the development of a legal entity's governance model and its legal consolidation.

The corporate governance model follows a monotypic principle, whereby a single corporate governance body (either a sole director or a board) is established. Technical terms will be explained when they are first used. If a corporation does not act on a permanent basis, a body for managing its affairs shall be elected by the general meeting of members. The corporate governance body's chairman will be chosen by the board of the corporation if it is collegial.

The low concentration of shareholder capital, combined with dispersed shareholdings among a large number of shareholders and significant stock market volatility, unequivocally indicate a poorly functioning general meeting. Consequently, the executive body – the management board, board of directors, sole director, etc. – must assume responsibility for proper corporate governance and civil transaction operations. The financial market objectively assesses a corporation's performance as a factor of its 'economic reliability'.

4.4.2. Dual Model of Corporate Governance

In contrast to the external capital structure of a corporation, the internal structure of a corporation in Germany, Japan and France excludes external factors that could affect its activities. This type of corporation is characterised by a high level of share capital concentration with a low level of dependence on external factors that could impact its economic development. In this case, the executive body of a corporation lacks independence while making management decisions, which is dissimilar to a corporation with a unitary model of corporate governance. The general meeting's predominant role presents a challenge to the corporate governance model, introducing an extra layer that aims to balance the corporation's shareholders' interests and its executive body. The general meeting nominates a supervisory board to oversee the activities of a corporation's executive body continuously. In this scenario, the supervisory board, which represents the interests of both the company's shareholders and stakeholders, regulates its performance and governance. However, the model of corporate governance is based on a binary principle and comprises not only the supervisory board as the executive body, but also the executive body of the second level of corporate governance, either a sole director or a collegial board. This governance model outlines the process for forming the necessary bodies. The supervisory board is appointed by the general meeting, and subsequently appoints the management board (director) as the second tier of corporate governance.

4.5. Morphology of the Corporate Governance Model

Despite the diversity of corporate governance models, they share a common structural principle. It is based on a specific corporate institution with its unique temporality of existence, which consolidates the interests of the corporation's members (founders). Such an institution is the general meeting. As the consolidated will of the corporation's members (founders), the general meeting determines the fate of a corporation and areas of its activities, however, beyond the scope of the corporation's autonomous expression of will. Among other things, the general meeting sets out the appropriate corporate governance model and forms executive bodies.

It is noteworthy that the corporate governance body's social and legal purpose is to collaboratively develop and make appropriate decisions on aspects of the legal entity's activities, based on the majority's agreement. This way of organising a social group is a conventional expression of democratic ideals, whereby an individual's viewpoint holds no authoritative power. The principle of the minority being subject to the majority's stance constitutes a micro-level manifestation of social interaction. This approach has been adopted by non-profit organisations, which are characterised by the concentration of interests of certain individuals. Their opinions are considered when making collective decisions. In contrast, for an entrepreneurial organisation with a capital concentration principle, the value of a member's will is established by the number of shares they possess in the authorised capital. When deciding, the shareholders' meeting of a corporation considers the total number of shares holding the same nominal amount of authorised capital, which includes those with share certificates that evidence their corporate rights. The formation and exercise of the governing powers of the corporate executive body depend on the general meeting's will. Consequently, an executive governing body must be established. Its purpose is to guarantee that a company operates in line with its aims and objectives and executes resolutions made by the general members' meeting of the company. The executive body of a legal entity, whether sole or collective, ensures its operations in the civil sphere, oversees ongoing operations within the primary sectors specified by the general meeting.

The executive body operates continuously, unlike the general meeting. This enables them to represent the corporation in third-party relationships without requiring a power of attorney. Additionally, the will of the executive body is represented by an official, while the general meeting represents a collective expression of will on legal entity corporate governance issues. The constitution, composition and proficiency of the executive body is set by a non-compulsory determination made by the general meeting of a corporation, which may additionally delegate some of its abilities to it.

The fundamental element of the structure entails the establishment and operation of the executive entity responsible for the execution of corporate governance resolutions. This level exists in various forms such as the supervisory board and management board. As a result, the general meeting has diversified competence in delegating special powers to individual governing bodies. The concept behind this division is twofold: firstly, to enhance management efficiency by establishing a permanent executive body that operates within the temporary framework of the general meeting, and secondly to eliminate two fundamental conflicts of interest in corporate governance. Established models of governance bodies vary, and the dual model of governance utilises a binary structure for corporate governance via interaction between two bodies. This algorithm serves as a defining characteristic. In such circumstances, the board of directors ensures equilibrium between the interests of all members of a company with regard to the actions of a collective *(board of management)* or individual *(director)* executive team, and takes on supervisory and executive management responsibilities. The unitary model of governance is defined by a uniform structure for forming the governing bodies of a legal entity, represented by either a collegial *(management board)* or sole *(director)* executive body fulfilling the corresponding functions of a corporation. The tool for guaranteeing interest equilibrium is the social self-regulation lever.

4.5.1. Binary Approach to The Structure Of The Governance Model

The development of the corporate governance model follows a binary approach to the structure of the executive body of a legal entity. This principle arises from the complexity of the operating structure of corporate governance. Unlike the monotypic approach, this binary nature guarantees the capacity of the corporation within two projections of its competence. Minority stakeholders in a corporation often face difficulties in influencing the executive body's decisions due to inadequate information and limited sources of power. The supervisory board acts as a means to safeguard the interests of all members, regardless of their level of representation within the corporation's executive structure. The purpose of this organisation is to manage and control the activities of the executive body, ensuring the interests of all members of a corporation are secure and not just those of a specific group.

The primary tier of governance is represented by the supervisory board, which functions as a body for formulating and executing vital decisions pertaining to the management of the corporate enterprise and its affairs. This includes ongoing supervision of the Management board (director), composed of non-executive and autonomous directors. *The second tier of corporate governance* entails a collegial body *(the Management Board)* led by its Chairman, comprising executive directors or a solo body *(the Director)* responsible for operational management of the company. The division within the executive body appears indispensable to resolving any inconsistencies that may arise in the relationship between the majority and minority members of the corporation According to Jensen, the board of directors is the optimal internal control mechanism to oversee the conduct of senior management (Aluchna 2013; Fama and Jensen, 1983;).

In such cases, it is advisable to reconcile discrepancies between the interests of the minority and the majority and exercise authority over the achievement of these interests by the pertinent governing authority of the corporation. Moreover, it is imperative that the activities of the supervisory board include the participation of the representative body of employees and other interested parties. It is worth noting that this practice is mandated by the legislation of numerous countries, such as France, as previously mentioned. In fact, the representation of employees is considered to be a characteristic feature of the legal system in Continental Europe.

4.5.2. The Monotypic Principle of Formation of Corporate Governance Bodies

The Monotypic Principle of Formation of Corporate Governance Bodies is based on the functioning of the executive body of a corporation within a single level of governance.

The absence of consolidation in interest or capital, characteristic of the unitary model controlled by a monotypic principle, results in concentration within the relevant executive body, as previously demonstrated. The objective non-existence of any ownership conflict (or conflict of interest amongst corporation members) renders the establishment of a supervisory board to mitigate its risk and resolution unnecessary. However, the possible presence of a conflict of control *(a conflict of interest between the members of the corporation and its governing body)* highlights the importance of guaranteeing openness and responsibility of the corporate executive body, whether it is a collective management board or an individual director. The executive body of a corporation, known as the management board, holds the highest permanent governing responsibility for policy development, strategy formulation and implementation. In this context, the management board of a corporation concentrates organisational and administrative functions through regular and systematic operation, thereby realising the legal capacity of a legal entity.

5. CONCLUSION

The interdisciplinary nature of the research emphasises the significance of incorporating economic considerations in crafting the corporate governance framework. Such considerations encompass investment resource mobilisation efficiency and transparency in the company's operations, enabling it to attract financial resources actively and accomplish its objectives. The flexibility of models allows for maintaining a balance of interests among all corporate stakeholders, including gender, age and profession. The regulatory structure of corporate governance can comprehensively ensure the interests of a corporation and its members by enshrining them in relevant instruments across various levels of regulation. The combination of these factors yields a comprehensive model for corporate governance that guarantees the interests of all parties. The analysis of the two models of corporate governance suggests that their structures are gradually converging. The unitary model is being supplemented with features of a multivariate model, indicating a dual model. Numerous countries have exhibited parallel trends in their legislation. Notably, China mandates corporations to establish three legal and obligatory corporate governance bodies. In the context of economic globalisation, unifying the corporate governance model is crucial as it enables the application of an optimal model that is clear to all involved parties.

REFERENCES

Aluchna, Maria (2013). "One tier board," *Encyclopedia of Corporate Social Responsibility*, pp. 1778–1790. https://doi.org/10.1007/978-3-642-28036-8_294.

Beslikoeva, E. (2005). Review of modern corporation: sociological analysis of property, power and management. *PhD Thesis*, Saint Petersburg State University. [Beslikoeva Elena Vladimirovna. Sovremennaja korporacija: sociologicheskij analiz sobstvennosti, vlasti i upravlenija : Dis. ... kand. sociol. nauk : 22.00.08 : Sankt-Peterburg, 2004 151 c. RGB OD, 61:04-22/635].

Edwards, J., and M. Nibler (2000). "Corporate governance in Germany: the role of banks and ownership concentration," *Economic Policy* 15(31): 238–267. https://doi.org/10.1111/1468-0327.00062.

Edwards, Jonathan R. (2007). *The International Journal of Accounting*, December. https://doi.org/10.1016/j.intacc.2007.09.001.

Fama, Eugene F., and Michael C. Jensen (1983). "Separation of ownership and control," *SSRN Electronic Journal* 26 (2): 301–325. https://doi.org/10.2139/ssrn.94034.

Guo, Liang, Clive Smallman, and Jack Radford (2013). "A critique of corporate governance in China," *International Journal of Law and Management* 55(4): 257–272. https://doi.org/10.1108/ijlma-10-2011-0012.

Khan, Humera (2011). "A literature review of corporate governance," http://www.ipedr.com/vol25/1-ICEME2011-A10015.pdf.

Kostruba, Anatoliy (2021). *Review of Corporation: Experience of Phenomenological Research*. Talkom . http://lib.pnu.edu.ua:8080/handle/123456789/11492. [Korporatsiya: dosvid fenomenologichnogo doslidzhennya : monografiya/A. V. Kostruba. – K. : Talkom, 2021. – 406 s.]

OECD (2015). *G20/OECD Principles of Corporate Governance 2015*. OECD Publishing. https://doi.org/10.1787/9789264236882-en.

Solomon, J. (2007). *Corporate Governance and Accountability*. Chichester, England; Hoboken, NJ: Wiley.

Vargas-Hernández, José G., and María Elizabeth Teodoro Cruz (2018). "Corporate Governance and Agency Theory: Megacable Case," *Corporate Governance and Sustainability Review* 2(1): 59–69. https://doi.org/10.22495/cgsrv2i1p5.

2. Regulating Anticompetitive Practices with Reference to the Digital Space: A Comparative Study

Dr. Saurabh Chandra
Associate Professor, School of Law, Bennett University, Greater Noida, India
Email: saurabhchandranls@gmail.com
ORCID ID : 0000-0003-4172-9968
Ms. Suparna Kundu
Legal Professional
Email: tulisuparnakundu37@gmail.com
ORCID ID : 0009-0000-5142-8945

ABSTRACT: Competition law is a body of law that seeks to promote fair competition in the marketplace by prohibiting anticompetitive practices, such as price fixing, bid rigging, and market allocations. Competition law is an integral part of a free market economy, where businesses compete to offer consumers the best prices and services. The emergence of cyberspace has presented new challenges to competition law. The internet has allowed businesses to operate across national borders, making it difficult to enforce competition law in multiple jurisdictions. Furthermore, digital technologies have enabled companies to collect and analyse vast amounts of data, which can lead to anticompetitive practices such as price discrimination or strategic alliances. Competition law has had to adapt to the digital age. Many countries have adopted laws that prohibit anticompetitive agreements between companies in the same industry, even if they are located in different countries. Additionally, authorities are increasingly using data-driven techniques to identify and investigate anticompetitive activities. In order to ensure that competition law is effective in cyberspace, it is important for businesses to be aware of the rules and regulations that apply to them. This includes understanding what types of activities are considered to be anticompetitive, as well as the potential penalties for engaging in such activities. Governments are also taking steps to ensure that companies comply with competition law, such as by introducing enforcement measures and bringing cases against companies that violate the rules.

Competition law emerged as a branch of law over the years so as to maintain a balance in the market by ensuring that there is a free

Chapter 2 DOI- 10.4324/9781003428213-2

and fair environment for all the stakeholders, including producers, manufacturers, and consumers. With the advent of globalisation and liberalisation in the early 1990s, countries around the world opened up their trading activities, as a result the importance of a free and fair market emerged for both the domestic and the international players. With this background, the laws emerged, however, over the recent years; instances of a number of anti-competitive practices have come to light especially in the cyberspace. This article attempts to identify these recent issues and analyse whether the present competition law has been effective in addressing such issues.

KEYWORDS: Anticompetitive practices, competition, cyberspace, market, regulation

1. INTRODUCTION

Otherwise known as antitrust law, competition law is a body of law that seeks to promote fair competition in the marketplace by prohibiting anticompetitive practices, such as price fixing, bid rigging, and market allocations. Competition law is an integral part of a free market economy, where businesses compete to offer consumers the best prices and services. The emergence of cyberspace has presented new challenges to competition law. The internet has allowed businesses to operate across national borders, making it difficult to enforce competition law in multiple jurisdictions. Furthermore, digital technologies have enabled companies to collect and analyse vast amounts of data, which can lead to anticompetitive practices such as price discrimination or strategic alliances. Competition law has had to adapt to the digital age. For example, many countries have adopted laws that prohibit anticompetitive agreements between companies in the same industry, even if they are located in different countries. Additionally, authorities are increasingly using data-driven techniques to identify and investigate anticompetitive activities. In order to ensure that competition law is effective in cyberspace, it is important for businesses to be aware of the rules and regulations that apply to them. This includes understanding what types of activities are considered to be anticompetitive, as well as the potential penalties for engaging in such activities. Governments are also taking steps to ensure that companies comply with competition law, such as by introducing enforcement measures and bringing cases against companies that violate the rules.

Competition law emerged as a branch of law over the years so as to maintain a balance in the market by ensuring that there is a free and fair environment for all the stakeholders, including, producers, manufacturers, and consumers. With the advent of globalisation and liberalisation in the early 1990s, countries around the world opened up their trading activities, as a result the importance of a free and fair market emerged for both the domestic and the international players. With this background, the laws emerged, however, over the recent years; instances of a number of anticompetitive practices have come to light especially in the cyberspace. This article attempts to identify these recent issues and analyse whether the present competition law has been effective in addressing such issues.

In general terms, competition law is made up of guidelines whose purpose is to safeguard the competitive process in an effort to promote consumer welfare. Due to the significant shifts in political and economic thought that have occurred globally in recent years, competition law has expanded at an astounding rate.

The ability of a firm or firms with market power to negatively impact consumer welfare through various means, such as decreasing output, raising prices, lowering the quality of products on the market, stifling innovation, and denying consumers of choice, is a key concern of competition law and policy. These issues cannot be described in a codified table of rules with specific application, as, for instance, tax laws or the landlord–tenant relationship may.

Market power must always be evaluated in order to analyse competition challenges, and this evaluation cannot be done without knowledge of the underlying economic theories. The same is true for the kinds of conduct that affect competition, such as cartelisation, predatory pricing, discrimination, and mergers. These are not issues that lend themselves to a straightforward rule-based analysis. Each case will depend on its unique circumstances but will frequently require both legal and economic input. Competition law is about the economic examination of markets inside a legal process.

In this article, the author aims to analyse the issues pertaining to competition laws with reference to cyberspace in the recent years. Furthermore, this article will also focus on the recent case studies that have come up with respect to anticompetitive practices in cyber space over the years.

2. COMPETITION LAW: CONCEPT AND HISTORICAL OVERVIEW

Early any economy's expansion depends on a dynamic and practical foundation for competition legislation. It aids in regulating a fair market free from any anti-competitive behaviour that is bad for both consumers and businesses. Competition law is a crucial tool to keep markets balanced by making sure that a small number of dominant players do not control everything alone. Instead, the market should function in a way that prevents unfair burdens from being placed on businesses, which would force them to engage in unfair practices in order to survive competition.

The former MRTP Act 1969, which previously oversaw India's competition law framework, has been replaced by the Competition Act, 2002 (the 'Act'). An important component of the Directive Principles of State Policy (DPSP) is socialism, and the MRTP Act was designed with this philosophy in mind. The main goal of MRTP was to prevent and limit the emergence of monopolies in the market. It was believed that any such concentration of power in the hands of a select few in a free market would harm consumer interests and economic growth and so needed to be curbed.

In order to address the shortcomings of MRTP and act as an effective piece of legislation to encourage fair trading practices in the Indian market, the 2002 Act was introduced. Abuse of dominant position, combinations, and anticompetitive acts are all prohibited and regulated by this Act. For proper implementation of the objectives of this legislation and regulation of the abovementioned agreements so as to ensure a free and fair market, the Act also established a specialised body known as the Competition Commission of India (CCI) under the provisions of the legislation.

3. CYBER SPACE: CONCEPT AND OVERVIEW

The study Cyberspace is a global network of interconnected computer-based processing systems, communications networks, and information technologies. It is really different from space since space is the lawyer's natural habitat and space is what our space looks like in the physical world. Understanding cyberspace is now more important than ever to prevent cybercrimes and commercial dominance.

With the increase in the use of networks and the introduction of internet, it has become almost an inevitable part of human lives. Markets have flourished with the rise in the use of internet as the globe is seen as one in today's time. The internet's phenomenal expansion is a prime example of network effects, a favourable demand side externality in which the value of a good or service to a particular user improves as the number of users rises.

Cyberspace is a term used to describe the virtual world of online networks, services, and systems that exist on the internet. It encompasses all forms of electronic communication, including social media, websites, emails, and other digital communications. As the use of digital technology has grown exponentially over the past few decades, so have the implications for competition law.

The goal of competition law is to safeguard consumers from anticompetitive actions like price-fixing and other contracts that restrict market competition. In the context of cyberspace, these same principles apply.

Companies must ensure that their online activities comply with applicable competition law, and that they take the necessary steps to protect the privacy of their customers. As the use of digital technology continues to grow, it is important that companies remain informed of the changing legal landscape and continue to take steps to ensure compliance with competition law.

Competition law as a branch of law emerged with the advent of liberalisation, globalisation and privatisation in India especially after 1991. Prior to this, significant importance was provided to competition within the market, however, with the increase in trade and free movement of goods and services across the borders, the nation realised the importance of a free and fair market equivalent for all the players. The MRTP Act, 1969 was subsequently replaced by the Competition Act, 2002 however it came into effect in 2009. R. Whish and D. Bailey reiterated the background and the circumstances which led to the amendments in the laws of competition over a period of time. The author also discusses the various anticompetitive practices which are prohibited by the competition laws over the world economies. One of such practices is the abuse of dominance.

It is significant to note that within the Indian laws, 'dominance' per se is not prohibited by the laws; rather the 'abuse' of such dominant position is prohibited under the Act. With the use of technology, competition matters have spread to the cyber/digital space as well. In today's world, everyone is dependent upon technology, online transactions, and businesses. Thereby, it becomes important to regulate competition matters in the digital space as well. H. Handa also discusses the importance of regulating the online space with the increasing instances of abuse of dominance position in such spaces. Cases of Google and BookMyShow are of recent significance which elucidates this aspect of competition law. I. Roy elaborates the issues pertaining to BookMyShow case and the stand of CCI in detail.

3.1. Competition Law and the Practices Controlled: An Overview

Practices that damage the competitive process are addressed by systems of competition law. Competition law is concerned with:

Anticompetitive practices: agreements which restrict competition as their goal or effect are illegal unless they have a justification, like increasing economic efficiency. A cartel agreement between rival businesses, such as one to regulate prices, share markets, or limit output, would be an example. Such agreements are harshly punished, and in some legal systems, they can even result in the imprisonment of the parties involved. When they may hurt competition, agreements between businesses at various levels of the market may also be illegal. Vertical agreements are, on the whole, significantly unlikely to hinder competition as compared to horizontal agreements.

Abusive behaviour: competition law can also be used to condemn the abusive behaviour of a corporation with significant market power that allows it to act autonomously on the market without consideration for competitors, customers, or ultimately consumers. An illustration of predatory pricing would be when a dominating corporation cuts its prices down below cost in an effort to push a rival out of the market or to prevent one from entering so that it can then charge higher prices.

Mergers: the ability to investigate mergers between companies that might harm the competitive process is provided by many competition law systems. It is obvious that if one competitor were to acquire its primary rival, the market might become less competitive, which could lead to consumers paying higher prices. Many systems of competition law provide that certain mergers cannot be completed until the relevant competition authority has given its approval.

3.2. Anti-Competitive Practices in Cyber Space: Issues and Challenges

In India, as it is well established from the above discussion that dominance per se is not prohibited in India, rather the 'abuse' of such dominance is prohibited under the Competition Laws of India.

Understanding the elements of an Act, such as the definition of a dominant position and the related relevant market, it is important for it to be considered 'abuse' in this context. The Act outlines the different characteristics of a dominating position, including size, market share, financial power and customer dependence on a certain business, as well as taking into account the size of competitors and the market.

This issue of abusing the dominant position has come to light in the recent years, especially in the cyber space with the advent of technology and network all over the world. In this section, for the purpose of analysing the issues pertaining to this 'dominance', it is significant to consider some of the recent case studies, including the case of Google and The Showtyme v. BookMyShow.

3.3. Google: A Case Study

With a big user base and a wealth of user data, Google is the best example of high technology in terms of search engines and social networking. As a result, Google is a dominant force in the rapidly evolving internet-based market. Consequently, it is reasonable for the courts to be concerned about how an alleged competitive behaviour would affect competition.

They essentially have influence over the market owing to their overarching strategies and goals. Regulators and the courts must distinguish between powerful corporations that are primarily benefiting from successful inventions' lawful economic gains and corporations that are unethically outlawing competition by taking advantage of the significant market power.

Due to its dominant position in internet surfing and its 90% market share in the European Union, Google has a huge market share. The other rivals accuse Google of tampering with customer search results in order to benefit the businesses that display advertisements on Google. It creates entrance obstacles for other advertising agencies trying to compete with Google in digital markets that depend on search.

By its order dated 8 February 2018, the CCI declared that Google has a dominating position in the relevant Indian market and has abused its position in violation of the Competition Act, 2002. Applying the proportionality principle and basing the fine on the pertinent turnover from the direct sales operations alone in India, the CCI issued a fine of USD 21 million.

3.4. The Showtyme v. BookMyShow Case: A Case Study

In this particular case, both the parties in question are websites that sell tickets online. BookMyShow is said to have a 90% market share even though Showtyme only entered the market in 2021. Showtyme's major defence is that BookMyShow has organised a cartel and is acting illegally, putting impediments in the way of other market competitors.

BookMyShow was the subject of an investigation by the CCI on 16 June 2022, for allegedly 'abusing its dominant position' in violation of Section 4 of the Act. A social worker who founded 'Showtyme', an online platform for purchasing tickets, said that BookMyShow had exploited its dominating market position by entering into exclusive contracts with theatres and multiplexes and using cash deposits and loans as leverage to forge an impenetrable market.

In this case, BookMyShow argued that they were only an intermediate platform that facilitated the purchase of movie tickets and that there was no distinct 'market' for online purchases because the market was too large to include purchases made in person at theatres.

In this regard, the CCI rejected the contentions of the party and recognised the existence of a separate market for e-booking of tickets. Further the commission also held that certain data ownership clauses in deals with theatres gave the platform a monopolistic position. Furthermore, by virtue of exclusive agreements, it was also apparent at first glance that BookMyShow was attempting to impose restrictions on new competitors and entrants to the market. With the escalating abuse of such power, it demotivates the rivals.

These abovementioned two case studies points towards the fact that over the years competition law is not restricted to physical markets only. In today's growing economy and digitalisation of the world, the common population of the world often chooses online platforms to conduct businesses and thereby it is important for the Governments over the world to ensure that the interests of the general public are protected. For such purposes, the Governments are required to enact sufficient legislations capable of taking into consideration, both physical and digital markets.

The abovementioned cases of 'Google' and 'BookMyShow' points towards the fact that often the 'dominant position' is abused by these big-techs, which results in prejudicing consumer choices and free market. In such scenarios a specialised body/commission is of utmost necessity to determine such abuses and thereby restrict these big-techs from violating the basic principles of competition law. In both these scenarios the CCI imposed hefty penalties on these organisations, which is an example of the fact that CCI also regulates the digital and cyberspace, and is not restricted to the physical markets.

However, it is important to note that with this global evolution of markets, it is the need of the hour to include digital and cyberspaces within the ambit of the Act explicitly so as to ensure proper regulation of these instances.

4. CONCLUSION

The Google and BookMyShow case studies demonstrate that competition law issues are increasingly relevant in the online space, and as the cyberspace continue to expand, the need for effective regulation will become increasingly necessary. Companies must be aware of the potential for antitrust violations and be prepared to take proactive steps to ensure compliance with competition laws. Additionally, regulators must stay abreast of the latest developments in the digital economy and ensure that competition law is enforced appropriately. With the right enforcement and regulations in place, companies can continue to innovate and deliver value to consumers, while ensuring fair competition in the digital world.

With globalisation and the advent of technology and networks, it has become increasingly important to regulate these e-platforms. In order to ensure such regulation, it is the need of the hour that the Indian Competition Laws provide explicit provisions to deal with such platforms. Even though the CCI has intervened in the recent instances, to ensure a free and fair market, however, there is an absence of any explicit provision under the laws.

If left unregulated, situations may arise wherein certain Big-techs may rule the entire market place which will prove to be a detriment for the interests of the other players and the consumers at large. It is essential to ensure that digital companies do not gain an unfair advantage over their competitors, as well as to protect consumers from unfair and deceptive practices. In addition, competition law can help to foster innovation and competition in the digital space, enabling companies to continue to bring new and innovative products and services to the market. By regulating digital space through competition law, we can ensure that the digital space is a safe, equitable, and beneficial environment for all users.

REFERENCES

Brockman, P., D. French, and C. Tamm (2014). "REIT organizational structure, institutional ownership, and stock performance," *J. Real Estate Portf. Manag.* 20(1): 2136.

Buts, Caroline (2017). "Competition policy's travel through cyberspace: EU and US enforcement of vertical restraints in online distribution," *Eur. Competition & Reg. L. Rev.* 1: 26.

Chawla, N.M. (2022). *Analysis of CCI's Order Against BookMyShow and The Increasing Accountability of* Intermediaries.

Gouri, Geeta (2023). "Conclusions: challenges for competition policy and law," *A Commissioner's Primer to Economics of Competition Law in India*, Singapore: Springer Nature Singapore, pp. 237–243.

Gouri, Geeta, and Kalyani Pandya (2020). "The Indian competition law experience–its history and its (digital) future," *Indian Law Review* 4(3): 276–300.

Handa H. (2018). *Abuse of Dominance in Cyberspace: A Critical Analysis, NJCSL.*

Kleinert, Jörn, and Daniel Piazolo (2002). "Governing the cyber space," *The New Economy and Economic Growth in Europe and the US*. Berlin, Heidelberg: Springer Berlin Heidelberg, pp. 271–292.

Newman, John M. (2019). "Antitrust in digital markets," *Vand. L. Rev.* 72: 1497.

Nishith Desai Associates (2015). *Competition Law in India*. https://www.nishithdesai.com/Content/document/pdf/ResearchPapers/Competition-Law-in-India.pdf.

Roy, I. (2022). *Abuse of Dominant Position-Analyzing The Showtyme v. BookMyShow Case.*

Whish, R., and D. Bailey (2015). *Competition Law*. Oxford University Press.

3. Decoding Business Environment: Company's Perspective

Pankaj Saini[1] and Deepak Singh[2]

[1]Department of Management, Bharati Vidyapeeth (Deemed to be University) Institute of Management & Research, New Delhi, India

[2]Department of Law, Bharati Vidyapeeth (Deemed to be University) Institute of Management & Research, New Delhi, India

ABSTRACT: This study aims to provide a conceptual framework for interpreting the elements of the business environment and their effects on an organisation's ability to operate. A corporate organisation must be able to interpret environmental data in a timely manner in order to recognise 17 early warning signs and commercial possibilities. In order to demonstrate the importance of the business environment, further rebuild the sequence from information decoding to organisational results and suggest a conceptual framework, case study method 22 has been employed. Research has covered the probable business impact for commercial organisations only and majorly focused on case study for Indian business environment. Secondary data have been used only for taking reference of cases. The cases from 1991 to 2023 have been covered only.

KEYWORDS: Decoding business information, IEMM environment framework

1. INTRODUCTION

Decoding the business environment is important because it helps companies to understand by identifying internal and exterior factors that can affect their operations. Organisations are able to plan ahead, anticipate changes and make well-informed decisions when they have a solid awareness of their environment. Additionally, it aids in their ability to recognise warning signs and potentially advantageous possibilities as well as the competitive environment. The environment of business has been defined as a set of all forces and factors that influence a company's operations and performance. Changes in the economy can affect an organisation's ability to access capital, hire employees and find customers.

Chapter 3 DOI- 10.4324/9781003428213-3

2. LITERATURE REVIEW

Foreign corporations tend to invest in countries with stronger overall business environments because they will draw more high-quality FDI inflows (Wang and Zhuang 2019). Geography matters for entrepreneurs to decide about location of business. Predominantly for industries that depend on heavily on natural resources, an area's inherent geographic advantages can be a major draw for business (Krugman 1993). In South Africa, Kirsten (2020) investigated the relationship between macroeconomic indicators and the uncertainty of economic policy. The findings demonstrated that a sudden rise in the uncertainty index led to a drop in industrial output and a depreciation in the cost of the currency. Policy uncertainty happens when economic agents have doubts about the economic effects of government policies. Artificial intelligence has changed traditional manufacturing into intelligent and sustainable manufacturing as the technological environment is always evolving (Bag et al. 2021; Chatterjee et al. 2021; Zeba et al. 2021). The transformative effects of AI in manufacturing show the applicability of intelligent agents, blockchain and IoT in the framework of Industry 4.0. (Culot et al. 2020; Dwivedi et al. 2022). Data analytics for large data sets have been used by educational institutions to carry out useful information for internal purposes. Manocha and Saini (2022). Global warming and extreme weather, according to Stott (2016), alter both natural ecosystem and human social structure. Consequently, the effects of the weather directly affect economic output (Minner 2001). One of the earliest and most extensively used strategy tools globally is the SWOT analysis.

There are few techniques available to study the business environment like SWOT (Stewart et al. 1965, p. 16) which is frequently used in retail to comprehend micro- and macro-settings. It's among the original frameworks for strategic planning. (Stewart 1963). Strategic planning has a wide range of possible advantages for organisations in determining future direction and profitability; nevertheless, no single definition of the subject is universally accepted due to its complexity and diversity (Piercy et al. 2012). Old traditional market scanning frameworks which managers use for external environment are 5-forces industry analysis (Porter 1989) and PESTEL tool (Aguilar 1967; Peteraf and Bergen 2003). The existing framework of business scanning has a gap of not providing information for environment which is internal to the organisation and lacks the current contextual example from industry. There exists a theoretical and conceptual research gap which will be filled with finding answers of questions based on objectives of study.

2.1. Objectives

- To provide a concise and meaningful review of the literature on decoding business environment from organisation's perspective in the backdrop of important factors of business information.

- To put out a fresh framework for commercial organisations to use in deciphering the business environment and make decisions.
- To analyse the influence of government regulations on the processes of a company in the changing business environment.

3. CONCEPTUAL FRAMEWORK

Table 1: IEMM environment framework (internal, external, micro and macro).

1-Internal Environment (Controllable factors)	**Company's Position**		
	Low	**Moderate**	**Highly Stable**
• Hierarchy • Integrity • Financial capability • Image of organisation • Marketing capability • Research and development • Physical assets • Human resources			
2-External Environment (Uncontrollable factors)	**Company's Strength and Response**		
	Low	**Moderate**	**Highly Stable**
Microenvironment • Customers • Competitors • Financiers • Market intermediaries • Publics pressure groups • Local government agencies • Suppliers			
Macroenvironment	**Company's Understanding and Preparedness**		
	Low	**Moderate**	**Highly Stable**
• Political and legal • Economical • Socio-cultural • Technological • Natural • Global			

Business environment can be studied and decoded by classifying into two subparts:

3.1. Internal environment

This refers to all internal forces that are more directly involved in the day-to-day operations of the organisation. Organisations are in charge of each of these aspects. The elements of the interior environment are as follows:

Hierarchy: The structure of the board of directors, organisational hierarchy, managerial tiers and professionalism are all significant determinants of corporate outcomes. While certain management structures and styles promote rapid decision-making, others delay it.

Integrity: Integrity or value system of an organisation includes the culture, ethics and norms of the organisation set by founders and management. The example of Kingfisher, case of Mr. Vijay Mallya, who defaulted 17 Indian banks about Rs. 9,000 crore, has been accused of fraud and money laundering. In contrary, Tata Group is known for their ethical working and setting highest moral example.

Financial capability: This is a reference to a business's solvency, liquidity and capacity to raise, use and manage capital flows. It is important for accomplishing organisational goals.

Image of organisation: Anything negative about company's products, employees, policies and office politics might lend the organisation in trouble. However, a good image always contributes in enhancing brand equity and sales of the organisation.

Marketing capability: Marketing capability is controllable by the firm and is the key differentiator for achieving organisational goals. There are many examples of companies which have achieved exemplary success for marketing of products like Fogg deodorant by Vini Cosmetics, Maggie by Nestle and Pizza by Dominos.

Research and Development: The company's capacity for innovation and competitiveness is determined by its technological capabilities, research and development. This is one of the important critical differentiators that determines how quickly a firm grows.

Physical Assets: Physical assets and facilities such as an office, an industrial plant, state-of-the-art machinery, manufacturing capacity, technology and a distribution network are some of the internal variables that affect an organisation's competitiveness.

Human Resources: The department of a company tasked with locating, hiring, screening and training job applicants is known as human resources (HR). Additionally, it manages employee benefit plans. In the 21st century, HR is critical to helping businesses adapt to a business climate that is changing quickly and to the increased demand for qualified workers. Out of many factors of organisation's success, the talented employees make the significant difference.

3.2. External environment

This encompasses all factors that indirectly affect the organisation's long-term operations. The two subsections that make up this are micro and macro.

***Microenvironment*:** This is used to describe the circumstances in a company's immediate surroundings that have an impact on its performance and decision-making. It is connected to a small area where the company operates. Following are the important variables of this task environment:

Customers: The major task of business organisation is to create and retain customers. Customers are considered as king of the market. Organisations need to decode their changing tastes and preferences to keep their products matching and exceeding their expectations.

Competitors: Competitors of a business include not just other businesses selling comparable goods but also anybody vying for clients' discretionary cash. There is fight among the companies and different industries to grab the maximum buying for their products from customers. Organisations need to monitor their competitors if they want to remain in business. Reliance Jio entry into telecommunication industry made other players to change pricing for their products.

Financiers: One additional important aspect of the microenvironment is the financial status of the company. They give businesses the money they need to launch, run and grow their businesses. Businesses cannot pay for personnel, commodities or equipment necessary to keep up everyday operations without sufficient funding.

Market intermediaries: They are companies, organisations or individuals that assist manufacturers with operations to distribute products to consumers. This is also important to decide kind of profit margins shared with them, and market intermediaries play key role in some industries to boost the sales of products. In insurance companies, there are direct agents who are not employees of the company but they get commission from the company for the business they generate. Majority of products sold by them are those wherein they get maximum commission not those products which are having less charges. So, their role becomes important.

Public pressure groups: A public pressure group can be one individual, NGO, media group, local publics and political opposition party. Tata Motors faced the farmer's protest against its nano-manufacturing plant in Singur, Hooghly district, West Bengal, which was supported by opposition party leader Mamta Banerjee at that time. Tata Company suffered approximately Rs. 10000 crore loss due to this protest and later on shifted its manufacturing plant to Sanand, Ahmedabad district, Gujrat.

Local Government agencies: Local government agencies like municipal committee, Nagar Nigam, issue NOC for construction, provide water connection and business operating license, and impose house taxes.

Suppliers: Suppliers are those who supply inputs like raw materials and components to the company. Companies dealing and selling daily-based food to customers like Mother Dairy and Amul need to maintain continuous monitoring of suppliers in comparison with companies into banking services.

Macroenvironment: It refers to all those forces that indirectly affect the business operation and working conditions. These factors are uncontrollable, and the organisation is not capable of exercising any control over them.

Political and Legal: This factor determines government influence on tax policies, trading agreements, FDI, international trade regulations and restrictions, monopolies, rules of mergers and consumer protection. This also includes role of legislature, role of judiciary, role of industry regulators and dispute resolution mechanism. Indian government adopted liberalisation, privatisation, globalisation (LPG) in 1991 and opened its economy to outside world. GST implementation by government in July 2017 had its positive and negative effects on organisations. Similarly, demonetisation in 2016 had its implications on business organisations. Companies which keep tracing business environment take advantage of information. Many insurance companies have come to India to tap highly potential insurance industry FDI for which was increased from 26 to 49 %. Business organisations functioning in India need to deal with following important legal laws:

Indian contract Act 1872: It specifies the conditions in which commitments made by the contractual parties are legally binding on them. Carlill v Carbolic Smoke Ball Company [1892] in UK is a good example. In this instance, the corporation ran product advertising claiming that anyone who consumed the smoke balls according to the recommended dosage would not become ill. If someone does, the corporation will give them 100 pounds right away. In an effort to demonstrate their earnestness with this proposal, the corporation put a thousand pounds into a public bank account. Despite taking the medication as directed, one Carlill customer purchased the medicine and yet had the flu. She brought legal action to retrieve the money that was promised in the advertising. The business said there was no contract between them and rejected the money. It was decided that a contract between the individual and the business resulted in Carlill receiving the 100 pounds.

Foreign Exchange Management Act 1999: It controls transactions involving foreign currencies and foreign securities. This law facilitates cross-border trade and cross-border capital flows and cultivates the environment for business in India and benefited GDP. Enforcement directorate (ED) has filed a case against BBC under this act in April 2023 for *foreign* direct investment (FDI) *violations* by the company.

Competition Act 2002: It is one such piece of law that seeks to eradicate anticompetitive behaviour by primarily prohibiting anticompetitive agreements and instances of market abuse of power. This act prevents small-scale business and gives them environment to grow by providing strict laws in given three areas: a-anti-competitive agreements including Cartels, b-abuse of dominance and c-mergers which have potential for anti-competitive effect. Competition Commission of India (CCI) passed an order in August 2016 imposing a penalty of over Rs. 6700 crore on eleven cement companies including big players like UltraTech, Binani, Ramco, JK Cement, ACC, Century, Shree Cement as well as their trade association Cement Manufacturers Association (CMA) for cartelisation.

Consumer protection Act 1986: It aims to safeguard the interests of consumers and ensure they are protected from unfair trade practices and exploitation. Organisations keep this in mind about this act while designing products and services for customers. The eight consumer rights are right to basic needs, safety, information, choosing, representation, redress, consumer education and healthy environment.

Companies Act 2013: It governs the incorporation of a company, its duties, its directors and its dissolution. In case of Satyam Computer Services Ltd. in 2008, fine of Rs. 5 lakhs on four directors was imposed along with simple imprisonment of six months under this act.

Indian Trademark Act 1999: In a larger sense, it promotes initiative and commercial enterprise by making their owners famous and wealthy. Trade mark protection also prevents dishonest competitors, like counterfeiters from using similar distinguishing marks to advertise subpar or unrelated goods or services. In the annals of Indian intellectual property rights history, the case Coca-Cola v. Bisleri International represents a seminal ruling. In India, Coca-Cola purchased the trademark for the mango drink MAAZA from Bisleri, the original owner of the property. Later, Bisleri began exporting mango drinks with the MAAZA name after submitting an application for trademark registration in Turkey. Coca-Cola filed a lawsuit in India, requesting damages and relief for trademark infringement under the MAAZA brand. Coca-Cola was successful in getting Bisleri to submit to an interim injunction for trademark infringement. ***Essential commodities Act 1955:*** It has been used to manage the supply, distribution and production of commodities termed as essentials. This act has been used by the Indian government to crack down on hoarders and black-marketers of essential commodities. It has been invoked many times to ensure adequate supplies and to protect consumers against irrational spikes in prices of essential commodities.

Economical: These variables might be large- or small-scale, and they are frequently outside of a company's control. An economic system is formed by the interaction of several factors such as inflation, interest rates, consumer behaviour and consumer spending. An essential tool for comprehending economic activity is the business cycle.

Socio-Cultural: Islamic banking in Middle East countries has emerged just because of corporate understanding of socio-economic environment. LG, South Korea-based company, made the world record in the year 2006 by selling and installing one million TV sets in ten days during Diwali time period just because it understood the culture of India and encased on this. In Indian real estate, companies avoid to give thirteen number to the flats and shops they sell just because some section of society believe that this number is inauspicious, even the Chandigarh city does not have any sector named as thirteen. Well-known Italian airline company (Alitalia) does not have this seat number. Some companies forget that certain cultures read from right to left, rather than left to right. In this situation, a hoarding in North America and India with three pictures from left to right in the order of a man with a headache looking sad and in pain, a man taking a pill and a man smiling without a headache will not have the same advertising effect in the Middle East.

Technological: Through many ways, technology keeps shaping the kinds of products offered by companies. In USA, electrical appliances are operated in 110 watts, whereas it is 220 watts in India. Nokia Company used to be the number one player in all parameters but lost the market share and it's identify just because of lack of identifying and adapting new technology. Technology makes the business products complex and it becomes difficult to decode to whom they need to compete in market. Exclusive camera manufacturers like Kodak and Nippon did not anticipate and they need to compete with mobile phone manufacturers like Samsung, Nokia, Apple and other players of same industry as phone is having camera as inbuilt feature in it.

Natural: Natural environment plays an important role in shaping the kind of progress for a particular type of industry in a particular geographical region. Mining depends on natural deposits, and due to this reason, mining industry is progressing in states like Jharkhand, Bihar and Odisha and few names of companies are Jindal Steel and Sail. Raw material like cotton and fabric is needed for textile manufacturing, and due to this, states like Punjab, Maharashtra and Tamil Nadu have cluster of such companies. Jeep and power bikes are more preferred in hill area in comparison with plain region. The demand of winter clothing is more there in hill area in comparison with sea regions.

Global: The whole world has seen the impact of COVID-19 which started from China in 2020 affected all countries and stopped all things including business. There was time when world shifted towards globalisation, but nowadays, there is a shift to de-globalisation. Most of the countries are now adapting protectionist approach for their domestic industry and economy.

4. CONCLUSION

The new IEMM framework studies environment by dividing it into internal and external part, wherein external environment further studies micro- and macro-aspects of it. The internal environment is controllable in nature, and this includes hierarchy, integrity, financial capability, image of the company, marketing capability, research and development, physical assets and human resources. Organisations need to know the position where they stand, that is low, moderate or highly stable for these variables. Microenvironment includes customers, competitors, financiers, market intermediaries, public pressure groups, local government agencies and suppliers. Industry in general operates in this task environment. Organisations need to check its strengths and response readiness for microenvironment, that is either low, moderate or highly stable. Macroenvironment covers political and legal, economical, socio-cultural, technological, natural and global variables which is very difficult to predict. Organisations need to check its understanding and preparedness for adapting changes for these variables of external environment, that is either low, moderate or highly stable.

REFERENCES

Bag, S., J. H. C. Pretorius, S. Gupta, and Y. K. Dwivedi. 2021. "Role of institutional pressures and resources in the adoption of big data analytics powered artificial intelligence, sustainable manufacturing practices and circular economy capabilities." *Technological Forecasting and Social Change*, (February), 163. doi: 10.1016/j. techfore.2020.120420.

Chatterjee, S., N. P. Rana, Y. K. Dwivedi, and A. M. Baabdullah. 2021. "Understanding AI adoption in manufacturing and production firms using an integrated TAM-TOE model." *Technological Forecasting and Social Change*, (September), 170 (5). doi: 10.1016/j. techfore.2021.120880.

Culot, G., G. Orzes, M. Sartor, and G. Nassimbeni. 2020. "The future of manufacturing: a Delphi-based scenario analysis on industry 4.0." *Technological Forecasting and Social Change*, (April), 157 (4). doi: 10.1016/j.techfore.2020.120092.

Dwivedi, A., M. A. Moktadir, C. J. Chiappetta Jabbour, and D. E. Carvalho. 2022. "Integrating the circular economy and industry 4.0 for sustainable development: implications for responsible footwear production in a big data-driven world." *Technological Forecasting and Social Change*, (November), 175 (4). doi: 10.1016/j. techfore.2021.121335.

Hitt, M. A., B. W. Keats, and S. M. DeMarie. 1998. "Navigating in the new competitive landscape: building strategic flexibility and competitive advantage in the 21st century." *The Academy of Management Executive*, (November), 12 (4): 22–42. doi: 10.5465/ ame.1998.1333922.

Kirsten, T. 2020. "Macroeconomic implications of uncertainty in South Africa." *South African Journal of Economic and Management Sciences*, (February), 23 (1). doi: 10.4102/sajems.v23i1.3350.

Krugman, P. 1993. "First nature, second nature, and metropolitan location." *Journal of Regional Science*, 33 (2): 129–144. doi: 10.1111/j.1467-9787.1993.tb00217.x.

Manocha, S. and P. Saini. 2022. "Insights of big data analytics in Education-challenges & opportunities – a review paper." *International Management Issues, Trenton, New Jersey, USA: American Scholars Press*, 18. http://www.americanscholarspress.us/journals/IMR/journal_previous_issues.php#collapse_70.\

Minner, S. 2001. "Strategic safety stocks in reverse logistics supply chains." *International Journal of Production Economics, Elsevier*, (May), 71 (1–3): 417–428. https://www.sciencedirect.com/science/article/abs/pii/S0925527300001389.

Peteraf, M. A. and M. E. Bergen. 2003. "Scanning dynamic competitive landscapes: a market-based and resource-based framework." *Strategic Management Journal*, 24 (10): 1027–1041. doi: 10.1002/smj.325.

Piercy, N. F., D. W. Cravens, and N. Lane. 2012. "Sales manager behvior-based control and salesperson performance: the effects of manager control competencies and organizational citizenship behavior." *The Journal of Marketing Theory and Practice*, (January), 20 (1): 7–22. doi: 10.2307/23243692.

Porter, M. E. 1989. "How competitive forces shape strategy." Edited by D. Asch and C. Bowman. *Readings in Strategic Management*. Palgrave, London. doi: 10.1007/978-1-349-20317-8_10.

Stewart, R. F. and M. O. Doscher. 1963. *The Corporate Development Plan (No. 183)*. Menlo Park, California, N.p.: Stanford Research Institute.

Stewart, R. F., O. J. Benepe, and A. Mitchell. 1965. *Formal Planning: the Staff Planner's Role at Start up (No. 250)*. Menlo Park, California, USA, N.p.: Stanford Research Institute.

Stott, P. 2016. "How climate change affects extreme weather events." *Science*, (June), 352 (6293): 1517–1518. doi: 10.1126/science.aaf7271.

Wang, M. and H. Zhuang. 2019. "How do firms in the private sector perceive constraints to doing business in China?" *Global Economic Review*, (February), 48 (2): 1–31. doi: 10.1080/1226508X.2019.1584762.

Zeba, G., M. Dabi'c, M. Cicak, T. Diam, and H. Yalcin. 2021. "Technology mining: artificial intelligence in manufacturing." *Technological Forecasting and Social Change*, (June), 171: 1–18. doi: 10.1016/j.techfore.2021.120971.

4. Critical Analysis of the Social Security Code 2020 in India: Assessing Its Implications and Challenges

Ms. Ishani Vaidya, Assistant Professor, Faculty of Legal Science, Shoolini University, Research Scholar, Department of Laws, HPU, Himachal Pradesh, India

Email: ivaidya3@gmail.com

Mr. Shubham Sindhu, UILS, HPU, Himachal Pradesh, India

ABSTRACT: Since the debut of the four new labour codes passed by the Indian Parliament in the year 2020, they have been the talk of the town and a topic of debate and discussion among the people regarding its implications and challenges. The new code aimed to restructure and amalgamate various existing labour laws related to social security, to provide a comprehensive framework for the welfare of workers. Nevertheless, like any crucial legislation, the Social Security Code is not without its flaws and challenges. This article critically analyses the Social Security Code 2020, exploring its repercussions on workers, employers and the overall socio-economic landscape of India.

KEYWORDS: New labour code, organised sector, social security, unorganised sector

1. INTRODUCTION

Making states accountable for providing protection and assurance to their citizens against certain life contingencies is the fundamental principle upon which the notion of social security is based. According to the International Labour Organization (ILO), social security is a form of insurance provided by society to individuals and households to provide access to healthcare and to provide assured financial stability, particularly in situations of severance, old age and job accident, maternity leave or loss of the only earner in the family. Two extensive social security programs are Social Assistance and Social Assurance. The streamlined Code on Social Security, 2020 (Social Security Code), which was based on the Standing Committee Report and passed by the Lok Sabha on 22 September 2020, and the Rajya Sabha on 23 September 2020, was one of three labour codes that the Lok Sabha introduced on 19 September 2020.

Chapter 4 DOI- 10.4324/9781003428213-4

The consolidation of 29 national labour laws into four codes – the Code of Wages, 2019 (2019 Code), the Industrial Relations Code, 2020 (2020 Industrial Code), the Code on Social Security (2020 Code) and the Occupational Safety, Health and Working Conditions Code, 2020 (2020 Occupational Safety Code) – marks a significant advancement for India as a labour-intensive nation. These codes are currently awaiting government enforcement. Additionally, the consolidation has led to the conversion of old laws, the elimination of redundant sections and authorities and an expansion of the application, ease of compliance, efficiency of execution and wisdom of penalties of several labour laws.

To provide individuals more security over their life, the Indian government has adopted the new Social Security Code of 2020 as a part of labour reforms. It is a comprehensive piece of legislation aimed at reforming and rationalising India's social security system. The code consolidates and amends various existing laws related to social security, including employee benefits, retirement funds, health insurance and occupational safety. The code consolidated nine central laws, including the Employees' Provident Funds and Miscellaneous Provisions Act, the Employees' State Insurance Act and the Maternity Benefit Act, among others.

2. LITERATURE REVIEW

In the course of the present study, the researcher has gone through a number of literatures related to labour migration in India and for doing so various books and articles are thoroughly analysed. An ICSSR Project research from 1987 focused mostly on the socioeconomic circumstances of dadan out-migrant labourers in the Orissa area of Ganjam. According to reports, these out-migrants (dadan sramik) are subjected to abuse and exploitation by agents. In his article, J. P. Singh has drawn attention to migration statistics from the Indian census and the NSSO Report while also emphasising international migration, which has its roots in excess labour and poverty. Regarding the human rights of the migrant workers, Penna L.Rao51 has discussed the origin of the modem Magna Charta of migrant workers and where the author tries to reflect about migration for employment has always been a matter of concern for the community of nations both the recruiters and the primary employers who hire them.

3. RESEARCH METHODOLOGY

The researcher in the present work has used a doctrinal method of research where in-depth analysis has been done on various provisions of statutes and reports. The data have been primarily taken from articles, books, reports of commissions, and relevant statutes.

4. CONCEPT OF SOCIAL SECURITY AND ITS SCOPE

Social security covers a wide range of things and varies from country to country. However, there are mainly two different kinds of social security programs: one is social insurance, in which workers and employees pay regular contributions and the money raised is then distributed to provide benefits based on the contribution made by them over a period of time, and social assistance, in which benefits are supplied by the government. The social security scope was divided into nine separate components by the ILO, which are further enlisted as follows:

Medical care: The medical care assistance includes preventive care, care from the general practitioner, provision of prescription-based essential medicines, dental care, pre-natal and post-natal care by the concerned practitioners along with complete medical rehabilitation, if required. Sickness benefits: A specific amount of fund is periodically provided to workers/employees who are incapable of working. This covers the funeral expenses as well in case of the death of the said beneficiary. Unemployment benefits: This component enshrines the provision of providing assistance to the worker who is capable of working but unemployed during a period due to the lack of appropriate employment opportunities. However, this component may be limited to cover the unemployment of 13 weeks annually. Old-age benefits: In this component, the payment depends on an individual's capacity to work before his retirement time. After a pre-set age, a fixed amount is paid, which is further continued till the death of the beneficiary. Maternity benefits: The maternity benefit component involves all medical care during the pre-natal and post-natal care provided by medical practitioners along with any assistance required from the hospital.

The fundamental idea that conceptualises (Deakin, Simon F. (2013).) the concept of social security in any geography is putting the responsibility of the protection of citizens on states while assuring citizens against specific life contingencies. It ensures that an individual is provided with much-needed financial help when he/she is not capable of earning a livelihood due to old age, disease or during the maternity period.

5. SOCIAL SECURITY FROM INTERNATIONAL PERSPECTIVE

The right to social security finds its foundation within the international human rights laws, especially within the International Covenant on Economic, Social and Cultural Rights (ICESCR) and the Universal Declaration of Human Rights (UDHR). Though several times, social security is portrayed as detrimental to the global economic dynamic and overall development, there is a huge scope and body of work that showcases the symbiotic relationship between sustained economic growth, development and prosperity and social security and welfare.

Such positive, symbiotic synergies have been retrieved quite recently by the advocates of the social security state. The confluence of thoughts recognising and acknowledging the social, political and economic requirement of social security resonates robustly with the entire international community, which made social security a very prominent agenda in the 2030 Agenda for Sustainable Development or 2030 Agenda.

There are many challenges we have yet to face to make the right to social protection a reality for all the workers but the historical trend shows a positive development which is a good factor to bank on. During the COVID-19 crisis, only 30.6% of the population of working age had legal coverage of a social protection system with a full range of benefits and more than half of the world's population had (Rajan, S. Irudaya, and R.B. Bhagat (2022).) no social protection and cash benefits cover, which highlights a stark gap in the social protection system. In recent decades, social assistance schemes have reached many more (Deakin, Simon, and Frank Wilkinson (1991).) people than before and this might be an important factor of right-based national social protection systems which provide coverage to the most vulnerable groups. However, coverage of adequate social protection for the working-age population is not provided by even the most narrowly targeted social assistance when they need it the most. Private health insurance and pensions are privatised and individualised market solutions that only a few privileged workers can afford.

During 1900–2000, there was a positive (ILO (2017).) development of social protection schemes throughout the world. During the COVID-19 pandemic, nearly half (53.1%) of the global population which is equal to 4.1 billion people were left without any social protection scheme to fall back on to. Many domestic workers as well as truly self-employed (farmers and street vendors) who were part of informal economy and are in employment relationship did not fare good specially the migrant workers have to face additional legal, administrative and practical challenges. Deakin, Simon, Colin Fenwick, and Prabirjit Sarkar (2014).

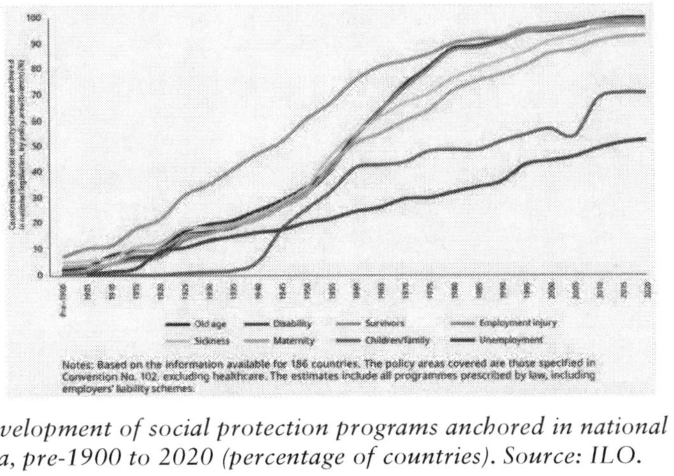

Figure 1. *Development of social protection programs anchored in national legislation by policy area, pre-1900 to 2020 (percentage of countries). Source: ILO.*

There are a lot of challenges in making the right to social security a reality for the workers. First and the biggest of them is the informal nature of economic units and employment. Nearly more than 2 billion men and women, which may be more than 60% of the global employed population, are a part of the informal economy who are majorly present in developing countries. Lack of adequate health care and income security is one of the major issues these workers and their families face, in addition to work deficits and social security. ILO conducted a survey of platform workers (12,000 in number) in 100 countries and found out that most platform workers with access to social protection are not covered through their economic activity they were covered through family members or tax-financed programs or their contribution to social insurance through other employment. Only 40% had health insurance, employment injury protection and old age pensions (ILO, 2021e). (Almutairi, Saad S. (2020).)

A recent study conducted in the year 2020 on the IMF programs Figure 1. across 148 countries, within the light of the key inclination of each country's global policy framework for macroeconomics during the COVID-19 pandemic, showed various recommendations on taxation with special focus on the expansion or the introduction of VATs or value-added taxes by either reducing exemptions or widening the base. This recommendation is there despite the recognition of VAT for its regressive nature by the IMF. Only a very few reports from a few states had positive recommendations to increase the rate of revenue collection in a direct form of taxes such as corporate income tax, personal income tax and property tax. It is worth mentioning that even when many states are capable enough to widen their fiscal area by increasing the tax-to-GDP ratio, only a fraction of the overall revenues are sanctioned for social protection schemes. Thus, it becomes critical to ensure that all social insurance schemes which are formulated for social protection and funded by both workers and employers are not only maintained but boosted as well. The question forming the bottom line how efficiently and effectively are these social security schemes have been able to attract the different categories of workers who were earlier a part of the informal economy and the major reforms required in these schemes to make them more inclusive.

6. SCOPE OF SOCIAL SECURITY IN INDIA

In India, the concept and scheme of social security enshrines a wide range of programs and schemes which are further governed by several regulations and laws. Some of the social insurances that are enlisted under the Indian Social scheme involve pensions after the retirement of individuals, various health benefits and medical insurance, benefits during the maternity tenure, benefits for disabled individuals and gratuity. All Indian citizens who are employees in the organised sector as defined by the laws, including the ones who are employees of foreign investors, are entitled to avail coverage and protection under all the above-mentioned schemes.

Since India is a labour-intensive nation, the state has taken immense progressive initiatives towards improving the concept of social security by consolidating the 29 national labour laws into 4 different codes which are: the Code of Wages, 2019 (2019 Code), the Code of Social Security (2020 Code), Industrial Relations Code, 2020 and the Occupational Safety, Health and Working Conditions Code, 2020, which are still in the pipeline from government's end to be implemented. Once this consolidation occurs, there would be an impressive impact on employees and employers alike. Aside from this much-required consolidation, the Indian government has also taken many initiatives to simplify and smoother the functioning of different legislations pertaining to social security and employment in India, thus ensuring the ease of carrying out business in the country.

On 23 September 2020, the Parliament of India enacted the Code on Social Security, with the aim of ensuring optimal social security coverage to the workforce across India's labour industry. This code brought together and subsumed the eight pre-existing central labour laws including the Employees' Provident Funds and Miscellaneous Provisions Act, 1952, Payment of Gratuity Act, 1972, Workers Cess Act of 1996, Employees' Compensation Act of 1923, Maternity Benefit Act of 1961, Cine Workers Welfare Fund Act of 1981, Building and Other Construction, Employees' State Insurance Act of 1948 and lastly, the Unorganised Workers' Social Security Act of 2008. Regulations and rules alone can't bring the compliance with principles of business and human rights (BHRs). Businesses must use these rules as the starting point to develop stringent reporting needs based on top-down compliance method and ethical standards to weave BHR compliance into the nano fabric of the organisations. This new Social Security Code entails different rules which further highlights contribution in the social security and payments aspects for employee benefits.

After the enactment of the Social Security Code in the year 2020, there was no fixed date from the Centre pertaining to the enforcement of the code. It is now under the umbrella of the State governments to take it further from here. Under this, several states have taken the liberty to chalk down the first draft rules of the Social Security Code as per the state's individual requirements. The states that have penned down the first draft rules are Arunachal Pradesh, Assam, Bihar, Chhattisgarh, Goa, Gujarat, Haryana, Himachal Pradesh, Jharkhand, Karnataka, Kerala, Madhya Pradesh, Maharashtra, Manipur, Odisha, Punjab, Telangana, Tripura, Uttarakhand, Uttar Pradesh, UTs of Andaman & Nicobar Island, Chandigarh, Jammu & Kashmir and Puducherry. However, rest of the states are still left with drafting the humongous task of drafting rules, pushing the enforcement of said act into the bosom of the future.

6.1. Scope Widening of the Term 'Wage' and its Synchronization with Social Security Code

In the newly launched Social Security Code, there was a significant widening of the scope of the definition of the term 'WAGE' (Aggrawal Tushar, 2014). With the expansion of the definition of 'wages' under the new code, the retired employees are expected to receive raised benefits. According to the new Wage Code, the basic salary can't be lesser than 50% of the net CTC, which directly affects deductions under PF contributions, while indirectly impacting the social security. All in all, this new change will have a substantial impact on the salaries, gratuity and provident fund (PF) of the Central employees while impacting the salary structure in the private sector as well. The term 'wage' in the code is now defined and explained in such a way that it covers a diverse range of activities which can be differentiated into three aspects:

Definition inclusivity: All and any remuneration which is expressed in financial terminology would be considered as stipend and this includes honey allowance, introductory pay and retaining allowance. Special exclusions: Pension and gratuity, PF, vehicle allowance and house rent and other such are not a part of the term 'stipend' if they are less than 50% of the entire remuneration paid. Benefits in kind: Benefits in kind would ensure that the different social security benefits are at least 50% of the entire compensation. This specific kind can be up to 15% of the total stipend provided. Social Security Welfare Scheme: The Central Government, under Section 16 of the Code, may notify several social security schemes for workers' benefits and involve various schemes including EPS, EPF and EDLI. Mansoor, Kashif, and Donal O'Neill (2020).

6.2. Significant Alterations in Contributions Amount

Now the EPS, EPF, ESI and EDLI schemes will be financed via an amalgamation of benefactions from the hand and employer in which both of them make 10% benefactions of the stipend, or similar other rate as confirmed by the government. For all other benefactions or motherliness benefits, gratuity, hand compensation, erecting worker's cess, the employer would be the responsible holder.

6.3. Social Security for the Indian Unorganised Sector

The Code also enshrines that the 'Central Government of India' shall regularly formulate and notify suitable and appropriate weal schemes for workers under the unorganised sector on important matters related to disability cover, health and maternity benefits, old age cover, life cover and any other benefit that may deemed by the Central Government for the workers of unorganised sector, platform workers and gig workers.

6.4. Corporate Social Security Organisation

After the revival of Social Security Code in India, it required the establishment of different bodies to supervise over the smooth implementation of different schemes. These bodies are as follows: Chaired by the Central Provident Fund Commissioner, a Central Board of Trustees to supervise the accurate administration of EPS, EPF and EDLI schemes. Chaired by the Chairperson appointed by the

Central Government, the Employee State Insurance Corporation to supervise the ESI scheme.

6.4.1. Maternity Benefits

For females, the Social Security Code of 2020 entails that every woman is entitled to the coverage of maternity benefits, with the employer being liable to pay so, the rate of the average diurnal pay covering the time of her absence from the office, which is the time before the delivery day to any day post the delivery and is subjected to other aspects of the law. (Chigater, Shraddha (2021)).

6.4.2. Gratuity for Employees

Earlier employees who completed five years of regular employment with one employer were entitled to the gratuity. Under the new code, all full-time employees can now avail of gratuity on a pro-rata basis, with the major change that now the employees only need to complete one year of service rather than five years.

6.4.3. Sanctions and Offences

The new Social Security Code is a stricter version of the previous ones as it has enlisted penalties on the basis of the account of non-compliance of any specific or all provisions under the code such as failure of payment of gratuity, contribution or any other liability and nature of offence. Moreover, if the contributor fails non-compliance in terms of paying cess, contribution, charges, gratuity, maternity benefits and any other compensation, the 2020 Code directs a minimum imprisonment of two years for the employer which can be further extended to 5 years along with a fine of Rs. 300,000.

6.4.4. Offence Compounding

Another change that the Social Security Code of 2020 witnessed was the addition of offence compounding. Under this provision, there's the substitute to compound any kind of offence which is punishable with fine only or by imprisonment which doesn't exceed more than one year along with paying the fine. The point to be noted is that it is a once in three year's opportunity and any employer cannot exercise this opportunity within the period of three years from the date of commissioning of a similar offence for which the employer was either convicted or compounded earlier.

6.4.5. Appeals and Inspection

In the new Social Security Code of 2020, the designated authorities have given powers to appoint facilitators-cum-inspectors to inspect different establishments under the Code and provide appropriate guidance to employees and employers in regards to the compliance.

6.4.6. Exemptions

The new Social Security Code of 2020 vests in Central Government the power to exempt certain establishments from some or all provisions of the Code while making Aadhar Card mandatory to receive any kind of benefit from the enlisted social security schemes.

7. IMPLICATIONS AND KEY CHALLENGES OF SOCIAL SECURITY CODE 2020

Being enacted in the year 2020, the Social Security Code has ushered a new era in the Indian labour and social welfare ecosystem. One of its significant implications is the streamlining and merger of several labour laws into a one, unified framework, which highly simplifies the compliance for both employees and employers. The code also expands the net of social security by bringing in a diverse range of workers including informal sector and gig workers, providing them access to benefits like gratuity, PF and maternity benefits which, in turn, improves financial security, thereby the living standards of the Indian workforce. There are several key challenges in the Social Security Code of 2020 which are listed as follows:

There is a lack of clarity in the provision of the Social Security Code for gig workers and workers who are using any online app-based platform to provide services. This lack of clarity creates confusion while applying specific schemes to different workers falling under this category and this also might create loopholes which can be further used by the employers. There are certain recommendations which are written in code but are not implemented such as: social security system should be applied to all units and establishments; functional integration of administration is necessary to implement existing schemes; to increase coverage of the wage ceilings which are now in existence should be removed. (Nishith Desai Associates (2022)).

The new recommendations were not implemented so the earlier setup with its threshold based on the size is now retained. Medical insurance and pension benefits are only mandatory for the units that have ten or twenty employees working for them so the units which have a lesser number of employees will come under the umbrella of discretionary schemes as the government notified. The code provides for an employee state insurance scheme which covers establishments having more than 10 workers. If any establishment wants to avail of this scheme with less than 10 workers, then there is a catch: this scheme will be provided to the establishments having less than 10 workers only if all the workers voluntarily opt for the scheme. For employees working in a hazardous place, it is mandatory for them to opt for this scheme but it's the responsibility of the employee only and it's up to them to apply for this scheme and employers do not get a say or responsibility for it. In India, the number of workers who are self-employed is large and a major source of income is home-based work. The code has no provision for providing social security benefits to such a class of workers. To receive social security benefits, this new code made it compulsory for the worker to provide his Aadhaar card number which is in contempt of ruling of honourable Supreme Court as in Puttswamy Case, it is clearly stated that Aadhaar number could only be made mandatory for use with a subsidy, benefit or service from the consolidated fund of India. But some of the benefits like gratuity and PFs are provided by employees and employers rather than consolidated funs of India and this may make requirement of Aadhaar to receive them against the law. The code states that in case of fixed-term employment, gratuity would be paid to employees on pro rata basis so gratuity becomes a burden to the employer and irrespective of their terms of services, employees get the gratuity benefits. But Industrial Relations Code states that to get the eligibility for gratuity, a fixed-term worker has to work for at least 1 year on a contract basis. This code does not provide these provisions which give rise to ambiguous situations. This bill gives the power to the government to exempt any new industrial establishment from all of the provisions of the Social Security Code, if it's in the public interest. It also extends the State Government the power to exempt any institution from its provisions if it's creating more economic activity and employment. Every factory will generate employment and will create economic activity and exemptions may be abused widely. In some cases, the authority and their actions may lead to aggrieved persons. This bill provides for an administrative appellate authority to be notified but it does not provide any judicial mechanism for hearing such disputes under the bill. This bill bars civil courts from hearing any disputes which come under the umbrella of the bill. The only thing an aggrieved person can do is file a writ petition directly before the relevant high court and this can deny the aggrieved person a chance to challenge certain issues before a lower court. This also makes the process a little more complex and will add more burden on the already over-burdened high courts of our country.

8. CONCLUSION

Our country has an extensive labour system with several defects and loopholes in it. Out of all, it still suffers from challenges and issues pertaining to migrant and permanent labours. However, laws are becoming stricter unlike countries like Dubai where the glamorous lifestyle has overpowered the harsh reality of the living conditions of migrant workers. However, even in India, this code needs a firm reassessment as there are certain challenges that can prevent the utmost impact of the code. The mandatory Aadhar-based registration to leverage the benefits of the Social Security Code is a direct violation of the acknowledgement of the right to privacy by none other than the Supreme Court of India as an integral part of life under Article 21 in one of the ground-breaking statements of 2016. Additionally, the code also restricts the judiciary and civil courts without mentioning the legal jurisdiction of industrial tribunals and labour courts. This needs to be tackled with and changed along with many provisions of benefits and compensation, compliance and policies requirements, human resources, redressal mechanism, workforce management, etc. and subsequent revisions should be done for effective and pragmatic implementation of the Social Security Code of 2020 to achieve the goal of providing the constitutional right of social security to all citizens of India.

REFERENCES

Agrawal, Tushar (2014). "Geschlecht und Kaste-ansässige Lohndiskriminierung in Indien: Einige Neue Beweise," *Journal for Labour Market Research* 47: 329–340.

Almutairi, Saad S. (2020). "Comparison of labour laws in different countries," *Journal of Critical Reviews* 908–916.

Chigater, Shraddha (2021). "Labour law reforms and women's work in India: assessing the new labour codes from a gender lens," Available at SSRN 3947175.

Deakin, Simon, Colin Fenwick, and Prabirjit Sarkar (2014). "Labour law and inclusive development: the economic effects of industrial relations laws in middle-income countries," *Institutional Competition between Common Law and Civil Law: Theory and Policy*, pp. 185–209. Berlin, Heidelberg: Springer Berlin Heidelberg.

Deakin, Simon F. (2013). "Addressing labour market segmentation: The role of labour law."

Deakin, Simon, and Frank Wilkinson (1991). "Labour law, social security and economic inequality," *Cambridge Journal of Economics* 15(2): 125–148.

ILO (2017). *World Social Protection Report 2017–19*. Geneva: ILO.

ILO (2018). *Women and Men in the Informal Economy: A Statistical Picture*. 3rd ed. Geneva: ILO.

ILO (2020). Promoting Employment and Decent Work in a Changing Landscape: Report of the Committee of Experts on the Application of Conventions and Recommendations (articles 19, 22 and 35 of the Constitution) Report III (Part B). ILC 109th Session.

Mansoor, Kashif, and Donal O'Neill (2020). "Minimum wage compliance and household welfare: an analysis of over 1500 minimum wages."

Mitchell, Richard, Petra Mahy, and Peter G. Gahan (2014). "The evolution of labour law in India: an overview and commentary on regulatory objectives and development," *Asian Journal of Law and Society* 413, 415.

Nishith Desai Associates (2022). New labour codes in India delayed. https://www.nishithdesai.com/NewsDetails/5436.

Patra Rath Gopal, C., and G.C. Parida (1989). "S.C. Dadan System of out-migration in Orissa," Prachi Prakashan, New Delhi.

Rajan, S. Irudaya, and R.B. Bhagat (2022). "Internal migration and the Covid-19 pandemic in India," *Migration and Pandemics* 164: 227.

5. Issues of Unorganised Migrant Workers during COVID-19 Pandemic under Indian Legal and Judicial Developments

Sonali Kusum
Assistant Professor, School of Law, Rights & Constitutional Governance, Tata Institute of Social Sciences Mumbai, Maharashtra

ABSTRACT: The 'migrant workers' working as 'daily wage workers' are included under the Social Security for the Unorganised Workers Act (UWSSA), 2008, largely regulated by the Inter-State Migrant Worker's Act (ISMWA), 1979. The migrating workers from other states were most adversely affected by the pandemic COVID-19, being deprived of livelihood, daily wages, food, ration, accommodation and transportation during the lockdown, leading to a mass exodus of nearly 30 million migrant workers walking on foot with their families, children towards their homeland, increasing spread of COVID-19 virus and violation of government regulations.

The Apex Court of India took cognisance of their plight in Suo Moto cases, and further, Government of India issues advisories and socio-economic assistance schemes for these workers, but due to lack of records, government identity cards and registration for the migrant workers under the UWSSA and ISMWA, the migrant workers could not avail the same. A strong need is felt for better safeguard of their rights and rehabilitation. Accordingly, the objective of the paper is to enumerate socio-legal issues faced by migrant labour during the pandemic, vis-a-vis the existing policy, legal and judicial developments and the way forward.

KEYWORDS: unorganised, migrant workers, social security act, pandemic covid-19

1. INTRODUCTION

The term 'migrant worker' is inclusive of 'wage worker' and 'unorganised worker'. Under the UWSS Act, 2008, 'wage worker' as ' a person under employment

Chapter 5 DOI- 10.4324/9781003428213-5

in unorganised or informal sector in return for wages payment or kind either recruited directly or through any intermediate agency as contractor for one or several employers, this encompasses casual or migrant or expatriate worker'.

These workers are commonly understood as 'inter-state migrant workers'. Migrant workers are originally inhabitants of their respective home towns and states but travel for work outside from their home town.

Migrant worker is included within the phrase, 'inter-state migrant workmen' means 'an individual appointed by a contractor in consultation with the employer in a given state under any written arrangement or otherwise to be working in other state, with respect to such employment' (ISMW Act).

The International Convention, namely the rights of migrants and their dependent families, 1990, defines a 'migrant worker' as 'a person who is to be engaged, is engaged or has been engaged in a remunerated activity in a state of which he or she is not a citizen'.

2. LEGAL FRAMEWORK ON EXISTING LABOUR LAW – CONSTITUTIONAL DIRECTIONS, STATUTORY ACTS AND CODES IN INDIA

The Indian Constitution, 1950*:* Under Part IV, State Policy Article 39, the government is directed to formulate policy to secure ' adequate means of livelihood' with 'equal pay for equal work for both men and women'. The DPSP, Article 41 provides for 'right to work' and Article 42 provides for 'provision for just and humane conditions of work' and 'maternity relief'.

The Constitution, Seventh Schedule, Labour falls within the concurrent list, empowering federal and the regional government jurisdiction to enact laws on the same.

Thereby the Supreme Court in Charanjit Lal Choudhary vs. Union of India (UOI), Gangaram vs. UOI, Chandra Boarding vs. State of Mysore and Bharatiya Dak Tar Mazdoor Munch vs. UOI directed for making special provisions for labour, making reasonable classification for labour representing a class interest.

The (ISMW) Act, 1979: The purpose of the act is to 'regulate the employment of inter-state migrant workmen and to provide for their conditions of services'.

The salient aspects of the ISMW Act are the right of migrant working community to avail 'displacement allowance' and 'a journey allowance', 'wages' to be paid from since their recruitment. The ISMW Act confers a 'suitable residential accommodation, to provide medical facilities, protective clothing to the workmen, residential accommodation' among others.

The Social Security Act for Unorganised Workers, 2008: The act registers informal or wage worker, that is workers from other states and 'an identity card' by the District Administration. The local self-government authorities in rural and the urban areas ensure 'record-keeping' on migrant workers. The government at the state level creates workers facilitation centres 'to disseminate information on social security schemes for the unorganised workers'.

The Labour Codes, 2019 – 2020: The 2nd Government Commission on Labour at national level recommended consolidation and simplification of around 29 central labour legislations. In 2019, the Labour Ministry introduced four labour codes, namely i. Wage Codes, ii. Industry – Labour Relation Code, iii. Social Economic Assistance and Security Code and iv. Work Health and Safety Code.

Wage Code (Central) Rules, 2019: The Indian government issued a gazette notification for the draft Wages Rules and provides for a minimum statutory wage, and it is mandatory for the employer to compensate the employee minimum rate of wages and nothing short of this, as notified by government. The code on wage covers contract labour includes migrant workers.

Code on Work Health, Safety and Occupation *(OSH), 2020:* This code casts responsibility on the contractor, principal employer to protect the health and terms of the workers. The OSH code permits migrant workers to benefit from the Government Food Security System either in their host state or others.

3. GOVERNMENT SCHEMES FOR MIGRATING WORKERS AMIDST COVID-19 PANDEMIC

'Garib Kalyan Yojana by the Pradhan Mantri (PMGKY)': The National Government started 'the Pradhan Mantri Garib Kalyan Ann Yojana (PMGKAY)' aegis of government, Food Security Act (FSA), for distribution of free food grains up to five kg of wheat and rice per month for poor including unorganised labour, migrant and informal labour, who were denied of livelihood due to lockdown following COVID-19 pandemic (Press Information Bureau, December 2022).

'PM CARES' (Prime Minister's Citizen Assistance and Relief in Emergency Situations) Fund: The government established a Rs 1,000 crore fund for migrant labourers under Prime Minister's 'Citizen Assistance and Relief in Emergency Situations' or the 'PM CARES, Fund' for 'welfare of the migrants and poor'. The first ever allotment under the PM CARES fund was utilised for procuring vaccines, ventilators and medical treatment of poor and migrant workers (Indian Express, May 2020).

National Database of Inter-State Migrant Workers: The Ministry of Labour and Employment is compiling a 'National Database of Unorganised Workers (NDUW)', including other construction and migrant workers.

4. CONTEMPORARY JUDICIAL DIRECTIONS AND SIGNIFICANT PUBLIC INTEREST LITIGATION (PIL)

The public interest litigation (PIL) filed in Harsh Mander Vs UOI, 2020, Anjali Bhardwaj Vs UOI, Jagdeep S. Chhokar Vs. UOI, Supreme Court of India, and Suo Moto in Re Problems, Misery of Migrants seeking Supreme Court (SC) directed the Central and Regional Government 'to ensure food security by framing insurance, assistance for providing free dry ration, allocation of additional foodgrains till the pandemic, cash transfers' by implementing 'One Nation One Ration Card' scheme within the time bound manner for migrant workers facing livelihood issues during lockdown following COVID-19 pandemic. The SC directed for a 'Government Database on Wage Workers to register all migrant workers'.

Alakh Alok Srivastava Vs Union of India was another writ petition demonstrating the plight of migrant workers, including women, small children, elders and differently abled persons found walking barefoot in metro cities back to their villages without basic services while pandemic for providing them with essential services such as nutrition, water, medicines, transportation arrangements and wage payment to the migrants.

The SC directed the governments 'to check the spread of contamination of further coronavirus (COVID-19)'. The SC directed the 'Public servants to strictly comply with the directions, advisories and orders' passed by the government for welfare of the community. The SC directed for disbursement of '*PMGKY* ' for poor, migrant workers to be provided with food grains.

The Gujarat High Court in Suo Motu vs State of Gujarat directed Gujarat state to comply with Ministry of Home Affairs and Ministry of Health and Family Welfare Guidelines in 'assisting the migration of stranded labourers from various states to their native states' through the 'Shramik Special Trains' following social distancing norms.

The High Court of Punjab and Haryana reiterated the order of SC in a Suo Motu writ petition in Nirmal Gorana Versus the State of Haryana and others and accordingly directed that 'all those migrant workers who are found walking on highways or roads shall be immediately provided transport to their destination and would also be provided with the facility of food and water etc'. The Haryana state 'issued helpline numbers to assist all the migrant workers' and 'simplified the registration process of stranded migrant workers'.

In Subhash Chandran K.R Vs State of Himachal Pradesh, Himachal Pradesh, the High Court directed the state government 'to formulate a standard operating procedure (SOP) for movement of migrant stranded labour' as per the Home Ministry Advisory to address 'the challenges faced by migrant labourers in Himachal Pradesh during the COVID-19 pandemic'. The court directed the state 'to ensure free screening or testing and free vaccination against COVID-19 for all migrant labour entering Himachal Pradesh territory to prevent further infection spread' and further to register all the migrant workers residing in relief/ shelter camps in the states.

5. ISSUES AND CHALLENGES – VULNERABILITY OF MIGRANT WORKERS DURING COVID-19 PANDEMIC

5.1. The Decline in Wages of Migrant Workers during the COVID-19 Pandemic

Most workers faced a decline of up to sixty per cent in the mean monthly income of labour, for instance, it was reported that in Lucknow, Uttar Pradesh, the wage has declined by 62% from Rs 9,500 per month in pre-pandemic times to Rs 3,500 per month, whereas in Pune, Maharashtra, the wage declined by a 54.5% from Rs 10,000 to Rs 4,500 (Mohan et al. 2021).

5.2. Inadequate Data on Unorganised Migrant Worker

It was reported that the government has inadequate data on migrant workers' deaths on their way back to their home states during the lockdown. The highest court of India issued directions to Labour Ministry to register unorganised workers", "to create a National Database for providing social security, and welfare measures while the pandemic. (Nath 2019)

5.3. Limitations in Availing PDS Schemes

The 'One Nation, One Ration Card' (ONORC)2020 provided free subsidies during the lockdown, but it faced limitations in reaching out to the migrant workers. This card is not uniformly implemented among the varied states in India. It was reported that certain states, namely Chhattisgarh, West Bengal, Assam and Delhi, have not implemented the ONORC scheme (The Economic Times 2021). Another problem related to accessing the ONORC is the prerequisite of 'biometric authentication, government identity cards such as Aadhaar cards', and hence, this scheme had limited coverage (PIB, Delhi 2022).

5.4. Lack of Awareness in Workers on Legislation and Social Security Scheme

Considering the socio-economic and educational background of the wage or expatriate workers, unable to read or access electronic or online information and comprehend the procedures related to same. The migrant workers also lack legal awareness of the rights accruing from the ISMW Act. Contrastingly, the migrant labourers are exploited by the contractors and mostly underpaid. Neither the contractors and the labour commissioners nor the local bodies conduct any awareness programme on the same (John et al. 2020).

5.5. Constraints for Migrant Women Workers to Utilise Child Welfare Services

The migrant women workers being pregnant or lactating their children were not able to procure from these child welfare schemes (Chakraborty 2022). The

Women and Child Ministry directed the governments to implement the scheme for migrant women population living in the vicinity of the worksites (Roy 2022).

5.6. Special Concerns of Women Migrating Unorganised Workers

Survey of several women workers migrating from twelve states, in India by the United Nation_Agency regarding the implications following pandemic on women migrant workers, indicated that these women faced a double burden of earning a livelihood and unpaid care work at home. These women faced decline by half percentage in incomes during the pandemic compared to pre-pandemic levels, lack of social security measures, dearth of food security, lack of cash assistance, health insurance and protection against domestic violence (Khasnobis and Chandna 2021).

5.7. Narrow Coverage of the ISMW Act

The ISMW Act applies only to 'a particular category of the migrant workers', The category of 'migrant workers who are not engaged by a contractor' or 'recruited by any other mode' in informal sector do not fall or thus excluded from the ISMW Act.

5.8. Legal Recognition to Inter-State Migrant Workers Vs Intra-State Migrants

Under the ISMW Act, the term migrant workers is defined by including 'inter-state migrant workers' with legal rights and welfare measures.

There is omission of an 'intra-state migrant workers'. Though both are included under the term 'unorganised labour' are placed as 'unorganised labour'.

5.9. State Rules not Formulated for Unorganised Workers Social Security Act (UWSS Act, 2008)

The Unorganised Workers Act provides for registry of unorganised, migrant workers. This act provides for insurance schemes to the migrant workers following the registration. However, several state governments, including the Delhi Government, have not framed state rules under this act. This lack of rules has caused the problem of non-distribution of benefits under the social security schemes. This was addressed by the Supreme Court (SC) in Shramajivi Mahila Samiti vs State of NCT of Delhi, wherein the court issued orders to those states (such as NCT Delhi) to formulate the rules under the same.

5.10. Non-Payment of Wages and Termination of Services of Migrant Workers

It is reported that approximately seven hundred or more complaints were received over the government 'Shramik helpline' from the migrant workers contending non-payment of wages, arbitrary termination of migrant workers. In response to the same, a ‘ Special Nodal Officer’ was designated to adjudicate complaints from migrant workers during the COVID-19 lockdown as reported in Shashank S. Mangal & Anr vs Government of NCT of Delhi & Ors.

5.11. Non-Implementation of Significant Provisions ISMW Act

The ISMW Act, 1979, provides for comprehensive record-keeping of all migrant workmen and the wages that they are paid. But most of these rights could not be guaranteed to the unorganised workers due to lack of record-keeping, government identity cards. In Shashank S. Mangal & Anr vs NCT, it was found that registration of licences under the 1979 Act is almost negligible if not nil. In Shramajivi Mahila Samiti v. NCT Delhi, the Indian government proposed for ‘NDUW’. It was submitted by the ‘Ministry of Labour and Employment that there is lack of government data on migrant workers who lost their jobs, lost their lives or during the COVID-19 lockdown’. There were no stagewise data on assistance provided to these workers. This surfaced during the parliamentary session during monsoon of the Lok Sabha (Nath 2019).

6. CONCLUSION

Given the above issues, it is inferred that despite the statutory enactments and regulations, the implementation of the law, judicial directions and social security schemes is yet overdue. Though the labour codes are progressive, however, this is dependent upon database and registration. The record-keeping and database ought to be updated. The government identity cards, necessary license permit and registration need to be augmented, and this is crucial for availing the government schemes.

The plight of workers should be understood and addressed holistically by including both inter-state and intra-state migrant workers. The awareness generation has to be undertaken. As per the constitutional directive, labour needs a welfare approach; accordingly, their welfare ought to be promoted.

REFERENCES

Alakh Alok Srivastava Vs Union of India, 2020, Writ Petition No. 468/2020.

Allard, J., M. Jagnani, Y. Neggers, R. Pande, S. Schaner, and C. T. Moore. 2019. “Indian female migrants face greater barriers to post–Covid recovery than males: evidence from a panel study.” Accessed September 5, 2023. doi: 10.1016/j.eclinm.2022.101631.

Anjali Bhardwaj Vs Union of India 2020.

Anun Dhawan & Ors. Vs. Union of India & Ors, 2019, IA No. 130084/2019.

Bandhua Mukti Morcha Vs Union of India & Others, 1984 SCR (2) 67.

Bharatiya Dak Tar Mazdoor Munch vs. Union of India 1987, 2003 (4) BomCR 189.

Chakraborty, R. 2022. “Of 25260 beneficiaries who migrated, all services under ICDS provided to 17337 through Maha MTS.” Accessed September 5, 2023. https://

indianexpress.com/article/cities/mumbai/maharashtra-women-child-development-interview-migrants-8279706/.

Chandra Boarding vs. State of Mysore 1970 AIR 2042.

Charanjit Lal Choudhary Vs. Union of India, 1950 SCR 869.

Gangaram vs. Union of India 1970 AIR 2178.

Hari Singh Rajpurohit Vs State of Rajasthan, 2020, D.B. Civil Writ Petition No.4281/2020.

Jagdeep S. Chhokar Vs. Union of India, 2020, W.P(C) Diary No(s). 10801/2020.

Jana Samparka Samithy Vs State of Kerala, 2020, WP(C).No.27148 of 2015(S).

John, J., N. J. Thomas, M. Jacob, and N. Jacob. 2020. "A Study on Social Security and Health Rights of Migrant Workers in India." Accessed September 5, 2023. https://nhrc.nic.in/sites/default/files/Approved_Health%20and%20social%20security%20ISMW_KDS-NHRC.pdf.

Khasnobis, B. G. and S. Chandna. 2021. "Socio-Economic Impact of COVID-19 on Women Migrant Workers." Accessed September 5, 2023. https://www.undp.org/library/dfs-socio-economic-impact-covid-19-women-migrant-workers.

Matter of Harsh Mander Vs Union of India (UOI) 2020.

Mohan, D., J. Mistry, A. Singh, and S. Sreedhar. 2021. "How daily wage workers in India suffered in the lockdown – and continue to struggle months later." Accessed September 5, 2023. https://scroll.in/article/989258/how-daily-wage-workers-in-india-suffered-in-the-lockdown-and-continue-to-struggle-months-later.

N. Malaikannu Vs State, 2020, W.P.(MD) No.6325 of 2020.

Nath, D. 2019. "Govt. has no data of migrant workers' death, loss of job." Accessed September 5, 2023. https://www.thehindu.com/news/national/govt-has-no-data-of-migrant-workers-death-loss-of-job/article32600637.ece.

Nirmal Gorana Vs State of Haryana and others, 2020, CWP-PIL No. 59 of 2020 (O&M) 02.06.2020.

Press Information Bureau. 2022. "One Nation-One Ration card benefitted the poor: Union Minister Shri Narendra Singh Tomar Centre distributed free food grains by spending Rs 3.90 lakh crore under the Pradhan Mantri Garib Kalyan Ann Yojana Record Rs 2.75 lakh crore food grains." Accessed September 5, 2023. https://pib.gov.in/PressReleaseIframePage.aspx?PRID=1885814.

Roy, E. 2022. "Centre focuses on access to anganwadi services for migrants." Accessed September 5, 2023. https://indianexpress.com/article/india/centre-focuses-on-access-to-anganwadi-services-for-migrants-7977880/.

Sharma, H. 2020. "Only 13% of allocated free food grain handed out to returning migrant workers, reveals govt data." Accessed September 5, 2023. https://indianexpress.com/article/india/only-13-of-allocated-free-food-grain-handed-out-to-returning-migrant-workers-reveals-govt-data-6485982/.

Shashank S. Mangal & Anr Vs Government of Nct of Delhi & Ors., 2020, W.P(C) 3324/2020.

Shramjeevi Mahila Samiti Vs. State of NCT of Delhi & Ors. 2012, SLP (Crl) 150/2012.

Subhash Chandran K.R Vs State of Himachal Pradesh, 2020, CWP 1402/2020.

Suo – Moto in Re Problems and Miseries of Migrant Labourers, Suo Moto Writ petition No.6 of 2020.

The Hindu Bureau. 2019. "Sugar-belt shocker: the financial and sexual abuse of Maharashtra's migrant workforce." Accessed September 5, 2023. https://www.thehindu.com/news/national/other-states/bombay-hc-takes-cognisance-of-article-in-the-hindu-on-exploitation-of-maharashtras-migrant-workers-in-sugar-belt/article66721933.ece.

The Economic Times. 2021. "SC asks states, UTs to implement 'one nation, one ration card' scheme." Accessed September 5, 2023. https://economictimes.indiatimes.com/news/india/sc-asks-states-uts-to-implement-one-nation-one-ration-card-scheme/articleshow/83436412.cms.

The Press Trust of India, New Delhi. 2018. "Domestic workers registration: supreme Court asks govt not to give funds to states." Accessed September 5, 2023. https://m.economictimes.com/news/politics-and-nation/domestic-workers-registration-supreme-court-asks-govt-not-to-give-funds-to-states/amp_articleshow/64404124.cms.

Workmen of Bharat Heavy Vs Union of India And Others, 1992 (3) KarLJ 610.

6. Arbitration Under Bilateral Investment Treaties: An Indian Perspective

R. Swathi[1] and MS. Sharmila[2]

[1]Research Scholar, School of Law, Vellore Institute of Technology, Chennai, India

[2]Associate Professor, School of Law, Vellore Institute of Technology, Chennai, India

ABSTRACT: The law governing foreign investments in the domestic economy is governed by treaties between two nations under which investors of one nation invest in the other, and this is due to the absence of a multi-lateral international framework to govern international investments. Where disputes arise pertaining to such investments, the treaties provide for arbitration as the preferred mode of dispute resolution governed mostly in consonance with the Convention on the Settlement of Investment Disputes between States and Nationals of Other States (ICSID Convention) or the UNCITRAL Arbitration Rules. In the Indian context, the first use of the BIT arbitration mechanism was concerning a retrospective tax provision under the Income Tax Law (Section 9 of the Income Tax Act) relating to the indirect transfer of shares of an Indian entity through the transfer of shares of holding companies abroad.

The proposed paper intends to analyse arbitration as the prescribed mode of resolution of disputes between state-to-state and investor-to-state disputes and further study the impact of bilateral investment treaties on domestic laws and explore the Indian saga of Cairn India BIT arbitration pertaining to retrospective taxation.

KEYWORDS: Bilateral investment treaty, arbitration, retrospective taxation, international framework.

1. INTRODUCTION

'Conflict is inevitable, but combat is optional' – Max Lucade.

Chapter 6 DOI- 10.4324/9781003428213-6

Arbitration has become an increasingly popular mechanism for resolving international investment disputes. This is particularly true in the context of bilateral investment treaties (BITs), which are agreements between two countries that provide protection for foreign investors. BITs typically include provisions that allow investors to bring claims against host governments for alleged violations of the treaty's protections. These claims can be brought before domestic courts or through international arbitration.

Despite these perks, many BITs include provisions that require disputes to be resolved through arbitration. In recent years, there has been a growing body of research on the effectiveness of arbitration as an investment dispute resolution mechanism. This research has generally been positive, with many studies finding that arbitration is a more effective and efficient means of resolving investment disputes than litigation in domestic courts.

For an instance, a 2019 study by the United Nations Conference on Trade and Development (UNCTAD) found that investors were more likely to win cases brought before arbitral tribunals than they were in litigation before domestic courts.

Another study by the International Bar Association (IBA) found that arbitrators tended to have more expertise in investment law and policy than judges in domestic courts.

Despite these positive findings, there are still some concerns about the effectiveness of arbitration as an investment dispute resolution mechanism. One of the main concerns is that arbitration can be seen as favouring investors over host governments, particularly if the arbitrators are perceived as being biased towards investors. Additionally, there are concerns that arbitration can lead to inconsistent outcomes, particularly if different arbitral tribunals interpret BIT provisions differently. This could lead to uncertainty and unpredictability in the outcome of investment disputes.

2. LITERATURE REVIEW

2.1. A Chronological Analysis of Vodafone and Cairn – A BIT-Ter Saga, Aayushi Singh

The current administration's use of retrospective taxation was rejected by Arun Jaitley, India's Finance Minister, from 26 May 2014 to 30 May 2019. He claimed that a permanent law in this area would not be possible and that the costs would be 'too heavy' if any future government undertook such a 'misadventure'. The comment was almost prophetic, considering what would subsequently befall the Indian Government.

The paper considers the rulings in the landmark cases of Vodafone International Holdings v. Government of India and Cairn Energy Plc v. the Republic of India chronologically while attempting to connect the dots between retrospective taxation and violations of the most-favourable-nation and fair and equitable treatment clauses.

2.2. The Constructive Role of General Principles in International Arbitration, Brianna Gorence

The article emphasises on the following:

1. Defining general principles of international law.
2. Illustrate their role, paying particular attention to their particular application in different international law contexts.
3. Ponder on the examples of FET, procedural norms and suspension of performance to show how general principles of international law are used in international arbitration.
4. Explain how they differ from general principles in domestic, public and private law systems.

Gabrielle Kaufmann, Kohler Michele Potesta, *European Yearbook of International Economic Law: Investor-State Dispute Settlement and National Courts*, Current Framework and reform options, 2020. (Switzerland: Springer Nature Switzerland AG)

In addition to WTO Law, External Trade Law for significant trading nations, significant Regional Economic Integration Agreements, International Competition Law, International Investment Regulation, International Monetary Law, International Intellectual Property Protection and International Tax Law, the EYIEL covers all areas of IEL. EYIEL Special Issues often cover specific contemporary problems in International Economic Law in addition to the usual annual volumes.

3. METHODOLOGY

The way to systematically address any research problem is through research methodology. Thus, the researcher proposes to incorporate the doctrinal method/ exploratory method for this research. The collection of material will be from E-library, acts, legislations, court rulings, articles, online and offline literature, books, and web sources. A study involving an analytical and critical approach is desired for this research.

4. ANALYSIS

An outlook on the bigger picture throws light on two inter-connected criticisms that are not in favour of investment treaty arbitration vis-à-vis domestic courts. It is contended that there is no need to confirm an international system to resolve investment disputes as investors reserve their right in any event, in the domestic laws, and such procedures are mostly presumed not established.

Many states have recently invoked principle of primacy of domestic courts over international tribunals in justification of anti-investment arbitration policies. The fundamental issue with parallel hearings is that they frequently result in inconsistent and contradictory legal rulings. Parallel proceedings are against the law, basic procedural rules and the right to a fair trial. It also has an impact on the parties' obligations and rights claims and refuses to grant them adequate judicial redress.

The 2 major cases that illustrated the difficult position of parallel proceedings shall be analysed to understand effectiveness of arbitration in investment treaty disputes.

4.1. Vodafone International Holdings Vs. Government of India – Re-visiting India's Tax Catastrophe

If it was because of the controversial retrospective tax reform or Vodafone's problematic revenue-sharing arrangement, Vodafone's experience in India has been mired in protracted legal battles. When Hutchison Telecommunications International Ltd. ('HTIL') sold CGP Investments to Vodafone International Holdings BV ('Vodafone'), the Vodafone Saga began.

The legal questions in the case concerned whether a transfer of shares between two foreign companies, which effectively transferred Indian assets while also transferring a foreign company's interest held by another foreign company, constituted a transfer of capital assets in India.

According to the Supreme Court, an interpretation of Section 9(1)(i) of the Income Tax Act did not include taxing indirect transfers and hence Hutchison-Vodafone was not liable under that section. Judges Swatanter Kumar, K.S. Radhakrishnan and Chief Justice S.H. Kapadia ruled that the taxpayer, Vodafone International Holdings BV, a Dutch corporation, was not subject to Indian taxation. Justice Radhakrishnan went ahead to note that the Income Tax authorities' demand for capital gains tax would 'amount to imposing capital punishment for capital investment since it lacks the authority of law'.

The Supreme Court noted that interposing investment in Indian companies through a foreign holding company based in the Cayman Islands or Mauritius was typical for tax and business purposes – primarily to avoid the approval and registration processes necessary for direct transfers. It is important to realise that this could inevitably result in hydra-headed evils like double taxation, tax evasion or other forms of tax avoidance.

The Court further went on to draw a distinction between tax evasion and tax planning, noting that this was an actual instance of strategic planning. Instead, the transfer of CGP shares by HTIL to VEL amounted to a transfer of capital assets as defined by Section 2(14) of the Income Tax Act and, as a result, was not subject to the Act's capital gains tax.

A Certificate of Residence provided by Mauritian authorities would be sufficient to establish tax residence and beneficial status under the Mauritius-India Double Tax Avoidance Agreement, according to prior instances. The Supreme Court in McDowell had stated that 'colourable devices cannot be part of tax planning and it is wrong to encourage or entertain the belief that it is honourable to avoid the payment of tax by resorting to dubious methods'. Vodafone continued by stating that the instances do not differ when it comes to issues like a forum, treaty shopping or tax evasion/avoidance.

The 2012 amendment to Section 9(1)(i) of the Income Tax Act resulted in the application of a retroactive tax on previous transactions. The change allowed for the addition of clarifications to the section. According to the clause, the word 'through' could indicate 'by means of', 'in accordance with' or 'by reason of'. The Income Tax Department cleverly issued Vodafone a tax demand for INR 14,200 crore, including taxes totalling INR 7,990 crore with interest. The Income Tax Department updated the tax demand in 2016 to INR 22,100 crore plus interest.

Vodafone BV, a subsidiary of VGP, questioned its legality and invoked Article 4(1) of the India-Netherlands BIT (national treatment and most-favoured-nation treatment) alleging a violation of fair and equitable treatment (FET) standard. India's natural defence, of course, challenged the jurisdiction of the Investment Court mainly because the BIT expressly excluded domestic tax law from FET protection.

However, more than Article 4(1) of the BIT, the heavily debated portion of the BIT was Article 4(4) which stated that the:

'Provisions of paragraphs 1 and 2 in respect of the grant of national treatment and most favoured nation treatment shall also not apply in respect of any international agreement or arrangement relating wholly or mainly to taxation or any domestic legislation or arrangements consequent to such legislation relating wholly or mainly to taxation'. This was criticised to be ambiguous and questionable on multiple grounds.

If, as stated, domestic tax law is solely barred from review for claims based on the national treatment and MFN treatment standard in paragraph 2, the reference to paragraph 1 (which deals with the FET criterion) in Article 4(4) becomes virtually unnecessary. To draw on interpretation principles stated in Article 31(1) of the Vienna Convention on the Law of Treaties, 'good faith' standards might be expanded to fully define the treaty's effect (effet utile). This should immediately extend to paragraph 1, removing domestic tax legislation from the net of fair and equal treatment, as well as comprehensive protection and security measures.

If India had to consider the elimination of tax measures from the jurisdiction of international treaties, then it also has to take steps to incorporate broader provisions in the treaty which cater to the same objective – exactly what Article 4(4) of the BIT failed to do.

The colossal issue is whether a retrospective change to the tax code would violate an investor's right to legitimate expectation. If we should consider the approaches laid down by Occidental and Enron, there must be no change in the legislation that can potentially affect the core of legitimate expectation, directly or indirectly. That being so, a riveting line of contentions can be built if the tribunal's reasoning in Enron is applied to Vodafone.

The retrospective tax was not explicitly targeted at Vodafone as it was a generic amendment. What became the problem was the carefully crafted timing of the legislation which reflected the implicit legal intention seemed absolutely wavering. A reform of the regulatory framework of the host state may, under certain circumstances, violate the investor's legitimate expectation since an investor frequently makes an investment in reasonable reliance on the stability of the regulatory framework of the host state. When the state actively communicates particular statements, guarantees or pledges to the investor at the time of the investment, the investor may have legitimate expectations that are based on those communications. The award demanded the Indian Government to reimburse Vodafone nearly 60% of its legal costs and half the cost borne by it for appointing an arbitrator on the panel. Thus, the liability in this case came around INR 75 crores.

Analogous to this PLC filed an arbitration independent of Cairn Energy PLC and Vedanta Resources, challenging the retrospective amendment of taxation laws, adding fuel to the fire.

4.2. Cairn Energy PLC and Cairn UK Holdings Limited (CUHL) Vs. Government of India

The conflict that Cairn PCA arbitration sparked began in 2006. The parties in question were Cairn Energy PLC (also known as 'CEP') and Cairn UK Holdings Limited (also known as 'CUHL'). The line of transactions resulted from a restructuring of CEP's Indian companies' shares, which were later transferred to CUHL, making CUHL the sole owner of all twenty-seven of CEP's Indian subsidiaries. Then, CUHL transferred these shares to Cairn India Holdings Limited (or 'CIHL'), a Jersey-incorporated subsidiary. Following the incorporation of Cairn India Limited (hence referred to as 'CIL') as a CUHL subsidiary in India, CUHL transferred its ownership of CIHL to CIL, thus (CUHL->CIHL->CIL). In an initial public offering, Cairn India Limited sold 30% of its shares and raised $931 million in December 2006. Vedanta UK acquired 59% of the remaining shares and gave them to Vedanta Limited, its wholly owned company in India. ('VL') After CIL and Vedanta Limited amalgamated in 2017, Cairn Energy received a 5% stake in VL.

An appeal against the proceedings was also initiated, without prejudice to the arbitration proceedings, before the Income Tax Appellate Tribunal. The Tribunal had earlier upheld the tax demand against CUHL in 2017 but did not stress on the imposition of interest thereupon. In the succeeding months of 2017, the Tax Department went forward selling the shares of CUHL in CIL which came up to 98.72 % of CUHL's shareholding in CIL/VL and other seized dividends and preference shares to CUHL.

India's main justification before the Permanent Court of Arbitration rested on its freedom to unilaterally change tax laws and those laws' inadvertent non-arbitrability under a BIT or otherwise. India placed its reliance on an implied exclusion of disputes arising in tax from the BIT in accordance with state practice. Further, India emphasised that in both The Indian and Dutch (Netherlands) transnational public policy, even if the parties consented to present arbitration, matters in taxation cannot be brought under the purview of arbitration under law.

A distinction was drawn by the Tribunal, between a tax dispute and a tax-related investment dispute. The former referred to the taxability of specific transactions and the amount thereunder, while the latter related to the violation of a BIT by a host state's measures related to taxation. A tax dispute concerns the domestic laws of a country and laws of multiple countries when international transactions are under consideration, eventually falling under the scope of a country's domestic laws as well as double taxation avoidance treaties with other countries.The latter would firmly fall under the purview of 'any dispute between an investor of one contracting party and the other contracting party'. The Tribunal adjudicated the dispute in hand to be a tax-related investment dispute. The issue was whether the host state's measure (regardless of its validity under municipal tax laws) was in violation of BIT and the international law obligations thereunder.

India further took a distinctive stance in understanding the UK-India BIT read with the India Double Taxation Avoidance Agreement (DTAA) taking into consideration Article 31(3).

Another barb of consideration was whether a dispute dealing with returns from an investment was taken as a dispute related to the investment since the problem in hand was specifically concerning the earned capital gains of the Claimants through the disinvestment of shares.

The retrospective application of the tax amendments brought in 2012 and the coerced sale of CUHL's shares resulted in invoking Article 3 (fair and equitable treatment, FET) and Article 5 (unlawful expropriation). Violation of Article 7 of the BIT was also raised, due to the restrictions embedded in it with regard to CUHL's right to transfer of remaining shares in CIL. Tantamount to Vodafone, the rudimentary change in taxation law leads to the bereavement of FET and breached the legal stability, predictability and legitimate expectations of the investors. It is widely caved in understanding that when the host state makes a certain administrative decision, the same has to be transparently communicated through notices to the investors concerned with the decisions. The change in the tax regime did not exhibit coherence with procedures being followed by the state.

While drawing nexus with non-enforceability of tax liability imposed on Vodafone and to set in motion action against Cairn succeeding to the enforcement of the 2012 amendments, clearly established the differential treatment candidly strengthening the claim of violation of FET. Thus, the Tribunal held that the retrospective taxation of the transactions carried out in 2006 was grossly unfair and was in violation of FET standards under Article 3 of the BIT.

4.3. The Causatum of Multiple Investment Arbitrations and the Disposition of India

On a more encouraging note, the Taxation Amendment Act, 2021, which sought to invalidate the tax assessments assessed on Cairn in January 2016 and ordered the refund of INR 7,900 crore collected from Cairn, was enacted subject to certain conditions. In order to notify the withdrawal, termination and/or discontinuation of various enforcement activities, Cairn would submit the relevant documents in accordance with Rule 11UF (3) of the Indian Income Tax Rules, 1962.

5. CONCLUSION

This may appear positive, but there are deeper problems that demand addressing. When compared to the carve-out in Article 4(3) of the India-UK BIT cited in Cairn and Vedanta, which was severely curtailed, Article 4(4) of the Vodafone treaty (the India-Netherlands BIT) showed a marginal improvement. The exclusion of claims involving treaty requirements other than MFN or National Treatment is not mentioned in Article 4(3) of the India-UK BIT (expropriation or fair and equitable treatment might still be argued with regard to taxation, for example).

A critical analysis of the Indian Model BIT's framework is required when we discuss arbitral awards in disputes arising out of international investments. Article 2.4 (ii) of the Model BIT stated that the host state's regulatory measures with respect to taxation cannot be adjudged by an investment tribunal. This puts any taxing measure outside the purview of the BIT. Consequentially, investors are handicapped as under no circumstance can they challenge any alteration in the nation's taxation laws, further limiting challenges under DTAA or FTAs. Such exclusion is potentially tricky as it vests the host state with unbridled power. If there is a similar dispute arising in the future, the exclusion ensures that the arbitral tribunal will be deprived of the power to adjudicate. Dismally, the distinction stated in the Cairn Award will have no relevance. From the perspective of investors, it is imperative that upcoming BITs and FTAs include this delineation.

Even though India has offered a compromise on its carelessly chosen taxation tactics through the Taxation Laws (Amendment) Bill, 2021, much more needs to be resolved from our lessons learned from the unfavourable awards to create a better investment treaty regime and a favourable environment for investors.

Overall, while there are some concerns about the effectiveness of arbitration as an investment dispute resolution mechanism, the evidence suggests that it can be a more effective and efficient means of resolving investment disputes than litigation in domestic courts. As such, it is likely to continue to play an important role in the resolution of international investment disputes in the years to come.

REFERENCES

2015. "Misadventure of retrospective taxation will be costly: FM." *Hindustan Times* (May 17 2023). 2296 HYPERLINK "2296%20file:/C:/Users/Hp/Downloads/5Issue1IntlJLMgmtHuman.pdf%20"file:///C:/Users/Hp/Downloads/5Issue1IntlJLMgmtHuman.pdf.

Bung, S. 2022. *Problem with Parallel Proceedings and Need for Embodying the Principles of Lis Pendens and Res Judicata in International Investment Arbitration.* International JL MGMT. & HUMAN.

Chen, C. R. 2021. "The substantive value of diversity in investment treaty arbitration." *Virginia Journal of International Law*, 431. file:///C:/Users/Hp/Downloads/61VaJIntlL431.pdf - substantive value of diversity in investment treaty arbitration.

Gorence, B. 2018. *The Constructive Role of General Principles in International Arbitration.* Leiden: Koninklijke Brill NV. file:///C:/Users/Hp/Desktop/BITs/General%20principles%20in%20int%20arbit.pdf.

Kaufmann, G., and K. M. Potesta. 2020. *European Yearbook of International Economic Law: Investor-State Dispute Settlement and National Courts, Current Framework and Reform Options.* Switzerland: Springer Nature Switzerland AG). www.springer.com/series/8848.

Lohchab, H. 2020. "Telcos, ILDOs spar over international termination rate revenue share." *Economic Times.* (accessed May 18, 2023) https://economictimes.indiatimes.com/industry/telecom/telecom-news/telcos-ildos-spar-over-international-termination-rate-revenue-share/articleshow/73913901.cms?from=mdr.

Paulsson, R. P. M. "Conflict Resolution in a Changing World Order." file:///C:/Users/Hp/Downloads/24TrinityCLRev95.pdf.

Singh, A. "A Chronological Analysis of Vodafone Case – A BIT-tire Saga."

7. A Study of Socio-Political Determinants of NOTA

Dr. Shilpi Sharma
Associate Professor, School of Law, AURO University
Email: shilpi.sharma@aurouniversity.edu.in

ABSTRACT: This research examines the interplay between elections and democracy in India, the world's largest democracy. It emphasises the importance of 'free' and 'fair' elections to maintain electoral integrity. India has faced challenges such as criminalisation of politics, electoral violence, and voter abstention. To protect voter privacy during the transition to electronic voting machines (EVMs), the Supreme Court introduced the 'None of the Above' (NOTA) option in 2013. This research focuses on the determinants of the NOTA voting in India, with a case study in Gujarat. Understanding these factors can shed light on NOTA's potential as a cleansing agent in Indian politics.

KEYWORDS: NOTA, election, voter, Gujarat elections

1. INTRODUCTION

Elections, fundamental in democratic systems, serve as the means to gauge the collective will of the people. In the pursuit of a robust democracy, electoral integrity is paramount, with 'free' and 'fair' elections serving as indispensable components. India, the world's largest democracy, governs its elections through the Representation of the People Act, 1951, and constitutional provisions found in Articles 324 to 329. Conducting elections in a country with a massive electorate presents inevitable challenges. As India's democracy has matured, it has grappled with various electoral issues, including the criminalisation of politics, electoral violence, voter abstention, and bogus voting. To address these concerns, numerous Committees and Commissions have been established to implement reforms and improve electoral processes. In India, the 'Right to Vote' is considered a constitutional entitlement, stemming from Article 326. This right is only meaningful when voters can cast their ballots without fear, coercion, or the compromise of secrecy. To address this, rules such as 41(2), 41(3) and 49-O of the Conduct of Election Rules 1961 were put in place, allowing voters to indicate that they do not support any candidate without revealing their choice to others. However, the introduction of electronic voting machines (EVMs) in 1989

Chapter 7 DOI- 10.4324/9781003428213-7

raised concerns about maintaining the secrecy of votes. In response, the Supreme Court directed the Election Commission in 2013 to include a 'None of the Above' (NOTA) option in EVMs, preserving voter privacy for those who opt not to vote for any candidate. The hope was that this would increase voter turnout and encourage political parties to field cleaner and more efficient candidates. Eight years after the introduction of NOTA in India, some electoral issues persist. The success of NOTA hinges on voter awareness and the myriad factors influencing a voter's decision to use it.

This research aims to explore the determinants of NOTA voting in India, where factors like caste, literacy, emotions and community pressures impact the voting process. Given India's vast size, the study primarily focuses on the state of Gujarat, which has experienced four elections with NOTA up to 2017, making it a suitable case for generalisation. Data collection began before the 2022 Gujarat Assembly elections, and the research relies on data up to the 2017 Assembly elections.

2. THE HISTORICAL ASPECTS OF ELECTIONS

India holds the distinction of being the world's largest democracy, with a strong emphasis on elections as a fundamental aspect of its governance. The Constitution of India places significant importance on elections, dedicating Articles 324 to 329 to the conduct of elections for various positions, including the Parliament, State Legislatures, the President, and the Vice-President. The Parliament is authorised to enact laws related to elections under Article 327, resulting in the Representation of People Act, 1950, the Representation of People Act, 1951, the Presidential and Vice-Presidential Elections Act, 1952, and the Conduct of Election Rules, 1961, with subsequent amendments reflecting evolving socio-political conditions. The historical roots of elections in India date back to ancient times, with examples found in Vedic and Buddhist literature and Hindu polity. Even during the British rule, elections were introduced through legislation like the Indian Council Act, 1909, and subsequent acts in 1919 and 1935.

The turning point in India's electoral history was the Cabinet Mission and the Constituent Assembly, which laid the foundation for electoral democracy. Elections are central to India's democratic ethos, as they serve as the mechanism for the people to choose their representatives. To ensure the sanctity of this process, the responsibility for conducting elections is entrusted to an independent body, the Election Commission. The term 'election' in the Indian context encompasses the entire electoral process, as ruled by the Supreme Court in *N.P. Ponnuswamy v. the Returning Officer*, Namakkal. The Court's judgement emphasised that 'election' includes the complete procedure leading to the selection of a candidate to the legislature. This interpretation has set a precedent for subsequent legal decisions and reinforced the idea that free and fair elections are vital to India's democratic functioning.

3. ELECTORAL CHALLENGES AND REFORMS TILL DATE

A just and impartial electoral process is an absolute necessity for a vibrant democratic system. India, as the world's most extensive democracy, conducts the largest electoral exercise globally. To maintain the integrity of this process and adapt it to evolving political and socio-economic aspirations, constant changes are essential. India's immense size leads to a complex electoral system, with an electorate larger than the combined total of voters in 35 other democracies worldwide. This massive voter turnout demonstrates the faith of the people in the electoral system and political democracy. In light of this privilege, it is the duty of the Election Commission to continuously evaluate the electoral system's functioning, identify challenges, and propose reforms to keep the electoral mechanism dynamic. Several concerns have emerged in the electoral system, including rising election violence, unfair and corrupt practices, unstable governments, defection, and low voter turnout. These challenges necessitate legislative and implementation reforms. The electoral process is considered an ongoing effort to strengthen democracy. To address these challenges, numerous committees and commissions have examined core issues and proposed remedies. These remedies have often involved new legislation or amendments to existing laws, the establishment of independent bodies, and stricter penalties for electoral offences. Some recommendations have been enacted, while others remain on paper. Notable committees and commissions include the Tarkunde Committee, Goswami Committee, Vohra Committee, Indrajit Gupta Committee, National Commission to Review the Working of the Constitution, Election Commission of India, Jeevan Reddy Committee, and the Second Administrative Reforms Committee. Rather than discussing electoral challenges and reforms chronologically, this discussion focuses on the implementation of reforms based on subject matter. The first category of reforms encompasses those achieved through constitutional amendments. Free and fair elections are fundamental to democracy, forming a basic structure of the Indian Constitution. The Constitution entrusts the Election Commission with the responsibility of ensuring the integrity of elections and increased citizen participation. Article 324(2) establishes the structure of the Election Commission, including the Chief Election Commissioner (CEC) and other Election Commissioners (ECs). The Goswami Committee recommended that the removal procedure for ECs should be brought in line with that of the CEC to enhance the independence of the Commission. The independence of the Election Commission can be preserved by charging its expenses to the Consolidated Fund of India, a recommendation made by the Core Committee on Electoral Reforms in 1990 and supported in the 255th Law Commission of India Report. Furthermore, the Core Committee suggested that the Election Commission should have independent authority to select its staff and Secretariat, improving transparency. Regulation of service conditions of the Secretariat by the President currently hinders the transparency of the Commission's operations.

Another essential aspect of electoral democracy is ensuring greater citizen participation, particularly in matters related to the Electoral Roll Challenges and anomalies were observed in this regard, including discrepancies in the right to register between husbands and wives. The 1990 Commission recommended extending this right to husbands residing with their wives at their posting location. Additionally, the Commission recommended specifically including the 'Air Force Act, 1950, and the Navy Act, 1957' in Section 20(8)(b) of the Representation of People Act, 1950, to encompass the subject of the Army Act, 1950 within the definition of 'service qualification.' Election expenses have been a concern in independent India, leading to provisions in the Representation of People Act, 1951. However, the Act did not allow for filing an election petition against someone found guilty under Section 123 but who lost the election. Amendments were proposed to address this gap. The Commission recommended setting expenditure ceilings for teachers', graduates', and local authorities' constituencies similar to those in Assembly and Parliament constituencies.

Lastly, the Commission recommended that candidates from registered parties who replace deceased candidates be allowed additional expenditure under the Conduct of Election Rules, 1961. In 2000, a punishment for filing false affidavits was introduced under Section 125A based on the 170th Law Commission Report from 1999. However, this amendment did not significantly reduce false information. The 244th Law Commission Report recommended further strengthening this provision by increasing the minimum punishment period to two years and eliminating fines as a form of punishment to address the issue of providing false information.

4. NONE OF THE ABOVE

In India, the right to vote is constitutionally guaranteed under Article 326, based on Universal Adult Suffrage. This right has evolved into a fundamental right within the electoral context. The Supreme Court has differentiated between the right to vote (a constitutional right) and the freedom to vote, a fundamental aspect of the freedom of expression under Article 19(1)(a). When a voter chooses to cast their vote, they exercise their fundamental right to free expression, which includes auxiliary fundamental rights such as the right to know a candidate's background. It is the state's obligation to create an environment where people can naturally exercise this fundamental right, which is ensured through the Representation of People Act, 1951. The right to vote freely, without coercion, hinges on the right to maintain vote secrecy, protected by Section 128 of the Representation of People Act, 1951, and related rules. However, this right was compromised when a voter abstained from voting for any candidate. In such cases, the Presiding Officer had to record these voters separately, revealing their choice not to vote for any candidate. Secrecy is essential to ensure voters are unburdened by constraints when exercising their franchise. With the introduction of EVMs, the 'NOTA' option was missing. The Supreme Court directed the Election Commission to include the NOTA button in every EVM, preserving vote secrecy and enhancing citizen participation, which aimed to encourage political parties to nominate better candidates. The concept of NOTA or 'negative voting' is not new and had been proposed in various reports and recommendations. Internationally, several countries, including Sweden, Brazil, Russia, Colombia, Spain, France, Italy, the United States and Canada, have recognised the 'blank ballot' or 'negative vote' option. The Supreme Court's 2013 judgement directed the inclusion of the NOTA option in EVMs, providing voters with a way to express their dissatisfaction with all available candidates. This move aimed to bring systematic reforms to India's electoral system and compel political parties to field cleaner candidates. The introduction of NOTA in the 2014 general elections marked a significant milestone in Indian democracy, allowing voters to reject all candidates if none met their expectations.

5. DATA ANALYSIS

5.1. 'NOTA' in Gujarat

Gujarat, established on 1 May 1960, was carved out of seventeen northern districts of the former Bombay state. It shares borders with Rajasthan to the northeast, Madhya Pradesh to the east, and the Union Territories of Dadra-Nagar Haveli and Daman & Diu to the south. Covering an area of 196,024 square kilometres, it boasts India's longest coastline at 1,600 km and is divided into 33 districts, with Kutch being the largest. South Gujarat encompasses seven districts, including Surat and Bharuch.

According to the 2011 census, Gujarat's population stands at 6.03 crores, constituting 4.99% of India's total population. Urban population makes up 42.6%, with the remaining 57.4% residing in rural areas. Over the decade from 2001 to 2011, there was a shift towards urbanisation, with a population growth rate of 19.17% and a sex ratio of 918.

Gujarat houses a substantial Scheduled Caste (SC) population of 4,074,447 and a significant Scheduled Tribe (ST) population of 8,917,174.

In terms of literacy, 87.23% of males out of 314,832,282 are literate, while 70.73% of females out of 28,901,346 are literate.

Politically, Gujarat has 411 General constituency seats, 84 Scheduled Caste (SC) seats, and 47 Scheduled Tribe (ST) seats out of a total of 542 Lok Sabha seats in 2019. In the 17th Lok Sabha, Gujarat was represented by 26 seats, with 20 in General constituencies, 2 in SC, and 4 in ST constituencies. In the 2017 Legislative Assembly, Gujarat had 182 seats, including 142 in General constituencies, 13 in SC, and 27 in ST constituencies.

As the study is based on the southern part of the State, demographic details of the region covering the major five districts are given in Table 1.

Table 1: District-wise demographic details.

District	Area	Total Population	SC Population	ST Population	Literacy Rate
Surat	7,657 km^2	6,081,322	158,115	856,952	85.53%
Vadodara	7,546 km^2	4,165,626	221,629	1,149,901	78.92%
Navsari	2,196 km^2	1,329,672	35,464	639,659	83.88%
Bharuch	5,246 km^2	1,551,019	62,235	488,194	81.51%
Valsad	2,947 km^2	1,705,678	38,237	902,794	78.55%

5.2. NOTA in Gujarat

Gujarat, a progressive Indian state, has seen two general elections (2014 and 2019) and the 2017 Assembly election with the introduction of the NOTA option. The researcher analysed NOTA votes in Gujarat compared to other states, aiming to determine whether Gujarat leads in NOTA preferences and the reasons behind this. In the 2017 Gujarat Assembly election, some constituencies recorded more NOTA votes than the winning margin. The comparative study included states like Rajasthan, Madhya Pradesh, Maharashtra, Kerala, Assam and Haryana. Rajasthan and Madhya Pradesh were chosen because they were early adopters of NOTA in assembly elections post the 2013 landmark judgement.

Table 2 presents the NOTA vote data in Gujarat and other states for the 2014 and 2019 general elections and previous assembly elections, along with the percentage of NOTA votes. Table 3 offers a comparative view of NOTA usage in Gujarat's Assembly election and other states. The graphic representation below illustrates NOTA votes in these states during the 2014 and 2019 general elections.

Table 2: Percentage of NOTA vote casted in 2014 and 2019 General Election (The Election Commission of India, 2020b).

State	2014 (NOTA/ Total votes)	NOTA Percentage	2019 (NOTA/ Total votes)	NOTA percentage
Gujarat	454,885/ 25,849,655	1.76%	400,932/ 29,128,364	1.38%
Rajasthan	327,911/ 2,713,376	1.21%	327,559/ 32,476,481	1.01%
Madhya Pradesh	391,837/ 29,648,105	1.32%	340,984/ 36,928,342	0.92%

State	2014 (NOTA/ Total votes)	NOTA Percentage	2019 (NOTA/ Total votes)	NOTA percentage
Maharashtra	433,171/ 48,740,403	0.89%	488,766/ 54,111,038	0.9%
Kerala	210,563/ 17,987,124	1.17%	103,596/ 20,397,168	0.51%
Assam	147,057/ 15,092,387	0.97%	178,353/ 17,992,753	0.99%
Haryana	34,220/ 11,501,251	0.30%	41,781/ 12,701,029	(0.33%)

Based on data observations from randomly selected states for this study, it is evident that Gujarat leads in NOTA votes during general elections compared to other states. Although there was a decrease in NOTA voting within Gujarat itself in 2019 compared to 2014, the state still outperformed others in both general elections. The study focused on the southern part of Gujarat, particularly five major districts in the region, to conduct a comparative analysis of NOTA voting. Table 4 illustrates the NOTA votes in these five districts during the 2014 and 2019 general elections and the 2017 assembly elections.

The table reveals varying NOTA percentages in different districts in different years, with notable highs in Valsad District in 2014, Navsari District in 2017 (with Bharuch following closely), and Valsad District again in 2019. Interestingly, these districts with elevated NOTA voting also tend to have a higher proportion of rural population. For example, Valsad has a population of 70.69% rural and 29.31% urban, while Navsari features 24.86% rural and 75.14% urban residents. Even in Navsari, where urban population slightly outweighs rural, this urbanisation is concentrated within the Navsari constituency, while surrounding areas remain predominantly rural. Bharuch comprises 72.47% rural and 27.53% urban residents, whereas Surat boasts a larger urban population at 71.83%, with 28.17% residing in rural areas. Vadodara strikes a balance, with 50.41% rural and 49.59% urban population. This trend implies that NOTA voting is more pronounced in rural areas, possibly because rural residents, with longer-term residence, scrutinise local issues more closely. Respondents in the researcher's survey have also indicated a preference for local issues when voting.

5.3. Literacy Rate and the NOTA

The researcher assumes that only literate individuals opt for NOTA due to their awareness of the option and understanding of the democratic process, allowing them to refrain from electing inefficient representatives. NOTA voting was analysed in light of the literacy rates in the studied districts, based on 2011

Table 3: NOTA votes in assembly elections from 2013 to 2021 (The Election Commission of India, 2020a).

State	NOTA Total Voters						
	2013	2014	2016	2017	2018	2019	2021
Gujarat (2017)				551,594/ 30,015,920 (1.84%)			
Rajasthan (2018, 2013)	589,923/ 30,860,626 (1.91%)				467,988/ 35,672,912 (1.31%)		
Madhya Pradesh (2018, 2013)	643,171/ 33,852,504 (1.90%)				540,673/ 38,137,528 (1.43%)		
Maharashtra (2019, 2014)		483,459/ 52,901,326 (0.92%)				742,135/ 55,150,470 (1.35%)	
Kerala (2016)			107,245/ 20,232,563 (0.53%)				
Assam (2021, 2016)			189,085/ 16,919,364 (1.12%)				219,578/ 19,222,600 (1.14%)
Haryana (2019, 2014)		53,613/ 12,426,968 (0.43 %)				65,672/ 12,520,177 (0.52%)	

Table 4: NOTA in 2014, 2017 and 2019 election ('Assembly Elections 2017' 2017).

District	2014 (NOTA)	2017 (NOTA)	2019 (NOTA)
Surat	10,936/948,383 (1.15%)	35,823/2,614,667 (1.37%)	10,532/1,069,253 (0.98%)
Vadodara	18,053/1,162,168 (1.55%)	28,273/1,694,024 (1.67%)	16,999/1,223,709 (1.39%)
Navsari	9,322/1,161,476 (0.80%)	13,767/717,568 (1.92%)	9,033/1,309,236 (0.69%)
Valsad	26,606/1,123,182 (2.37%)	14,838/848,898 (1.75%)	19,307/1,261,364 (1.53%)
Bharuch	23,615/1,061,060 (2.23%)	15,797/824,912 (1.91%)	6,321/1,150,658 (0.55%)

census data. Table 5 displays literacy rates and NOTA voting in South Gujarat during the 2014 and 2019 general elections. Two graphical representations below depict literacy rates and NOTA voting in both general and assembly elections.

Table 5: Literacy rate and NOTA voting in General and Assembly Elections ('Gujarat Population 2022 | Sex ratio and literacy rate 2023' 2022) (The Election Commission of India, 2020).

District	Literacy Rate	NOTA Voting in General Elections		NOTA Voting in Assembly Election
		2014	2019	2017
Surat	85.53%	1.15%	.98%	1.37%
Vadodara	78.92%	1.55%	1.39%	1.67%
Valsad	78.55%	2.37%	1.53%	1.75%
Bharuch	81.51%	2.23%	.55%	1.91%
Navsari	83.88%	.80%	.69%	1.92%

Examining literacy rates and NOTA voting, it becomes evident that literacy does not significantly impact NOTA choices. Districts with higher literacy rates tend to have lower NOTA voting. Possible factors include awareness that NOTA does not impact the results, strong party or candidate preferences, or a gap between general literacy and political awareness.

5.4. General Voting Behaviour and the NOTA

5.4.1. The Cast Factor

The study delves into the voting behaviour and reasons for opting for NOTA in the surveyed districts. While analysing the national NOTA pattern, it is evident that it is more prevalent in reserved constituencies. Focusing on the research area, the study reveals that reserved constituencies in the districts exhibit higher NOTA voting compared to unreserved ones. For instance, in Surat district, ST constituencies have higher NOTA percentages in the 2017 Assembly elections, with Bardoli constituency breaking this trend by having 2.34% NOTA votes. In Navsari and Valsad districts, reserved constituencies like Vansda, Gandevi, Dharampur, and Kaprada show higher NOTA percentages than unreserved ones. Surprisingly, Vadodara's SC constituency has lower NOTA votes than many unreserved constituencies. The data suggests that caste and class affinity do not significantly influence the voting decisions, as voters in reserved constituencies still opt for NOTA, even if no candidate from their caste or tribe is available. Only 10.2% of the surveyed voters consider caste, community, or religion when choosing a candidate to vote for, based on the data collected by the researcher. This indicates that voters prioritise other factors over caste or class when making their choices.

5.4.2. The Party Factor

India's political landscape reflects strong party–voter loyalty, often overshadowing individual candidate backgrounds and leading to electoral irregularities. This loyalty hinders the use of NOTA, as voters typically favour their chosen party. A study investigated voting behaviour in the surveyed region, revealing that an equal number of respondents considered both party and candidate factors. Nonetheless, most assessed the party's past performance. For those prioritising candidates, the candidate's party affiliation also mattered. Therefore, in voting scenarios where party loyalty prevails, NOTA is less appealing to voters.

5.4.3. The Wave Factor

Indian elections have witnessed waves favouring or opposing political parties, often driven by emotional or issue-based factors. Historic elections like 1977 (anti-emergency wave), 1984 (post-assassination sympathy wave), and 2014 (Modi Wave) are examples. These waves can influence the NOTA use as voters may prioritise party affiliation over candidate backgrounds. In elections without significant waves, voter turnout has generally increased. The study region showed rising turnout in the 2014 and 2019 general elections. Comparing NOTA votes to turnout, there was a decrease in 2019 compared to 2014. Respondents who used NOTA indicated they might not vote if NOTA were not an option. The data does not conclusively link NOTA usage to electoral waves or high turnout in Table 6.

Table 6: Voter's turnout in 2009, 2014 & 2019 General Elections ('Constituency-wise detailed results – General Election 2009' 2018).

District	2009 (Voter's Turnout)	2014 (Voter's Turnout)	2019 (Voter's Turnout)
Surat	49.01%	63.87%	64.58%
Vadodara	49.02%	70.90%	68.18%
Navsari	46.66%	65.78%	66.4%
Valsad	56.11%	74.22%	75.48%
Bharuch	57.14%	74.79%	73.55%

5.4.5. The NOTA Literacy Factor

The Supreme Court's order to introduce the NOTA (None of the Above) option in voting machines emphasised the importance of educating voters about NATO's purpose. Effective use of NOTA relies on voters' understanding. The researcher sought to gauge electoral literacy and specifically awareness of NOTA among voters in the studied region. Most respondents affirmed their knowledge of NOTA when asked. To assess NOTA literacy, the researcher checked if respondents who were aware of NOTA also understood that it does not affect election outcomes. The data showed that out of 204 respondents familiar with NOTA, only 87 knew it does not impact the final election result. This suggests a low level of NOTA literacy among voters. Ignorance regarding NOTA's limited influence may explain why some voters choose it, incorrectly thinking it significantly affects their constituency's election outcome.

6. CONCLUSION

Based on the data collected and analysed, several conclusions can be drawn from this research study.

1. Gujarat demonstrates a higher utilisation of the NOTA (None of the Above) option in general elections compared to other randomly selected states.
2. NOTA usage is more prevalent in rural constituencies than in urban areas, primarily due to higher population mobility in urban settings.
3. The research does not establish a clear correlation between the literacy rate of the region and NOTA voting in the state.
4. While there is a higher incidence of NOTA usage in reserved constituencies, there is no definitive evidence to conclude that caste plays a significant role in either general voting behaviour or NOTA voting.

5. In voting patterns where loyalty to a political party is prominent, NOTA is less preferred by voters. No concrete evidence supports the idea that NOTA positively impacts voter participation.
6. There was a decrease in NOTA voting in the 2019 elections compared to 2014, but the available data does not allow us to conclude whether high voter turnout due to wave phenomena leads to increased NOTA voting.
7. The research highlights a low level of NOTA literacy among voters, which influences the utilisation of the NOTA option.

Given the lack of definitive factors for NOTA voting and the relatively low NOTA percentages, the study suggests maintaining NOTA as an option in EVMs, serving as a guarantee for voters to express their rejection of all candidates, consistent with the fundamental right of free expression. Enhanced electoral education programs by the Election Commission of India could potentially make NOTA a tool to increase voter participation, aligning with the principles of a healthy democracy.

REFERENCES

Election Commission of India (2017). "Assembly Elections 2017," https://eci.gov.in/assembly-election/ae-2017/.

Election Commission of India (2018). "Constituency wise detailed result - General Election 2009," https://eci.gov.in/files/file/2857-constituency-wise-detailed-result/.

Election Commission of India (2020a). "NOTA votes in Assembly Elections from 2013 to 2021," https://eci.gov.in/general-election/general-election/.

Election Commission of India (2020b). "Percentage of NOTA vote casted in 2014 & 2019 General Election," https://eci.gov.in/general-election/general-election/.

Population Census (2011). "Gujarat population 2022 | sex ratio & literacy rate 2023," 2022. https://www.census2011.co.in/census/state/gujarat.html.

8. Influence of International Environmental Norms in Domestic Laws: Indian Experience

Aneesh V. Pillai
Assistant Professor, School of Legal Studies, Cochin University of Science and Technology, India

ABSTRACT: The global attention towards the conservation and maintenance of the natural environment has only surfaced in recent years. The Stockholm Conference in 1972 is considered as a major milestone in the development of international norms for protection of environment. In the aftermath, the international community has established multiple norms with the objective of safeguarding and enhancing the environment. The Stockholm Declaration, the Montreal Protocol, WCED Report, Rio Declaration, Biological Diversity Convention, etc. are noteworthy international agreements and declarations that have significantly contributed to the field of environmental governance. These influential documents have played a pivotal role in shaping global environmental policies and promoting sustainable development practices. Though most of these norms do not set forth specific obligations as well as non-binding, nonetheless, they have influenced the domestic legal framework of various states. The effectiveness of international regulations designed to protect and preserve the natural environment is contingent upon the degree to which states adhere to these norms and their subsequent integration into national legal systems. Thus, it becomes crucial to comprehend the magnitude of influence exerted by these international environmental norms on different states, enabling the formulation of new legislation and the revision of existing laws, thereby attaining the ultimate objective of such international norms. This study aims to explore the impact of international environmental norms on the formulation of domestic legislation in India. It also investigates the role of the judiciary in interpreting and expanding the reach of existing laws based on these global norms.

KEYWORDS: Environment, treaties, biodiversity, judiciary, stockholm, incorporation

Chapter 8 DOI- 10.4324/9781003428213-8

1. INTRODUCTION

The emergence of worldwide awareness regarding the safeguarding and preservation of the natural environment is a recent occurrence. The Stockholm Conference held in 1972 is considered a pivotal moment in the establishment of international norms for environmental protection. Following this, the international community has developed a range of standards to safeguard and improve the environment. The Stockholm Declaration, the Montreal Protocol, WCED Report, Rio Declaration, the Biological Diversity Convention, etc. are notable international agreements that have played a significant role in shaping environmental policies and promoting sustainable development. These influential documents have provided a framework for addressing pressing environmental issues and have guided nations towards a more harmonious relationship with the natural world. Despite the absence of specific obligations and their non-binding nature, these norms have significantly impacted the domestic legal systems of different states. It is widely acknowledged that the adoption of globally agreed norms does not automatically result in their incorporation into domestic legislation (Thilakarathna and Jayarathna, 2021).

The triumph of numerous global norms established to safeguard and preserve the natural environment is reliant on the response of states to these norms and their integration into their domestic policies. Hence, it is necessary to know how far these international environmental norms influence in different states for making new laws and modifying existing laws thereby achieving the ultimate goal of such international norms. This chapter endeavours to analyse the significant influence of international environmental norms on the domestic laws of India. The first part of this chapter examines the relationship between Indian law and international law. The latter part of this chapter scrutinises the impact of international environmental norms on the Indian legal system.

2. INTERNATIONAL NORMS AND DOMESTIC LAWS

The relationship between international norms and domestic laws of different states has always been fundamental in analysing the influence of international laws into their domestic laws (Chandra, 2017). Upon a state's expression of consent to participate in a treaty, the manner in which the treaty's provisions will be implemented within its domestic sphere becomes a matter of inquiry. The integration of customary international laws into municipal law has similarly been a topic of examination within numerous judicial institutions (Baker, 2010). According to the fundamental tenets of international law, it is incumbent upon states to uphold both customary and treaty laws, and they are compelled to ascertain their application through their legal, executive and judicial establishments (Erasmus, 1989/90). Nevertheless, international law does not proffer any directives on the manner in which these obligations should be assimilated into domestic law by states. The discretion to make suitable determinations based on their sovereignty and internal circumstances rests solely with individual states, resulting in significant disparities among them when it comes to the implementation of international obligations (Marian, 2010). Thus, the relationship between customary and treaty law in international law and municipal law poses a classic challenge within the field of international law. The recognition and application of international law within domestic legal systems depend on whether the rules of international law are automatically incorporated into municipal law, thereby directly affecting citizens and the courts, or if a process of transformation is necessary (Schaffer, 1983). Theoretical examinations of this issue typically revolve around the theories of monism and dualism, with different legal scholars contributing to the discussion (Jackson, 2008).

Eminent jurists, including Emile Durkheim, Leon Duguit, Kelsen, Kunz, Scelle, Verdross and Wright, have extensively discussed the theory of monism. According to this theory, all rules of international law ultimately govern the behaviour of individuals. However, the challenge lies in attributing the consequences of such conduct to the State in the international arena (Mutubwa, 2019). These scholars argue that both in the international and municipal spheres, law functions as a command that binds individuals regardless of their will (Brochard, 1990). Consequently, municipal law and international law are not fundamentally distinct but rather constitute a unified normative order. The binding force of municipal law is derived from the delegation of authority from international law. As a result, both legal systems share common sources and subjects (Schaffer, 1983).

In contrast to the concept of monism, proponents of dualism argue that international law and municipal law are distinct and separate entities. Notable figures such as Tripel, Anzilotti and Oppenheim have championed the theory of dualism (Gaja, 1992; Starke, 1936). According to this theory, international law and municipal law consist of separate sets of legal norms, originating from different sources, applying to different subjects and pertaining to different objects (Margolis, 1995). Dualists contend that international law is not applicable to individuals but rather exclusively addresses states. As sovereign entities, states possess the authority to make decisions that best suit their interests without interference from other states, and international law exerts minimal or no control over municipal law. Professor Oppenheim asserts that "international law and municipal law are fundamentally distinct bodies of law that share no common ground, except for their classification as branches of the legal system" (Bochard, 1940). Dualists argue that while international law is based on the collective consent of multiple states, domestic law relies solely on the unilateral consent of a single state. Consequently, international law establishes rights and obligations among states, and each individual state determines how it adheres to these obligations (Shyllon, 2018). Therefore, environmental norms endorsed by dualist states do not become enforceable until they are incorporated or transformed into domestic law. It is worth noting that the practices of states regarding the relationship between international law and municipal law demonstrate that both monism and dualism hold practical significance and are not merely theoretical constructs. Countries such as Austria, Chile, China, Colombia, Egypt, France, Germany, Japan, Mexico, the Netherlands, Poland, Russia, South Africa, Switzerland, Thailand and the United States adhere to the theory of monism, while Australia, Canada, India, Israel and the United Kingdom adopt the dualist stance.

3. INTERNATIONAL NORMS AND DOMESTIC LAWS: INDIAN CONTEXT

The presence of a written Constitution in a State plays a significant role in determining the status of international law within its municipal legal system. In the context of the Indian Constitution, the relevant provisions pertaining to this matter can be found in articles 51, 53, 73, 77, 246, 253, and Entries 10–19 of List I (Union List) of the Seventh Schedule. Article 51(c) specifically highlights that the State has an obligation to undertake measures to promote adherence to treaty obligations and other international law. It is important to note that the term "state" as used in Article 51 corresponds to the definition provided in Article 12, which includes not only the Government and Parliament of India but also the respective governments and legislatures of all the States, as well as any local or other authorities under the control of the Government of India (Alexander, 1952). Within the Indian context, legislative powers are divided between the Central Government and the state governments through three lists outlined in the seventh schedule. Therefore, when the Central Government accepts an international obligation through a treaty, the concerned states in India possess the authority to enact appropriate legislation or measures to implement the treaty's provisions. However, it is important to highlight that if the Central Government chooses not to be a party to a particular treaty, the state governments in India lack the competence to enact legislation for the implementation of associated international norms.

According to the Constitution, the executive branch of the government holds the authority to engage in treaty-making and other international agreements, as stated in Articles 53, 73 and 77. Conversely, the power to enact laws pertaining to matters listed in the Union List of the Seventh Schedule is exclusively vested in the Parliament, as per Article 246. Specifically, Entries 10–19 of the Union List enumerate the matters that hold significance under international law. Additionally, Article 253 grants the Parliament the power to enact laws for the implementation of treaty obligations within the territory of India. Despite these provisions addressing certain aspects of international law, the precise position of international law within India remains unanswered. Nevertheless, the Indian judiciary has provided clarity on this matter through various judicial decisions. Notably, the Indian Courts have distinguished between customary international law and treaty international law when applying them to domestic law. The judiciary has explicitly declared that customary international law forms an integral part of the legal framework in India. In the case of Vellore Citizens Welfare Forum v. Union of India and Ors (AIR, 1997), the Court acknowledged that "the rules of customary International Law which are not contrary to the municipal law shall be deemed to have been incorporated in the domestic law and shall be followed by the Courts of Law".

The Court's observation in the Jolly George Varghese case (AIR, 1980) regarding international treaties emphasised that the positive commitment of States Parties does not automatically make the International Covenant enforceable in India's legal system. However, the Supreme Court's approach was slightly modified in the ADM, Jabalpur v. Shiv Kant Shukla case (AIR, 1976), where it was stated that any provision that conflicts with the Constitution cannot be enforced in India. The subsequent Gramophone Co. of India v. Birendra Bahadur Pandey case (AIR, 1984) clarified that international law rules can be accommodated in municipal law without express legislative sanction, as long as they do not conflict with Acts of Parliament, in accordance with the comity of nations.

It has been observed in the case of Vishaka & Ors v. State of Rajasthan & Ors (AIR, 1997) that international conventions and norms should be incorporated into domestic law in the absence of any conflicting enacted domestic law. This principle of judicial construction has been widely accepted and recognised in India, where international law is considered to be equivalent to domestic law as long as there is no inconsistency between them. Indian courts may also refer to international conventions as an external aid for the interpretation of national legislation, whenever necessary. Furthermore, it is a fundamental principle of statutory interpretation in Indian domestic law that statutory provisions must be interpreted in a manner consistent with India's international obligations (SCC, 1995).

The Stockholm Conference played a crucial role in shaping the environmental frameworks in India. Following the UN Conference on Human Environment, the Central Government established a committee on Human Environment under the leadership of Dr. Pitambar Pant. Based on the recommendations of this committee, the National Committee on Environmental Planning and Co-ordination (NCEPC) was established in the Department of Science and Technology in February 1972 (Dwivedi, 1997). This led to the creation of the Department of Environment by the Ministry of Science and Technology, which was later transformed into the Ministry of Environment and Forests in 1985 (Pachhauri, 2012). In 2014, recognising the significance of climate change mitigation and related measures, the Ministry of Environment and Forests was renamed as the Ministry of Environment, Forest and Climate Change (Sharam, 2018).

Within two years of the Stockholm Conference, the Water (Prevention and Control of Pollution) Act, 1974 was enacted by the Central Government in order to address the issue of water pollution and ensure the preservation and restoration of water quality. In 1976, the Constitution of India underwent an amendment through the 42nd Amendment Act, which introduced two specific provisions aimed at safeguarding the environment. Firstly, Article 48A imposes a duty on the state to protect and conserve the environment, forests and wildlife within the country. Secondly, Article 51A (g) imposes a fundamental duty on all citizens to protect and enhance the environment, including its various components such as wildlife, forests, rivers and lakes. Additionally, it emphasises the importance of showing compassion towards all living beings. Consequently, this constitutional amendment established a responsibility for both citizens and the state to protect and improve the natural environment. As a result of this constitutional obligation and the influence of international environmental instruments, India has developed a comprehensive environmental legal framework. These developments can be categorised into two main areas: legislative initiatives and the role of the judiciary.

4. LEGISLATIVE INITIATIVES

India, like numerous other nations, has demonstrated its consent by voluntarily ratifying or officially signing international agreements to incorporate various international norms into its domestic legislation. Consequently, the Indian Government has implemented a range of legislations and policies to establish an environmental governance framework that aligns with international environmental standards. One notable legislation, enacted directly influenced by an international treaty, is the Air (Prevention and Control of Pollution) Act of 1981. The primary objective of this Act is to establish a legal framework for the prevention, control and reduction of air pollution. It was enacted as a means for India to fulfil its responsibilities outlined in the Stockholm Declaration, particularly in relation to the regulation of air pollution and the preservation of air quality. Subsequently, to fulfil its obligations under the Stockholm Conference, India enacted the Environment (Protection) Act of 1986, which aims to provide a legal framework for the protection and enhancement of the environment.

The CITES, 1973, also known as the Convention on International Trade in Endangered Species of Wild Fauna and Flora, has had a significant impact on the legal framework in India. Its primary objective is to prevent the extinction of wild animals and plants resulting from international trade in their specimens. India signed and ratified this Convention in July and October 1976, respectively. Consequently, the responsibility of managing CITES in India was assigned to the Director of Wild Life Preservation. To aid in the implementation of CITES, the Ministry of Environment and Forests established a CITES Cell in 2010. Furthermore, the Wildlife Protection Act, 1972 and the Customs Act, 1962 were modified to align with the provisions of CITES.

The Basel Convention, 1989, also referred to as the Basel Convention on the Control of Transboundary Movements of Hazardous Wastes and their Disposal, aims to safeguard human health and the environment from the adverse effects of hazardous and other wastes. As a result of this Convention, the Government of India introduced several rules and regulations under the Environment (Protection) Act, 1986. These include the Hazardous Wastes (Management & Handling) Rules, 1989; Bio-Medical Wastes (Management and Handling) Rules, 1998; Recycled Plastics (Manufacture and Usage) Rules, 1999; Environment (Sitting for Industrial Projects) Rules, 1999; and the Municipal Solid Wastes (Management and Handling) Rules in 2000. The Convention on Biological Diversity, 1992, establishes an international framework for the conservation of biological diversity, the sustainable use of its components, and the fair and equitable sharing of benefits derived from the utilisation of genetic resources. To create a legal framework for the conservation and sustainable utilisation of biological diversity, India has taken various measures.

The mandatory insurance established by the Public Liability Insurance Act, 1991 serves as an immediate relief for victims of accidents resulting from hazardous activities. Principle 13 of the Rio Declaration on Environment and Development, 1992 emphasises the need for national laws regarding liability and compensation for victims of environmental damage, which the Public Liability Insurance Act, 1991 fulfils by providing a legal framework for claiming compensation in certain situations. The National Environment Tribunal Act, 1995 was enacted to ensure strict liability for damages caused by handling hazardous substances and to establish a National Environment Tribunal for efficient disposal of related cases. In 2010, the National Green Tribunal Act replaced NETA, establishing a new body for speedy disposal of environmental cases and providing different reliefs. The combined impact of the Water Act, Air Act, Environmental Protection Act, Biological Diversity Act and National Green Tribunal Act demonstrates India's commitment to fulfiling its obligations under international treaties.

5. ROLE OF INDIAN JUDICIARY

The Indian Judiciary has been recognised for its proactive stance in safeguarding the environment and natural resources. In instances where the political or executive branches of the government have failed to fulfil their duty to protect the environment, the judiciary has demonstrated its concern towards the environment. Through its proactive role, the judiciary has embraced international environmental norms for the preservation and protection of the environment and natural resources in the country. Notably, the Indian Judiciary has adopted several significant international environmental norms, including Sustainable Development and intergenerational equity, Public Trust Doctrine, Polluter Pays Principle and the Precautionary Principle. In the case of Rural Litigation and Entitlement Kendra and Others v. State of Uttar Pradesh and Others (AIR, 1987), the judiciary in India acknowledged the concept of sustainable development. The Court emphasised that while natural resources must be utilised for social development, it is crucial to exercise caution and care to prevent any adverse impact on the environment and ecology. The Court further emphasised the importance of long-term planning to ensure the preservation of national wealth, which is a permanent asset of mankind and not intended to be exhausted in one generation.

The concept of intergenerational equity asserts that the natural environment of our planet is a shared resource among all members of the human species, including past, present and future generations. As present members of society, we are entrusted with the responsibility of preserving the earth for future generations while also benefiting from its use. This means that the present generation, acting as a trustee, has the right to utilise the natural resources that constitute trust property (Singh, 2005). The Supreme Court of India has upheld this principle in various cases, including State of Himachal Pradesh vs. Ganesh Wood Products & Ors (SCC, 1995) and Bombay Dyeing & Mfg. Co. Ltd. v. Bombay Environmental Action Group (SCC, 2006).

The Public Trust Doctrine, an ancient legal theory developed by the Roman Empire, holds that certain common properties such as rivers, seashores, forests and the air are held in trusteeship by the government for the use of the common man. As such, the State is legally obligated to protect natural resources as a trustee (Mehta, 1997). The Supreme Court of India has recognised the public trust doctrine as part of its jurisprudence, as seen in the case of M. C. Metha v. Kamal Nath (SCC, 1997). Through this doctrine, the Court has reaffirmed the State's duty to safeguard natural resources.

The principle of intergenerational equity emphasises that the natural environment of our planet is a shared resource among all members of the human species, including past, present and future generations. As present members of society, we are entrusted with the responsibility of preserving the earth for future generations while also benefiting from its use. This means that the present generation, acting as a trustee, has the right to utilise the natural resources that constitute trust property (Singh, 2005). The Supreme Court of India has upheld this principle in various cases, including State of Himachal Pradesh vs. Ganesh Wood Products & Ors (SCC, 1995) and Bombay Dyeing & Mfg. Co. Ltd. v. Bombay Environmental Action Group (SCC, 2006). The Public Trust Doctrine, an ancient legal theory developed by the Roman Empire, holds that certain common properties such as rivers, seashores, forests and the air are held in trusteeship by the government for the use of the common man. As such, the State is legally obligated to protect natural resources.

The precautionary principle, rooted in Principle 15 of the Rio Declaration, emphasises the widespread application of the precautionary approach by States to safeguard the environment, taking into account their respective capabilities. It asserts that when there are potential threats of significant or irreversible harm, the absence of complete scientific certainty should not serve as a justification for delaying cost-effective measures aimed at preventing environmental degradation. The Indian Supreme Court has also embraced this principle, albeit with certain modifications. In the case of Indian Council for Enviro-Legal Action v. Union of India (JT, 1996), the Court elucidated that this principle has given rise to the distinctive burden of proof in environmental cases, wherein the onus lies on those seeking to alter the existing state of affairs to demonstrate the absence of detrimental effects resulting from their proposed actions (AIR, 1996).

The Polluter Pays principle posits that when an activity is inherently hazardous or dangerous, the individual responsible for carrying out such activity is legally obligated to compensate any other person who suffers losses as a result, regardless of whether reasonable care was exercised during the activity (JT, 1996). This principle has been acknowledged as a binding tenet in the case of Indian Council for Enviro-Legal Action v. Union of India (JT, 1996). It is noteworthy that both the precautionary principle and the Polluter Pays principle are recognised as customary international law. Given India's adherence to the theory of monism in matters pertaining to customary international law, these principles are considered integral components of the domestic legal framework. This perspective was affirmed by the Supreme Court in the case of Vellore Citizens Forum v. Union of India (SCC, 1995), which held that once these principles are acknowledged as part of customary international law, their incorporation into domestic law poses no difficulty.

6. CONCLUSION

India actively participates in international discussions on the protection of environmental law. As a result, the country responds pragmatically to international environmental norms. One significant response by India is the incorporation of environmental concerns into its Constitution, making them a part of the law of the land. This amendment was made immediately after the Stockholm Conference, making India the first country to include environmental concerns in its Constitution. The participation in the Stockholm Conference and other international conferences has raised awareness about the importance of environmental protection, leading to the enactment of various legislations in India, such as the Water Act, Air Act, Environmental Protection Act, Biological Diversity Act and more. The judiciary in India has also played an active role in citing international environmental norms to protect and preserve the environment when necessary. Therefore, it is evident that India fully recognises and acknowledges international environmental norms, regardless of the different approaches to the relationship between international law and municipal law.

REFERENCES

ADM, Jabalpur v. Shiv Kant Shukla, AIR 1976 SC1207.

Alexander, C. H. (1952). International law in India. *The International and Comparative Law Quarterly*, 1(3), 289–300.

Baker, R. B. 2010. Customary international law in the 21st century: old challenges and new debates. *European Journal of International Law*, 21 (3), 173–204.

Bombay Dyeing & Mfg. Co. Ltd. v. Bombay Environmental Action Group, 2006(3) SCC 434.

Chandra, A. (2017). *India and international law: Formal dualism, functional monism. Indian Journal of International Law,* 57 (1), 25–45.

Dwivedi, O. P. (1997). India's environmental policies, programmes and stewardship. 1st ed., New York: St. Martin's Press.

Erasmus, G. (1989/90). The Namibian constitution and the application of international law. *S. Afr. Y.B. Of Int'l Law*, 15, 81.

Gaja, G. (1992). Positivism and dualism in Dionisio Anzilotti. *EJIL*, 3, 123–138.

Gramophone Co. of India v. Birendra Bahadur Pandey, AIR 1984 SC 667.

http://www.eurocapacity.org/downloads/Consolidation_and_Devolution_final.pdf (accessed June 27, 2023)

Indian Council for Enviro- Legal Action v Union of India, J.T. 1996 (2) 196.

Jackson, P. T. (2008). Foregrounding ontology: dualism, monism, and IR theory. *Review of International Studies*, 34 (1), 129–153.

Jolly George Varghese v. Bank of Cochin, AIR 1980 S.C. 470

M. C. Metha v Kama Nath, 1997(1) SCC 388.

Marian, B. (2007). The Dualist and Monist Theories: International Law's Comprehension of these Theories. *The Juridical Current*, 1-2, 16–27.

Mehta, G. S. (2017). Role of traditional practices in conserving environment: a case of Manesar Village. *IOSR-JHSS*, 22 (11), Ver 10, 10–16.

Mutubwa, W. (2019). Monism or dualism: The dilemma in the application of international agreements under the South African Constitution. *Journal of CMSD*, 3(1), 27–37.

Official website, (July 6, 2018, 10.00 pm.). http://www.moef.nic.in/division/ international-conventions (accessed June 27, 2023)

Official website, (July 6, 2018, 10.00 pm.). https://www.cites.org/eng/disc/what.php (accessed June 27, 2023)

P.N. Krishanlal v. Govt. of Kerala, (1995) Sup. (2) SCC 187.

Pachhauri, S. (2012). *Environmental Education*. 1st ed. London: Pearson.

Rural Litigation and Entitlement Kendra and Others v. State of Uttar Pradesh and Others, AIR 1987 SC 359.

Sandholtz. (2015). How domestic courts use international law. *Fordham International Law Journal*, 38, 595.

Sarma, Dr. Nimisha. (2015). Environmental Awareness at the Time of Vedas. *Veda-Vidyā*, 26, 221–224.

Schaffer, R. P. (1983). The inter-relationship between public international law and the law of South Africa: an overview. *Int'l & Comp.* L.Q. 32, 277–283.

Sehrawat, V. (2021). Implementation of international law in Indian legal system. *Florida Journal of International Law,* 31 (1), Article 4.

Shyllon, Ololade O. Monism/Dualism or Self Executory: The Application of Human Rights Treaties by Domestic Courts in Africa www.web.abo. fi/instut/.../Shyllon_Monism%20 Dualism%20or%20Self%20 Executory.pdf (accessed June 27, 2023)

Singh, Gurdeep.2005. *Environmental Law in India.* MacMillan India: New Delhi.

Sloss, D. Domestic application of Treaties. http://digitalcommons.law.scu.edu/ facpubs/635 (accessed June 27, 2023)

Starke, J. G. (1936). Monism and Dualism in the Theory of International Law. *Brit. Y.B. Int'l L.* 17, 66–81.

State of Himachal Pradesh v. Ganesh Wood Products & Ors, 1995(6) SCC 363.

Thilakarathna, K. A. A. N., and Jayarathna, N. (2021). Theories involved in recognizing and implementing international law in domestic contexts. *Journal of Law, Policy and Globalization*, 109, 80–85.

Vellore Citizens Forum v. Union of India, (1996) 5 SCC 647.

9. Green Collar Crime – A Quest for Environmental Criminal Jurisprudence

Shrabana Chattopadhyay
Assistant Professor, Department of Law, IEM-UEM, Kolkata, India
Email: shrabana.uem@gmail.com; Orcid Id: 0000-0001-7648-6535
Dr. Ripon Bhattacharjee (Corresponding Author)
Assistant Professor, National Law University, Tripura, India
Email: ripon.bhattacharjee69@gmail.com

ABSTRACT: Development ruined the planet. Global and Indian green collar crime exists nowadays. Environmental and animal crimes are green collar crimes. India punishes green collar crime the same as other offences. Unusual circumstances are involved. Crimes should trump civil law. Enterprises and factories should be prosecuted for most environmental crimes. Can Environmental Criminal Law fix the ecological imbalance generated by hazardous waste from numerous economic sources and the callousness of the perpetrators? The article analyses the current criminal law framework and extra-legal data on investigation agency and trial court pendency rates, charge-sheeting, conviction and acquittal rates and sentence trends. Detailed wildlife crime trends are investigated. This analysis supports the creation of a separate environmental criminal law jurisprudence.

KEYWORDS: Green collar crime, criminal liability, ineffective investigation agency, need for environmental criminal jurisprudence

1. INTRODUCTION

There are exceptions to India's 45-year-old environmental criminal statute. Law and academia oppose it. Attention shows that trial court decisions rarely reach higher courts. Moti Lal v. Central Bureau of Investigation, AIR 2002 SC 1691; Sansar Chand v. State of Rajasthan (2011) 10 SCC 604; and Manoj Kumar Upadhyaya v. State of Andhra Pradesh, Cr. indicate that higher courts rarely investigate legal ideas that may have affected environmental crimes Appeal Environmental law was decided by the Supreme Court in civil cases. Legal schools teach Apex Court civil law theory in environment law. Environmental criminal law is taught less than civil law theory. Environmental crime law in India is new.

Chapter 9 DOI- 10.4324/9781003428213-9

Environmental offences are crimes that contain criminal procedure. Environmental crimes include wildlife trafficking, ozone-depleting substance and hazardous waste smuggling, illicit, unregulated, unreported fishing, unlawful logging and wood trading (UNICRI, 2021). These crimes reduce living standards, disrupt nature and challenge whether 'rule of law' works in any government.

Any act that decreases a person's 'right to life' harms it without official regulation. Mute animal, unknown secondary victim, or faceless victim without cypher 'right to life' damage may also be unlawful. Unsupervised behaviour that reduces life quality violates 'right to life'. Who should be criminally accountable for affecting a mute (animal), unknown (secondary victim), or faceless (water bodies or glaciers) victim's 'right to life' without it? Environmental crimes affect multiple generations, making victim identification difficult. Air pollution is illegal. Industrial air pollution was not dangerous for years. Environmental crime rarely harms, while air pollution kills hundreds of life (Perappadan, 2021). Stigma makes governments and police ignore 'victimless' and low-priority crimes (Review of Environmental Crime: A Threat to Future, 2021).

This study investigates how seriously Indian law enforcement addresses environmental offences. Environmental crimes in India centre on wildlife. Without animal activists, wildlife crime victims are unrepresented. Bird and animal traffickers operate globally. According to the WCCB website, Myanmar and Bangladesh dominate worldwide animal and component trafficking. The low arrest risk and big cash incentive entice criminals. EIA, an international environmental NGO, found billions in wildlife. Ecocrime is profitable, thus organised crime targets it. Interpol estimates billions in wildlife crime, whereas measuring environmental crime is difficult. WCCB, EIA and UNEP enforce environmental crimes, while WTI, PETA and WWF protect animals. Environmental justice implies applying laws and regulations equally regardless of race, ethnicity, or money. Morally and ethically, environmental law, regulation and policy should include all races, colours, nationalities and incomes. This study examines species-protecting environmental crime enforcement.

2. JURISPRUDENCE OF ENVIRONMENTAL CRIME

In the 'socio-legal approach', civil jurisdiction is emphasised, while 'environmental criminal law' focuses environmental offences. Civil and criminal environmental damage reduction methods differ. Civil environmental law uses 'polluter-pays', 'precautionary principle' and 'public trust doctrine'. Specific actions are punished under environmental crime.

Ecology crimes have many traits. The Supreme Court has repeatedly upheld the right to a fair trial, the assumption of innocence and the burden of proof in criminal proceedings. Rule of law affects environmental crime. The law alone can punish the defendant, protect his constitutional rights and administer the suitable penalty. Environmental criminal law procedure and penalties are examined in this research.

Crimes are punished by retribution, deterrence, or recompense. Criminal justice should seek retribution or deterrence, while civil justice tackles environmental law compensation. The culprit should suffer like the victim, thus punishment should match. Environmental neglect causes unidentified grief. Individual and environmental damage is hard to quantify. Thus, environmental crime penalties go beyond revenge. Although more research is needed, deterrent penalty appears to be the only environmental criminal law investigation alternative.

Punishment deters criminals. H.L.A. Hart believes 'the fundamental focus of punishment should be deterrence and other consequentialist goals', but the well-known principles that only the criminally guilty should be punished and that punishment should match the crime should limit specific punishment. 'Due process of law' should govern environmental offences. The Indian criminal justice system addresses environmental crime. Like all criminal laws, this one is rational and fair (Hart and Gardner, 2009).

3. ENVIRONMENTAL CRIMINAL LAW IN INDIA: EXPLORING ITS APPLICABILITY

The Wildlife Protection Act (1974), Air (Prevention and Control of Pollution) Act (1974), Water (Prevention and Control of Pollution) Act (1981) and Environment Protection Act (1986) prohibit environmental harm in India. This restriction must be tightened as environmental risks rise. So these laws won't help.

Timely trials, the rule of law, environmental justice and punishment deterrence are examined in this study. These issues are fixed: Environmental experiments typically last how long? Time of trial affects environmental justice? Does punishment or a swift trial dissuade environmental criminals? Some are unanswered.

The post answers with wildlife crime data. Environmental criminals' conviction and acquittal rates were examined in this study.

3.1. Status of Reporting of Offences under Various Laws for Protection of the Environment

After a crime has been reported, the criminal justice system is immediately put into action. The informant's knowledge and comprehension of the crime must be accepted as truthful and correct by law enforcement at all times. At the time of reporting, the informant's account of events is taken as truthful, and his knowledge of the topic is assumed to be accurate. Table 1 provides data on environmental infractions that have been reported.

Table 1: List of offences under various laws for protection of the environment.

Year	Number of Environmental Offences (Including Wildlife Offences)		Number of Offences Committed to Wildlife		Total Arrest	
	Number of Offences	Crime Rate	Number of Offences	Percentage of Offences Against Environmental Laws	Offences Against Environment	Offences Against Wildlife
2021 (NCRB, 2021)	64471	4.7	615	0.95	65381	1208
2020 (NCRB, 2020)	61767	4.6	672	1.08	60263	1096
2019 (NCRB, 2019)	34671	2.6	618	1.8	36237	1087
2018 (NCRB, 2018)	35196	2.7	782	2.2	37408	1295
2017 (NCRB, 2017)	42143	3.3	826	2	40720	1497

Source: National Crime Records Bureau.

As per Table 1, NCRB reported 64,471 environmental crimes in 2021 (CRIME IN INDIA – 2021). It covers offences under the Indian Forest Act, Forest Conservation Act, Wildlife Protection Act, Environmental Protection Act, Air (Prevention & Control of Pollution) Act, Water (Prevention & Control of Pollution) Act, Cigarette & Other Tobacco Products Act, Noise Pollution Acts and National Green Tribunal From 2017 to 2020, 42,143 reports were filed, 35,196 in 2018, 34,671 in 2019 and 61,767 in 2020. Crime rates grew from 3.3 in 2017 to 2.7 in 2018, 2.6 in 2019, 4.6 in 2020 and 4.7 in 2021. Two times as many incidents as 2017, 42,143 and 64,471. Around 5,000 reports were made annually before 2017. NCRB reports did not cover environmental violations until 2016. The NCRB began tracking Cigarette and Other Tobacco Products Act violations in 2016, however that changed in 2017.

Within five years (2017–2021), wildlife crimes have decreased. In 2017, 828 wildlife crimes occurred, 782 in 2018, 618 in 2019, 672 in 2020 and 615 in 2021. Animal offences remained 2% of environmental crimes. Wildlife crimes may have fallen slower than other environmental crimes. Thus, wildlife crime reporting may not be affected by environmental crime reporting reductions.

Since reporting is the first step in criminal proceedings, accurate records of all incidences are essential. Without reliable instance reporting, charging and conviction/acquittal rates cannot be statistically evaluated. The NCRB published an environmental violation book in 2017. Environmental crime statistics were poorly kept until recently, according to the NCRB.

Since reporting is the initial step in criminal proceedings, all incidents must be recorded accurately. Statistical study of charge-sheeting or conviction/acquittal rates requires instance reporting. Since 2017, NCRB has charged environmental offences separately. The NCRB discovered that environmental crime reporting records were poorly preserved until recently.

3.2. Status of Disposal of Cases by Investigating Agency

Since reporting is the initial step in criminal proceedings, keeping detailed records of all incidents is crucial. Without reliable instance reporting, charging and conviction/acquittal rates cannot be statistically studied. The NCRB created an environmental violation book in 2017. The NCRB noted that environmental crime reporting statistics were poorly kept until recently.

Table 2: List of disposal of cases by investigation agency.

	Disposal of Cases by Investigation Agency					
	Number of Cases where Charge not Framed Because of Insufficient Evidence Though the Case was Genuine		Rate of Charge-Sheet		Rate of Pendency of Cases	
Year	No. of Cases	Wildlife	No. of Cases	Wildlife	No. of Cases	Wildlife
2021 (NCRB, 2021)	850	66	98.1	90.4	65.4	91.7
2020 (NCRB, 2020)	459	70	98.9	82.7	22	35.5
2019 (NCRB, 2019)	310	68	98.6	84.2	17.9	30.8

Year	Disposal of Cases by Investigation Agency					
	Number of Cases where Charge not Framed Because of Insufficient Evidence Though the Case was Genuine		Rate of Charge-Sheet		Rate of Pendency of Cases	
	No. of Cases	Wildlife	No. of Cases	Wildlife	No. of Cases	Wildlife
2018 (NCRB, 2018)	493	91	98.1	82.8	15.2	28.1
2017 (NCRB, 2017)	389	96	98.4	83.6	13.9	27.3

Source: National Crime Records Bureau.

After receiving a criminal complaint, the investigative agency investigates and reports about the crime. The investigation may find no crime, a crime with sufficient evidence to prove the accused's guilt or a crime with inadequate evidence despite investigators' best efforts. As per Table 2, NCRB records suggest wildlife crimes may not be prosecuted due to insufficient evidence. Wildlife offences accounted for 7.76% (66) of the 850 insufficient evidence reports in 2021; 2018: 18.4% (91 out of 493), 2019: 21.9 percent (68 out of 310) and 2020: 15.2% (70 out of 459).

Among all environmental offences, wildlife infractions averaged 7% between 2021 and 2017. Insufficient evidence exists in ~32% of inquiry scenarios. International animal crimes may explain weak evidence collecting. Indian authorities cannot enter the nation to obtain evidence or question witnesses if wildlife is unlawfully exchanged and moved over the border.

Charge-sheet data from the investigating agency are in this table. The charge-sheet rate per case currently undergoing investigation is calculated by dividing the two numbers by the total number submitted in a year. A slow charge-sheet pace indicates a lengthy investigation. Wildlife infractions have a lower charge-sheet rate than other environmental offences, according to NCRB data. In 2017, it was 83.6 compared to 98.4, in 2018, 82.8 compared to 98.1, in 2019, 84.2 compared to 98.6, in 2020 82.7 compared to 98.9 and in 2021 90.4. Thus, wildlife crimes take longer to investigate than other environmental offences. Because wildlife crime is global or intriguing, the investigation may take longer than intended. If the victim cannot talk and the crime was committed in a remote region, witnesses will be difficult to find. The police department's pendency rate is high, however wildlife crimes were charged at 90.4 percent in 2021, up from 83.6 percent in 2017.

This allegation is supported by the investigative agency's pendency rate. The 'pendency rate' is the percentage of cases open a year later. A case is closed when the investigating agency issues its final report. The investigative agency must suggest that the Magistrate close the case if the offence did not occur or if no proof was found. NCRB data show that wildlife offences take longer to prosecute than other environmental crimes. It was 27.3 compared to 13.9 in 2017, 28.1 to 15.2 in 2018, 30.8 to 17.9 in 2019, 35.5 to 22.0 in 2020 and 91.7 to 65.4% in 2016.

3.3. Status of Disposal of Environmental Criminal Cases by the Trial Court

After the investigating agency submits its report, the magistracy must ensure that justice is served quickly without compromising criminal law. This section shows trial court resolutions.

Table 3: List of disposal of environmental criminal cases by the trial court.

Year	Disposal of Environmental Criminal Cases by the Trial Court					
	Total no of Pending Cases		Total no of Cases Where Conviction Awarded		Total Number of Cases, Compounded	
	Total	Wildlife	Total	Wildlife	Total	Wildlife
2021 (NCRB, 2021)	65.4	91.7	98	54	71	0
2020 (NCRB, 2020)	N/A	87.8	N/A	59.7	22	0
2019 (NCRB, 2019)	61.4	92.9	95.8	54.9	180	0
2018 (NCRB, 2018)	60.7	93	95.9	60.8	109	2
2017 (NCRB, 2017)	58.5	88.1	96.3	65.5	51	0

Source: National Crime Records Bureau.

In comparison to all environmental offences, NCRB data (Table 3) show that trial courts have a higher rate of wildlife law violation cases pending. It was 88.1 compared to 58.5 in 2017, 93.1 to 60.7 in 2018, 92.9 to 61.4 in 2019, 87.8 to 85.9 in 2020 and 91.7 to 65.4 in 2021. Wildlife crime recidivism is predicted to be ~90% from 2017 to 2021. After the matter is presented to the trial court, the investigation delay cannot be used to postpone the trial. A delayed trial may lower the conviction rate due to witnesses being absent, their examination being postponed, or their recollections deteriorating, making them untrustworthy. Considering the inverse relationship between 'pendency rate' and 'conviction rate' confirms the fact. The low pendency rate (61.4% in 2019, 85.9% in 2020 and 65.4% in 2021) directly affects the higher conviction rate (95.8 in 2019, 80.1 in 2020 and 98.0 in 2021).

Wildlife law violations have a lower conviction rate than environmental crimes, according to NCRB data: only 65.5% in 2017, 60.8% in 2018, 54.9% in 2019, 57% in 2020 and 54.0% in 2021. Instead, all environmental infractions were 96.3% in 2017, 95.9% in 2018, 95.8% in 2019, 80.1% in 2020 and 98.0% in 2021.

Fewer wildlife crime cases were compounded or settled in plea bargains, according to NCRB statistics. Compounding 51, 109, 180, 22 and 71 environmental offence cases in 2017, 2018, 2019, 2020 and 2021 indicates a trend. These offences were either not compounded or not documented before that time.

The Wild Protection Act's Proviso provision in Section 54 prohibits compounding an offence punishable by Section 51. A Central or State Government official having the necessary power can compound a crime, subject to the Proviso clause of said Section. The preceding data suggest that wildlife crimes should also be compoundable due to the rising rate of environmental offences being compounded. More convictions will result. The criminal justice system never seeks conviction, but it will have a bigger influence on environmental justice.

In court-supervised plea negotiating, the prosecution drops charges in return for a guilty plea. This strategy reduces wait times and ensures justice, even if it seems doubtful. Section 265-A76 of the Code of Criminal Procedure allows plea negotiations for crimes punishable by up to seven years in jail. The Wild Life Protection Act allows plea negotiating for crimes with a seven-year maximum sentence. The prosecution should identify cases with inadequate evidence against the accused to facilitate plea discussions. According to section 265-C of the Code, the trial court judge must ensure that both parties plead willingly. It ensures environmental justice is speedy.

Table 4: Data on determination of the accused by the court.

Year	Determination of the Accused by the Court					
	No. of Discharged Cases		No. of Acquittal Cases		No. of Conviction Cases	
	Total no. of Cases	Wildlife	Total no. of Cases	Wildlife	Total no. of Cases	Wildlife
2021(NCRB, 2021)	53	10	878	145	45,068	182
2020 (NCRB, 2020)	51	3	624	96	24,951	94
2019 (NCRB, 2019)	251	48	1,695	139	31,496	205
2018 (NCRB, 2018)	220	8	1,474	119	31,290	268
2017 (NCRB, 2017)	227	5	1,664	231	32,888	329

Source: National Crime Records Bureau.

The date in Table 4 shows that Wildlife cases yielded 18.86% (145 of 873) acquittals in 2021, according to NCRB data. In 2020, it was 15.38% (96 of 624), in 2019, 8.07% (119 of 1,474), in 2018, 13.8% (231 of 1,664) and in 2017, 9.6%. The conviction rate was 0.40% (482 out of 45,068), 0.38% (94 out of 24,951 in 2020), 0.6% (205 out of 31,496 in 2019), 0.8% (268 out of 31,290 in 2018) and 0.01% (329 out of 32,888 in 2017).

According to the pattern, wildlife violations are less likely to result in a conviction than other environmental offences. Wildlife offences have a higher arrest and acquittal rate than other environmental offences, but a lower conviction rate. One would also think a faster inquiry would strengthen the prosecution's case and increase convictions.

3.4. Present Extent of Sentence Awarded by the Trial Courts

Justice is served when the guilty are proved guilty and punished accordingly. The legislation prescribes penalty based on the type and severity of the offence, but the trial court judge must evaluate the case's facts and circumstances. Giving the trial judge such discretion is part of a legislative goal to guarantee that criminals receive fair and proportionate punishments for their cases. Environmental criminal law's punitive mechanism is meant to deter criminals, hence trial courts' environmental crime sentences should be examined. Trial court verdicts on wildlife violations are the focus of this article's inquiry.

Table 5: Extent of sentences awarded by the courts.

Present Extent of Sentence Awarded			
Number of cases	57		
Number of convicted	154		
	Award of Sentence		**Fine Imposed**
	(Convicted persons in number —191)		(Convicted persons in number —191)
Extent of Sentence	**Crimes with Imprisonment up to 3 years**	**Crimes with Imprisonment up to 7 years**	**Crimes with Maximum Fine of Rs. 25,000/-**
Maximum (number of convicted people)	46 (46%)	13 (14%)	0
Less than maximum sentence (number of convicted people)	53 (53%)	79 (86%)	191 (100%)
Total	79 (100%)	82 (100%)	191 (100%)

Source: National Crime Records Bureau.

Table 5 summarises 57 wildlife trial court judgments. Trial courts have penalised 154 defendants in these 57 judgements 191 times. A total of 191 punishments affected 154 convicted parties. Prisoners receiving sentences and fines outnumber prisoners due to their multiple crimes. The Wildlife Crime Control Bureau's website provided information on lower court rulings (*List of Convicts in Wildlife Cases* 2021).

Even though the maximum term for the detainees' crimes was three years in prison, only 46% of the detention orders were that long. This number reduces to 14% when a seven-year sentence is possible. Only 14% of sentence rulings in such cases were for the maximum 07-year prison term, demonstrating that trial judges are more careful when sentencing such crimes.

Despite the high profits in illegal wildlife trading, trial courts have never given maximum sanctions. Trial courts consider non-crime factors while sentencing. Criminal history, age and court conduct determine a defendant's fine. In Swarn Singh v. State of Punjab (1978) 10 SCC 111, the Supreme Court ruled that a fine or compensation must consider the crime's seriousness, the victim's injuries, the compensation claim's legitimacy, the defendant's financial capabilities and other factors. In Hari Singh v. Sukhbir Singh & Ors., AIR 1988 SC 2127; Surendra Pal Shivbalakpal v. State of Gujarat (2005) 3 SCC 127; and Sushhil Kumar v. State of Punjab (2009) 10 SCC 434, the Supreme Court stressed socioeconomic position in sentencing.

In illegal wildlife trading, middlemen connect the killer to the highest bidder. Global elites profit from illegal wildlife trade. Interestingly, the foreign trader does not kill a scheduled animal or bird. He bought wildlife products from a middleman who paid a destitute tribe member to kill them. Brokers sold foreigners goods.

The main illegal merchant is rarely caught, suggesting impoverished local tribal are more likely. This evidence supports (i) considering the offender's socioeconomic position when deciding sanctions and (ii) imposing minor fines. The convict's past may support this. This was possible only by digging through case files.

4. CONCLUSION

The 'nature' of environmental crime is unique. Environmental crimes are unrelated to society, family, or feelings. Like theft, avarice may drive it. Animal and bird slaughter is never motivated by anger or sexual desire. Industrial, automotive and water pollution are also 'nature'-specific offences. It covers community-wide crimes. These factors imply academics and attorneys must separate environmental law and policy. This has been our practise for decades.

Indian civil law courts have tightened environmental laws in recent decades. Environmental civil law is explained by Supreme Court opinions. No criminal case law exists for environmental breaches, thus courts and investigators cannot aid. Without structure or guidelines, trial court judges rarely punish environmental violations seriously. Environmental crimes are punished less. The study found that greater charge-sheet rates and lower investigation and trial pendencies increase convictions.

Current environmental laws transcend government rules. The new legislation enable courts try and sentence offenders like other crimes. Environmental criminal law doctrine helps trial courts and investigators accomplish environmental justice. Environmental criminal laws from decades ago are becoming increasingly essential.

REFERENCES

Hart, H. L. A., and John Gardner (2009). *Punishment and Responsibility: Essays in the Philosophy of Law*. Oxford; New York: Oxford University Press, pp. 8–13.

Nayak, R.S. v. A.R. Antulay, AIR 1984 SC 684.

Perappadan, Bindu Shajan (2021). *1.7 Million Deaths Were Attributable to Air Pollution in India in 2019* (blog) March 11, 2021. https://www.thehindu.com/news/national/17-million-deaths-in-india-were-attributable-to-air-pollution-in-2019.

Rabindra Kumar Dey v. State of Orissa, AIR 1977 SC 170.

Review of Crime in India (2017). https://ncrb.gov.in/en. New Delhi: National Crime Records Bureau. https://ncrb.gov.in/uploads/nationalcrimerecordsbureau/custom/1653885719_Crime%20in%20India%202017%20-%20Volume%202_0_1.pdf.

Review of Crime in India (2018). https://ncrb.gov.in/en. New Delhi: National Crime Records Bureau. https://ncrb.gov.in/uploads/nationalcrimerecordsbureau/custom/1653734519_Crime%20in%20India%202018%20-%20Volume%202_1_0.pdf.

Review of Crime in India (2019). https://ncrb.gov.in/en. New Delhi: National Crime Records Bureau. https://ncrb.gov.in/uploads/nationalcrimerecordsbureau/custom/1653730632_CII%202019%20Volume%202.pdf.

Review of Crime in India (2020). https://ncrb.gov.in/en. New Delhi: National Crime Records Bureau. https://ncrb.gov.in/uploads/nationalcrimerecordsbureau/custom/1653720991_CII%202020%20Volume%202.pdf.

Review of Crime in India (2021). https://ncrb.gov.in. New Delhi: National Crime Records Bureau. https://ncrb.gov.in/uploads/nationalcrimerecordsbureau/post/1679310741CII2021Volume2.pdf.

Review of Environmental Crime: A Threat to Future (2021). *Environmental Impact Agency*. https://www.unodc.org/documents/NGO/EIA_Ecocrime_report_0908_final_draft_low.pdf. ISBN: 0-9540768-5-0

Review of List of Convicts in Wildlife Cases (2021). *Wildlife Crime Control Bureau*. http://wccb.gov.in/Content/Convicts.aspx.

Sidharam Satlingappa Mhetre v. State of Maharashtra & Ors., (2011) 1 SCC 694.

Singh, Hari v. Sukhbir Singh & Ors., AIR 1988 SC 2127

Surendra Pal Shivbalakpal v. State of Gujarat, (2005) 3 SCC 127,

Sushhil Kumar v. State of Punjab, (2009) 10 SCC 434,

State of Rajasthan v. Abdul Mannan, (2011) 8 SCC 65,

Swarn Singh v. State of Punjab, (1978) 10 SCC 111,

UNICRI (2021). Review of *Environmental Crimes*. March 11, 2021. http://www.unicri.it/topics/environmental.

10. Examining the Role of the Supreme Court in Imparting Environmental Justice in India while Implementing the Polluter Pays Principle

Anjum Dadasha Shaha

Assistant Professor, School of Law, Auro University, Surat & Research Scholar at The Post Graduate Teaching Department of Law, Ph.D. Cell, RTMNU, Nagpur. Email: advanjumshaha@gmail.com

Adhara Deshpande

Assistant Professor, RTMNU's Dr. Babasaheb Ambedkar College of Law, Nagpur, Maharashtra

Email: dradharadeshpande@gmail.com

ABSTRACT: The protection of the environment is an essential part of the protection of human rights in India. The right to live in a pollution-free environment is not only protected under Article 21 of the Constitution of India but also protected under International Human Rights Law across the globe.

The Honourable Supreme Court of India has invoked several principles of justice to protect the Indian environment from being degraded. Among these principles, the Polluter Pays Principle stands supreme in not only protecting the environment but also in punishing the polluters.

The present paper tries to examine the approach of the Indian Supreme Court towards the protection of the environment. An empirical study, from the year 2003 to 2022 of the judicial decision pronounced by the Supreme Court ensuring environmental justice in India by invoking the principle of Polluter Pays, has been conducted. The efforts taken by the National Green Tribunal to curtail environmental pollution and penalise polluters also need to be appreciated.

The researchers have raised concern over the large quantum of pollution being generated in India, which is constantly damaging the pristine environment. The present empirical study draws attention towards the urgent necessity to use the Polluter Pays Principle by the Judiciary and the Authorities in curbing the fast-growing pollution levels of our country and to cause a deterrent effect by heavily punishing the polluters in order to bring back the serenity of the environment.

Chapter 10 DOI- 10.4324/9781003428213-10

KEYWORDS: Environment, human rights, Polluter Pays Principle, sustainable development, Supreme Court

1. INTRODUCTION

The Polluter Pays Principle is an environmental principle that asserts that the party responsible for producing pollution or environmental damage should bear the costs associated with it. In other words, those who pollute or harm the environment should pay for the negative impacts they cause. The principle is an offshoot of the Sustainable Development principle and is based on the idea that polluting activities impose secondary costs on the society, such as expenses incurred on health issues, restoration of the degraded environment, and the need for clean-up or remediation efforts. The Polluter Pays Principle seeks to internalise these costs by making the polluters financially responsible for the damage they cause. By doing so, it aims to encourage industries and individuals to adopt cleaner and more sustainable practices.

The implementation of the Polluter Pays Principle can take various forms depending on the specific context and the legal framework of a country. It may involve the imposition of fines, taxes, fees, or liability in the form of obligations on polluters. These financial measures are intended to create a deterrent effect on polluters so that they reduce their emissions and/or invest in pollution control technologies. The principle of Polluter Pays is often incorporated into environmental policies and regulations at national and international levels. It is seen as a way to promote the environmental responsibility and sustainability by shifting the burden of pollution from society as a whole to the entities responsible for its creation.

2. ORIGIN OF POLLUTER PAYS PRINCIPLE

The Polluter Pays Principle is considered as a fundamental concept in environmental law and economics. The origin of the Polluter Pays Principle can be traced back to the early 1970s when it emerged as a guiding principle in international environmental discussions. It gained significant attention and support following the United Nations Conference on the Human Environment held in Stockholm in 1972. The Stockholm Conference highlighted the growing concern over environmental issues and the need for global cooperation to address them. One of the key outcomes of the conference was the adoption of the Stockholm Declaration, which emphasised the responsibility of nations to protect and improve the environment. Within the Stockholm Declaration, Principle 16 stated: 'National authorities should endeavour to promote the internalisation of environmental costs and the use of economic instruments, taking into account the approach that the polluter should, in principle, bear the cost of pollution, with due regard to the public interest and without distorting international trade and investment.' This principle laid the foundation for the

Polluter Pays Principle, asserting that the party responsible for pollution should bear the costs associated with it. The idea behind this principle was to incorporate the environmental costs of pollution into economic decision-making processes and promote sustainable development. Since the Stockholm Conference, the Polluter Pays Principle has been widely recognised and adopted by many countries and international bodies as a fundamental principle of environmental law and policy. It has been incorporated into various international agreements and treaties, prominent among which is the Rio Declaration on Environment and Development (1992). Rio Declaration not only reaffirmed Polluter Pays Principle but further developed the principle making it stricter.

The Polluter Pays Principle originated from the growing awareness of environmental issues and the need for a fair and sustainable approach to addressing pollution and its impacts on society and the environment. This principle has been applied in various cases around the world to address environmental damage and hold polluters accountable for their actions.

The Polluter Pays Principle has been applied in several areas such as:

2.1. Oil Spills

In cases of major oil spills, such as the Exxon Valdez oil spill in 1989 and the Deepwater Horizon oil spill in 2010, the principle of Polluter Pays Principle had been invoked and the responsible parties were required to pay for the clean-up costs, compensate the affected communities, and to restore the environment.

2.2. Industrial Pollution

The principle was applied to industries that released pollutants into the air, water, and soil. Governments and regulatory agencies often impose fines, fees, or taxes on polluting industries to internalise the environmental costs and encourage pollution control measures. For instance, the European Union's Emissions Trading Scheme (EU ETS) has been imposing a cap-and-trade system on greenhouse gas emissions, where companies are required to purchase allowances for their emissions.

2.3. Waste Management

The Polluter Pays Principle is often used in waste management practices. Governments are authorised to impose taxes or fees on producers, importers, or retailers of products that generate significant waste that is difficult to recycle. These financial measures incentivise waste reduction, recycling and the development of more sustainable product designs.

2.4. Environmental Damage Assessments

The principle of Polluter Pays is applied in assessing the damages caused by pollution or environmental harm. When a polluting incident occurs, experts evaluate the extent of the damage and calculate the costs associated with it. The responsible party may then be required to compensate for the damages, such as in cases of chemical spills or contamination of natural resources.

2.5. Carbon Pricing

Carbon pricing mechanisms, such as carbon taxes or cap-and-trade systems, are examples of the Polluter Pays Principle applied to greenhouse gas emissions. By putting a price on carbon emissions, these policies aim to incentivise emission reductions and promote cleaner energy sources.

It is important to note that the application of the Polluter Pays Principle can vary depending on the legal frameworks and policies of different countries. The specific mechanisms and implementation methods may differ, but the underlying principle remains the same: those responsible for pollution should bear the costs and take responsibility for their actions.

3. PATH BREAKING CASES AND JUDGEMENTS ON POLLUTER PAYS PRINCIPLE

3.1. Bhopal Gas Tragedy (1984)

Following the devastating industrial accident at the Union Carbide pesticide plant in Bhopal, India, legal proceedings took place to determine liability and compensation. The Polluter Pays Principle played a significant role in holding Union Carbide Corporation accountable for the disaster and the subsequent environmental damage (Satinath, 2002).

3.2. Prestige Oil Spill (2002)

The Prestige was an oil tanker that sank off the coast of Spain, causing one of the largest oil spills in European waters. Spain pursued legal action against the ship's owner and the classification society responsible for certifying the vessel's seaworthiness. The case involved applying the Polluter Pays Principle to hold the responsible parties liable for the environmental and economic damages caused by the spill (Castanedo, 2006).

3.3. Minamata Disease Case (1956–1968)

Minamata Disease is a neurological disorder caused by methylmercury poisoning. The Japanese company Chisso Corporation was found responsible for discharging mercury into the Minamata Bay, leading to widespread contamination and health impacts. The case highlighted the importance of the Polluter Pays Principle in holding industries accountable for their pollution and compensating affected communities (Yorifuji, 2014).

3.4. Costa Concordia Shipwreck (2012)

When the cruise ship Costa Concordia ran aground off the coast of Italy, causing environmental damage and loss of life, legal proceedings ensued to determine liability and compensation. The case involved applying the Polluter Pays Principle to hold the ship's operator responsible for the environmental and socio-economic impacts of the accident (Andrea, 2016).

3.5. Vellore Citizen Case

The Vellore Citizen Case, also known as the Vellore Environmental Pollution Case, is a landmark environmental litigation in India. The case was filed in 1996 by the Vellore Citizen's Welfare Forum, an environmental organisation, against various industries and the Tamil Nadu Pollution Control Board (TNPCB). The litigation primarily focused on the issue of industrial pollution in the Vellore district of Tamil Nadu. The Vellore Citizen's Welfare Forum alleged that several industries in the Vellore district were causing severe pollution, including air and water pollution, leading to detrimental health effects on the local population and damage to the environment. Pollution was attributed to factors such as untreated effluents, emissions from industrial chimneys, and improper waste management practices (Choudhary, 2019).

The Vellore Citizen Case played a pivotal role in establishing important legal precedents and guidelines for environmental protection in India. It emphasised the Polluter Pays Principle and the constitutional right to a clean environment, reinforcing the responsibilities of industries to prevent pollution and bear the costs associated with environmental degradation.

This case contributed to the development of environmental jurisprudence in India and set a precedent for subsequent environmental litigation in the country. It showcased the role of citizen activism in holding polluting industries accountable and promoting environmental justice. These examples illustrate how the Polluter Pays Principle has been invoked in various legal cases to assign responsibility, seek compensation, and promote environmental accountability.

Several environmental pollution cases invoked various legal provisions, including the constitutional right to a clean and healthy environment and the principle of 'strict liability' for industries causing pollution. The Polluter Pays Principle was also cited as a guiding principle in seeking compensation and remedial measures. The Supreme Court of India took up the case and issued several significant directives and judgments. The court ordered the closure of certain polluting industries, the installation of pollution control devices in others, and the strict enforcement of environmental regulations by the TNPCB.

4. THE NATIONAL GREEN TRIBUNAL AND POLLUTER PAYS PRINCIPLE

The Green Tribunal, officially known as the National Green Tribunal (NGT), is a specialised judicial body in India that handles cases related to environmental protection and conservation. It was established in 2010 under the National Green Tribunal Act. The NGT has been instrumental in applying and enforcing the Polluter Pays Principle in various environmental cases. It plays a crucial role in ensuring that polluters are held accountable for their actions and that the costs of environmental damage are internalised.

4.1. Here's How the NGT and the Polluter Pays Principle are Interconnected

4.1.1. Adjudicating Environmental Cases

The NGT has the authority to hear cases related to environmental pollution and degradation. It addresses issues such as industrial pollution, waste management, air and water pollution, deforestation, and more. In these cases, the NGT often relies on the Polluter Pays Principle to determine liability and impose penalties on polluters.

4.1.2. Imposing Fines and Compensation

The NGT has the power to impose fines, penalties, and compensation orders on polluting industries or entities found to be in violation of environmental laws and regulations. These financial measures aim to ensure that the polluters bear the costs of environmental damage and restoration, as per the Polluter Pays Principle.

4.1.3. Remedial Measures

The NGT can order specific remedial measures to be undertaken by the polluters to mitigate environmental damage and prevent further harm. This can include the installation of pollution control devices, implementation of environmental management plans, or adoption of cleaner production techniques – all in line with the Polluter Pays Principle.

4.1.4. Environmental Compliance and Monitoring

The NGT oversees the compliance of industries and entities with environmental norms and standards. It plays a role in monitoring their activities and ensuring that they adhere to pollution control measures. By doing so, it upholds the principle of the Polluter Pays by holding polluters responsible for meeting environmental requirements. The NGT serves as an important institution for the application of the Polluter Pays Principle in India. It plays a significant role in adjudicating environmental disputes, imposing penalties, and promoting environmental justice by enforcing the principle that those who pollute should bear the costs of pollution.

The Polluter Pays Principle states that those responsible for pollution should bear the costs associated with it, aiming to promote environmental responsibility and sustainability. It holds industries, individuals, and entities accountable for the negative impacts they cause, using fines, fees, taxes, liability obligations, or compensation orders. Originating from the 1972 UN Conference on the Human Environment, the principle is recognised and adopted in international agreements and national laws. Courts and environmental tribunals, like India's National Green Tribunal, enforce the principle through legal proceedings, penalties, and ensuring compliance. The principle applies to industrial pollution, oil spills, waste management, and environmental damage assessments, guiding liability determination, environmental justice, and internalising pollution costs.

4.2. Here is How the NGT and the Polluter Pays Principle are Interconnected

Table 1 depicts the statistical data of the last 20 years, i.e. from 2003 to 2022.

Table 1: Cases decided by the Supreme Court from 2003 to 2022.

Year	Total reported cases of SC	Total Environmental Law cases	Polluter Pays Principal Cases of the SC	Year	Total reported cases of the SC	Total Environmental Law cases
2003	1,369	14	4	2003	1,369	14
2004	1,213	14	6	2004	1,213	14
2005	941	15	3	2005	941	15
2006	1,229	31	5	2006	1,229	31
2007	1,561	20	1	2007	1,561	20
2008	2,825	22	1	2008	2,825	22
2009	2,218	22	6	2009	2,218	22
2010	1,381	15	8	2010	1,381	15
2011	1,271	26	8	2011	1,271	26
2012	849	22	9	2012	849	22
2013	1,077	22	7	2013	1,077	22

Source: Author's compilation.

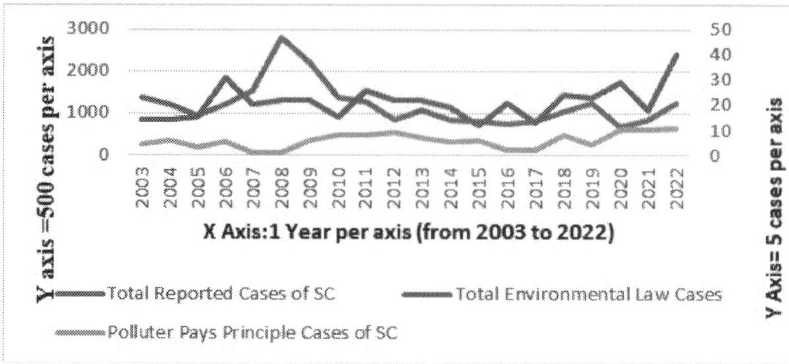

Figure 1. *Graphical representation of the cases decided by the Supreme Court (2003–2022). Source: Author's compilation.*

The abovementioned data and graph indicate that very few cases have been decided on the issue of environmental pollution. The data reflects the apathy of people towards environmental protection. It has been observed that very few cases are filed every year in the Apex court with regard to polluted air, water and environment. For curbing pollution mostly writ petitions are filed either in High Court or Supreme Court. When the matter is grave, of national importance or affects many people, public interest litigations are filed in the Apex Court. Green Tribunals also play a large role in containing pollution in India as they too are delivering strong and bold judgements. But the recent trend reveals that people are indifferent towards environmental protection and have a lethargic approach in filing cases. Out of the total reported cases of the Supreme Court (which includes appeals from High Courts and National Green Tribunal), only a handful are pertaining to environmental protection. This makes it clear that people, in general, are not bothered about the air, water, soil and the environment around them. They have either compromised with the conditions of the environment surrounding them or are simply not concerned about it being polluted. As the courts are overburdened by the cases probably, they have no time to take suo-moto cognizance of the growing pollution levels in India.

The data published by the Central Pollution Control Board speak volumes about the pitiful and deplorable conditions of the Indian environment. According to the 2021 World Air Quality Report, India is home to 63 of the 100 most polluted cities, with New Delhi named the capital with the worst air quality in the world. The study also found that PM2.5 concentrations – tiny particles in the air that are 2.5 micrometres or smaller in length – in 48% of the country's cities are more than 10 times higher than the 2021 WHO air quality guideline level (Martina, 2023). The Air Quality Index (AQI) data over the period of the last 20 years shows a steep decline in the air quality of various cities in India. Vehicular and industrial emissions along with thermal power stations and stubble burning contribute heavily towards air pollution. According to the data published by World Bank in 2021, the air pollution levels in India are among the highest in the world, posing a heavy threat to the country's health and economy. Around 1.4 billion of India's people are exposed to unhealthy levels of ambient PM 2.5. Constant exposure to this level of pollution can cause deadly illnesses such as lung cancer, stroke, and heart disease. Ambient and indoor air pollution is estimated to have caused 1.7 million premature deaths in India in 2019. The health impacts of pollution have also created a heavy cost to the Indian economy. Lost labour income due to fatal illness from PM 2.5 pollution in 2017 was in the range of $30–78 billion, equal in magnitude to about 0.3–0.9% of the country's GDP.

Although India has shown unprecedented development in the last two decades, however, it comes with huge environmental costs. Besides air, India has also seen a rise in water pollution levels. Despite the efforts taken by the government in cleaning major rivers like the Ganga, the majority of the small and large water sources have remained devoid of attention. The lakes, ponds and rivulets have become extremely polluted which has turned about 70% of the surface water unfit for human consumption. Illegal dumping of trade and sewage effluent and the absence of proper wastewater management have contributed immensely towards the contamination of water bodies beyond their self-sustenance. Water pollution costs the Indian government between USD$6.7 and $7.7 billion a year and is associated with a 9% drop in agricultural revenues as well as a 16% decrease in downstream agricultural yields (Martina, 2023). Besides losses in revenue, pollution also causes an adverse impact on human health and affects productivity further.

Pollution damages the health of crops and livestock. Land pollution lowers the fertility and productivity of the soil. Pollution causes loss of biodiversity and in turn, affects the national health and lowers the national GDP, which is important for the nation. The principle of Polluters Pays helps in checking all kinds of pollution and protecting the environment. The Supreme Court invokes this principle not only to protect the environment but also to penalise polluters so that a deterrent effect is caused amongst the polluters in society. However, from the above statistics, it is clear that the Apex Court has not had many cases before it to invoke this principle and conserve the environment from being damaged.

5. LIMITATIONS OF THE STUDY

The researchers have collected the data that are provided by the software and online sources like Manupatra, Indian Kanoon, SCC online etc. The data published by these sources vary so an average has been calculated and taken for the purpose of study. Further, the data which have been taken for study have been extracted from these sources using filters that have been developed by software engineers.

6. CONCLUSION

The Pölluter Pays Principle is the cornerstone of environmental law and policy, which emphasises the responsibility of polluters to bear the costs and take proactive measures to prevent pollution and mitigate environmental harm. By holding polluters accountable, this principle contributes towards the protection and preservation of the environment for present and future generations. With such a dynamic and effective principle at hand, the courts and the tribunals have a strong weapon against the polluters of the environment. However, this weapon is underused as there are not sufficient cases being filed before the court. The data of the last twenty years reflect that Polluter Pays Principle has been meagrely put into service by the Supreme Court to save the environment and is largely unemployed. The large quantum of pollution that people are producing every day is causing a severe threat to the Indian environment. So, a need is felt that the principle of Polluter Pays has been extensively used by the courts and the authorities to prevent environmental damage and to restore the lost pristinely of nature.

REFERENCES

Andrea, Ciampalini (2016). "The Costa Concordia last cruise: the first application of high frequency monitoring based on COSMO-SkyMed constellation for wreck removal," *ISPRS Journal of Photogrammetry and Remote Sensing* 37–49.

Castanedo, Raúl Medina, Losada Iñigo, Vidal César, Méndez Fernando, Osorio Andrés, Juanes José and Puente Araceli (2006). "The prestige oil spill in Cantabria (Bay of Biscay). Part I: operational forecasting system for quick response, risk assessment, and protection of natural resources," *Journal of Coastal Research* 1474–1489.

Choudhary, Anjali (2019). "Analysis of the effectiveness of the polluter pays in India," *Journal of Emerging Technologies and Innovative Research* 1–4.

Martina, Igini (2023). EARTH.ORG. April 30. Accessed May 01, 2023. https://earth.org/environmental-issues-in-india/.

Satinath, Dinham, and Barbara, Sarangi (2002). "The Bhopal Gas Leak Tragedy 1984 to ? Evasion of Corporate Responsibility," *CORPORATE CULPABILITY* 1–11.

Yorifuji, T., and T. Tisuda (2014). "Minimata," *Encyclopedia of Toxicology* 340–344.

Zou, H., and M. B. Adams (2008). "Corporate ownership, equity risk and returns in the People's Republic of China," *J. Int. Bus. Stud.* 39(7): 11491168.

11. Legal Construction of Human Rights Jurisprudence and Judicial Gerrymandering: An Overview

Sanjay Sindhu[1], Nandan Sharma[2], and Palak Sharma[3]
[1]Professor, Faculty of Law, Himachal Pradesh University, Shimla H.P. India
[2]Professor, Faculty of Legal Science, Shoolini University, Solan (H.P.). India
[3]PhD Research Scholar, Faculty of Legal Science, Shoolini University of Biotechnology and Management Sciences, Solan H.P., India

ABSTRACT: In a changing society, judicial activism is a vigorous process of changing the judicial outlook towards the public at large. It is a judicial ideology that encourages judges to reject established precedents in favour of novel social theories and legislative initiatives. Judicial activism doesn't carry any statutory definition. Thus, the term 'Judicial Activism' is used for the unconventional role played by the court when it gives value judgement and grants relief to the aggrieved person or persons according to its moral and social sense of justice in a situation where statutory law is silent or even contrary. Positively speaking, judicial activism is the process by which new legal theories are developed to modernise the law, bring it into line with societal demands and ultimately further the constitutional goal of advancing the public interest under the rule of law. This is a process where the judiciary is supposed to discharge their duties to expand and develop the law as to respond to the needs, hopes and aspiration of the citizens who are looking at the courts to give relief, life and content to law. The landmark innovation of public interest litigation (PIL) is of highest importance when it comes to judicial activism. In this regard, the judiciary has made several attempts to highlight the development regarding liberalisation of the doctrine of locus standi and to provide an introspection of the emergence of new dimensions of human rights jurisprudence under Indian legal system through public interest litigation.

KEYWORDS: Judicial activism, human rights, PIL

Chapter 11 DOI- 10.4324/9781003428213-11

1. EVOLUTION OF THE CONCEPT OF JUDICIAL ACTIVISM AND PUBLIC INTEREST LITIGATION

Retrospectively, honourable courts are taken to be an institution that prefers no innovation and are contended to decide issues on case-to-case basis under broad framework of either legislation or precedent. They have nothing to do or very little to do with social change. They feel to be just a safety device for the vindication of individual grievances. The common law struck to this view and left society to change itself and at the most left for the legislation to do it single-handedly. Their role, if any, is sometimes to block or retard the social change for the sake of legality, constitutionality or otherwise. Contrary to this, the courts in common law countries are assuming activist's role and evolving the idea of activist jurisprudence. This new character of the judges may make them an instrument of social change through law, for example legal aid and legal advice have revolutionised socio-legal structure of many countries. The most notable change in the functioning of court in present paradigm is social interest litigation. Thus, social interest litigation is popularly known as public interest litigation. It is a development of the latter half of 20th century and is an emerging jurisprudence of access to courts for justice.

Public interest litigation, an expression of judicial activism, has introduced one new dimension regarding judiciary's connection in public administration. It is persistent to acknowledge that Indian judiciary's proactive, inventive and nearly explosive efforts to alleviate the suffering of the majority led to public interest litigation. All the cases brought before the court through public interest litigation, the sanctity of locus standi and the difficulties of the legal process are completely sidestepped.

2. JUDICIAL ACTIVISM AND EMERGING DIMENSIONS THROUGH PUBLIC INTEREST LITIGATION UNDER INDIAN LEGAL SYSTEM

The concept of PIL which is attributable to the modern trends of judicial activism emerged as a dynamic and unconventional approach by the courts in India to the problems they required to tackle, in comparatively of recent origin.

The Indian Courts gave new dimensional change through judicial activism by the process of public interest litigation. The court has played a major role in shaping Indian jurisprudence in the domain of social and economic ordering of Indian society.

3. JUDICIAL ACTIVISM AND NEW APPROACH TO ARTICLE 21 OF THE INDIAN CONSTITUTION

The notion of personal liberty for the first time was decided in the Supreme Court in *A.K. Gopalan vs. State of Madras*. With its dynamic approach, the judiciary has given Article 21 life and blood. In Maneka Gandhi v. Union of India, the Supreme Court stated that rather than attenuating the meaning or content of basic rights by a process of restrictive judicial interpretation, the court should aim to expand their reach and range.

As per the dimensions of Article 21, that is right to life and personal liberty were elucidated and it was observed that this right doesn't only mean the continuance of a person's and animal's existence, but a quality of life. In the current stage of our civilisation, it refers to 'the fullest opportunity to develop one's personality and potentiality to the highest level possible'. It inevitably refers to the freedom to live a respectable life as a citizen of a civilised community. Thus, the judiciary in various decisions has provided an extended connotation to the 'right to life'. This includes right to live with dignity, right to reputation, right to livelihood, right against sexual harassment of women at work place, right to shelter, right to unpolluted environment, right against noise pollution, right to sustainable development, right to be educated, right to know or right to information, right to a secure future, right against honour killing, health rights, right to preserve life and no right to take your own life or to commit suicide.

Article 21 of the Constitution of India envisages under it a plethora of rights which are duly necessary for the well-being of various individuals. The court has over the years interpreted this article in a positive way which has invariably opened the way for many rights to be included in its ambit. The recent privacy judgement gave a very extensive interpretation of the article, and privacy rights were included under Article 21. Over multiple years, various rights such as travelling abroad, prisoner rights, women rights and child rights have found their way into Article 21.

Thus, it is evident from the above innovative acknowledged approach that the Apex Court of India has virtually heralded a revolutionary era in the realm of judicial functioning to render justice and ameliorate the miseries of masses. In the recent time, public interest litigation may be called an instrument manufactured by the apex court to give justice to the poor, ignorant and downtrodden who remained neglected for long. The former cases decided by the Supreme Court during the past three and half decades reveal that entertaining public interest litigation cases has multiplied on a very large scale giving an opportunity to court to render justice to women, children, bounded labour and host of other oppressed section of the society.

3.1. Other Arenas of Judicial Activism through Public Interest Litigation

There are abundant cases to show the court's attitude in entertaining public interest cases. Some of the relevant cases are of great significance. In the case of State of *Himachal Pradesh vs. Umed Ram*, the case was a writ petition and the high court under its power directed the Superintendent of PWD department to complete the road construction within the stipulated time. The honourable high court in this case observed that in hilly areas the right to have good and proper roads was an ancillary to better and decent life quality is necessary for the self-esteem of a person given under the Indian Constitution.

In another case, an advocate from Nader in West Bengal made the court aware through a letter with news items published in Amrit Bazar Patrika relating to sexual exploitation of girl's students, and in *Pratul Kumar vs. State of Orissa,* court had directed the Chief Judicial Magistrate to make an enquiry. In Janaki *Nathu Bhai and Another vs. Sardar Nagar Municipality and others*, the esteemed court took upon itself and played a major role by taking great initiative of allowing a letter written by two citizens regarding the poor conditions of drainage in the areas adjoining the city to be considered as a petition. The court, after hearing the case, issued directions to the department concerned for interim relief and to find a permanent solution to the problem at hand.

In *Bhopal Gas Peedith Mahila U. Sangatha vs. Union of India*, the honourable supreme court took cognisance of the people who were victims in Bhopal gas leak tragedy who were promised medical facilities, but even after the span of almost 15 years, the victims were empty-handed. The court issued orders directing for the quick completion of work and make the hospitals fully operational.

Considering prison reforms, in *R.D. Upadhyay vs. State of A.P.*, a public interest lawsuit claimed that about 73% of the inmates were found to be awaiting trial. Apex Court ordered attorneys representing various states and union territories to persuade the concerned administrations to take action within six weeks of the order's date for filling challans and reports, particularly in cases involving minor offences for which defendants have been imprisoned for some time. The Constitution's open-ended language in Articles 32 and 226 has also been exploited by the courts. These articles provide the courts with the freedom to alter existing remedies or even create new ones to uphold rights. The philosophy of compensatory jurisprudence was started from *Rudul Shah vs. State of Bihar*, where the court not only set free, but also asked the state to compensate the person for their unlawful detention with Rs. 30,000. against the growing inclination of the state's executive branch to act irresponsibly, which is creating a state of 'government lawlessness' in which the rule of law is not given much weight and the traditional legal remedies available to combat this evil appear to be insufficient. The situation has been addressed by the Supreme Court. Chandra Chud, the Chief Justice at the time, observed the following:

> *'It is true that Article 32 cannot be utilized to replace the effective enforcement of rights and obligations which in the normal turn of events the normal civil and criminal court processes. Therefore, a lawsuit filed in a lower grade court that is qualified to hear it must be the subject of a monetary claim and be litigated there. But the crucial*

> *issue under consideration is whether this court can issue a judgement ordering the payment of money if such a judgement is compensation for the violation of a fundamental right under the writ authority set forth in Article 32'.*

The instant case is of the examples of such cases. After being declared not guilty in a fully clothed trial, the petitioner was unlawfully held in prison for more than fourteen years. He requested his release from unauthorised custody by filing a Habeas Corpus petition with the court. He was relieved. The court believed that his incarceration following his acquittal was completely unwarranted.

Thus, logically to create dimensional compensatory jurisprudence the Apex Court through numerous cases creatively through judicial activism opened new vistas under Indian legal system. Furthermore, the Supreme Court under Article 32 and the High Court under Article 226 have the authority to seek judicial remedies for any legal wrong or injury inflicted to any of these individuals or a specific class of individuals in the event that any of their fundamental rights are violated.

In *People's Union for Democratic Rights vs. Union of India*, generally known as *the Asiad Labour Case*, a writ petition was presented by People's Union for Democratic Rights for the purpose of protecting democratic rights of the individuals. Moreover, in *Bandhua Mukti Morcha vs. Union of India,* the Bonded Labour System (Abolition) Act of 1976's provisions were not being implemented properly in Haryana, so the Supreme Court took up a case involving the release of bound labourer's and quarry workers. The case was brought to court through a group dedicated to the release of bound laborers. The court opined that PIL is not in adversarial litigation, but rather is a challenge and an opportunity for the administration and its officers to give meaning to the rights of the underprivileged and vulnerable sections of the community and to provide them with social and economic justice.

Moreover, when it comes to the menace of ragging in Special Leave Petition No 24295 of 2006, *University of Kerala Council of Principals of Colleges*, the honourable Apex Court of India was pleased to order the formation of a committee under the guidance of Shri R.K. Raghavan, a former Director of the Central Bureau of Investigation, to make recommendations regarding how to eliminate ragging in educational institutions. Despite its concern in the interim order for Vishwa Jagriti Mission through President vs. Central Government through Cabinet Secretary and Others, the Apex Court of India expressed its disappointment that 'practically very little has been done to prevent the menace of ragging in educational institution'. The court ordered the committee to identify ways that the laws already in place in many states and new laws that are needed to avert the threat can be effectively drafted to do so.

4. JUDICIAL ACTIVISM VIS-A-VIS LEGISLATIVE ACTIVISM: CONSEQUENTIAL EFFECT

As a consequential effect, to protect the fundamental human rights, the Indian parliament and state legislature have enacted several acts, ordinance, rules and regulations for the people of this country. The various important acts are as follows: The Prohibition of Smoking and Non-Smoker Health Protection Act, 1997; The Protection of Women form Domestic Violence Act, 2005; The Right to Information Act, 2005; The Protection Against Sexual Harassment at Workplace Bill, 2010; The National Green Tribunal Act, 2010, The Anti-Ragging Regulation; and The Right to Free and Compulsory Education.

5. EFFECTIVENESS OF JUDICIAL ACTIVISM AND SOCIAL CHANGE:

Public interest litigation is the most striking innovation in the recent years in regard to the delivery of the legal system. Because public interest litigation (PIL) is a byproduct of judicial activism, the two practices are closely related. It is true that it is common to use activism and restraint with reference to the operation of the judiciary. It is evident from observation that the judiciary has entertained, in public interest, certain matters and has given justice to the people who live hand to mouth for their existence and are illiterate and unorganised. At the same time, there has been a growing notion that individuals agitating for personal grievances under the guise of public interest are abusing PIL's.

After this horrific incidence that shook the country, the then finance minister announced setting up of Nirbhaya Fund, where government contributed Rs.1000 crores for safety and empowerment of women and girl children. Five fast track courts were set up for expeditious adjudication of cases related to sexual assault. Judiciary played an enormous role for contributing to women's safety and upholding death penalty in Nirbhaya's case.

In *Arjun Gopal v. Union of India*, it was held by Supreme Court that the matter pertaining to the firecracker ban has been resolved. It gave a thorough ruling, considering its earlier directives in this area, and imposed other rules pertaining to the usage and sale of firecrackers. It established rules such as prohibiting the sale of firecrackers through online retailers, specifying the appropriate time and location for exploding firecrackers, examining the composition of firecrackers, requesting the Central and State Pollution Control Boards to monitor the situation, and instituting the usage of green crackers.

The Delhi High Court's decision to commission women into the Army on a permanent basis was recently upheld by a Supreme Court Bench in *Defense Secretary v. Babita Puniya and Others*. The Supreme Court ruled that excluding women from command positions based only on their physical characteristics and domestic duties is unreasonable. The court further declared that women's complete exclusion is unlawful and in violation of Article 14 of the Indian Constitution.

In *National Legal Services Authority v. Union of India*, the Supreme Court acknowledged the right to self-identify one's gender and held that transgender community have the right to be treated as their individuality rather than their assigned gender at birth. This is a landmark judgement for the fight against transgender community in India. This judgement recognised the legal identity of transgender individuals and their right to self-identify as male, female or third gender.

In addition, the court ordered the administration to take action to eliminate the prejudice and marginalisation of the transgender minority and guarantee its access to fundamental freedoms and opportunities. The case sparked efforts to address these problems through policy and social reform and raised awareness of the prejudice and marginalisation transgender people experience in India.

6. CONCLUDING OBSERVATIONS

Thus, the observations reveal that judicial activism is more of a description of performance of duty consistently with the change in time. This concept is conceptualised as a corrective to inaction or failure of the government machinery to provide clean, competent and citizen friendly governance. In reality, the observation further depicts that the activism shown by the judiciary is the outcome of the judicial creativity when it awakened to the existing realities of the socio-economic conditions of the people, and as such, it intends to implement vigorously the social goal through the instrumentalities of equality amongst people outlines in constitution as null as legislature enactments. It is appropriate to mention here that in the Indian Constitution all the three organs of government are not separate from each other but work in coordination and are accountable to each other.

Furthermore, it is also clear that public interest litigation is a byproduct of judicial activism. It is a technique, a tool, a court procedure and a system that introduces the humanitarian idea of protecting the less fortunate in society by providing them with preferential treatment in the administration of justice. The substance of public interest litigation is secure justice, social, political and economic within the parameters of existing law. Thus, public interest litigation has opened new doors of judicial function. It is a multidimensional expansion. The doctrine of *locus standi* was loosened and the judiciary becomes the protector and guarantor of the fundamental rights of the people in India, most of whom are ignorant, illiterate, poor, have not's or downtrodden. Judicial activism's primary goal is to develop new legal theories in order to modernise the law and bring it into compliance with societal demands. This serves to further the constitutional goal of advancing the public interest under the rule of law. It is, therefore, obvious that judicial activism rightly understood and practised with judicial restraint is the felt need of the present times, and it has gained acceptability of the people, the ultimate sovereign, because it subserves the constitutional objective of public good and public interest.

Undoubtedly, the Indian judiciary has won a fervent prose by touching problems affecting the masses at large. The judiciary, more specifically the Supreme Court, has been very assertive and has forcefully reminded the executive of its obligation to the citizen. It is pertinent to mention here that the concept of judicial activism doesn't have its legitimacy if the three pillars of the government have failed. That is the only reason for judicial activism bordering on excessive. Even if other wings of the administration function efficiently, judicial activism will be required to acknowledge and defend the rights of marginalised minority. To sum up, it is, therefore, imperative to promote judicial activism with certain legitimate restraints.

REFERENCES

A.K. Gopalan vs. State of Madras AIR 1950 SC 27.

Agarwal, S. K. 1985. *PIL in India: A Critique*. N.M. Tripathi. 6.

Ahmad, A. M. 2003. "Dimensions of judicial activism." *Journal*, 1–2.

Apparel Export Promotion Council vs. A.K. Chopra, AIR 1999 SC 625, Vishake vs. State of Raj, AIR 1997 SC 3011.

Arjun Gopal v. Union of India 2019 13 SCC 523.

Bandhua Mukti Morcha vs. Union of India AIR 1984 SC 802.

Bhatia, K. L. 1999. "Judicial activism and social change." 242.

Bhopal Gas Peedith Mahila U. Sangatha vs. Union of India (2000) 9 SCC 281.

Centre for Public Interest Litigation vs. Union of India, AIR 2001 SC 80.

Chamel Singh vs. State of U.P., AIR 1996 SC 1051.

Constitution of India, 1950, Art 16.

Consumer Education and Research Centre vs. U.O.I., AIR 1995 SC 922.

D. K. Basu vs. State of W. B., AIR 1997 SC 3017.

Defense Secretary v. Babita Puniya and Others, Civil Appeal No. 1210 of 2020.

Ektra Hawkers Union vs. Maharashtra Corp. Greater Mumbai, AIR 2004 SC 416.

Essar Oil Ltd. vs. Halar Utkarsh Samiti, AIR 2004 SC 1834; R.P. Ltd. vs. Proprietors Indian Express Newspapers, Bombay Pvt. Ltd., AIR 1989 SC 190.

Francis Coralie vs. U.T. of Delhi, AIR 1981 SC 746.

Gian Kaur Vs State of Punjab AIR 1996 SC 946.

Himachal Pradesh vs. Umed Ram (1986) 2 SCC 68.

Hindustan Paper Corporation Ltd. vs. Ananta Bhattacharjee, (2004) 6 SCC 213.

Janaki Nathu Bhai and Another vs. Sardar Nagar Municipality and others AIR 1986 Guj. 49.

Kamala Devi vs. State of Punjab, AIR 1984 SC 1895.

Kamboj, N. S. 1999. "Human rights and judicial activism." *Journal of the Indian Law Institute*, 41 (1): 111.

LIC of India vs. Consumer Education and Research Centre, AIR 1995 SC 1811.

M. C. Mehta vs. Union of India, AIR 1987 SC 965.

M. C. Mehta vs. Union of India, AIR 1988 SC 1115.

M.C. Mehta vs. U.O.I. Air 1987 SC 965.

Mahesh Chand Bisht vs. Union of India, AIR 1999 SC 1575.

Maneka Gandhi vs. Union of India AIR 1978 SC 597.

Marbury vs. Madison I Cranch 137 (1803).

Motuni Jain vs. State of Karnataka, AIR 1992 SC 1858.

N.D. Jayal vs. U.O.I. AIR 2004 SC 867.

National Legal Services Authority v. Union of India AIR 2014 SC 1863; (2014) 5 SCC 43.

Nilabati Behera vs. State of Orissa, (1993) 2 SCC 746; AIR 1993 SC 1960.

Nirbhaya Fund, Press Information Bureau Government of India, 29 November 2019. https://pib.gov.in/newsite (accessed February 12, 2023).

Olga Telles vs. Bombay Municipal Corporation, AIR 1986 SC 108; Maharashtra.

P. Rathinam vs Union of India AIR 1994 SC 1844.

Parmanand Katara vs. U.O.I., AIR 1989 SC 2039.

People's Union for Democratic Rights vs. U.O.I. AIR 1982 SC 1973; Sanjit Raj v. State of Raj. AIR 1983 SC 328.

People's Union for Democratic Rights vs. Union of India AIR 1982 SC 1473.

People's Union for Democratic Rights vs. Union of India, AIR 1982 SC 1473.

Pratul Kumar vs. State of Orissa AIR 1989 SC 1783.

R.D. Upadhyay vs. State of A.P (2000) 10 SCC 255.

Ratlam Municipality vs. Vardhi Chand, AIR 1980 SC 1622.

Re: Noise Pollution, AIR 2005 SC 3136.

Rudul Shah vs. State of Bihar AIR 1983 SC 1086.

Rural Litigation and Entitlement Kendra vs. State of U. P., AIR 1989 SC 594.

Sheela Barse vs. Union of India, AIR 1986 SC 1773.

Sheela Barse vs. Union of India, AIR 1986 SC 1773.

SLP No.24296-24299 of 2004, W.P (Cri) No. 173/206 and SLP © No. 14356/2005.

State of Maharashtra v. Public Concern for Governance Trust, AIR 2007 SC 777.

State of Punjab vs. Baldeo Singh, AIR 1999 SC 2378.

Sujit Kumar vs. State of U.P., AIR 2002 NOC (Allahabad).

Sushila Gothala vs. State of Rajasthan AIR 1995 Raj 90, Gaurav Jain vs. Union of India AIR 1990 SC 292, M.C. Mehta vs. State of T.N. AIR 1991 SC 417 etc.

Tripathi, G. P. 2012. "Law and social tansformation." 12.

Unni Krishnan vs. State of AP, AIR 1993 SC 2178.

Veena Sethi vs. State of Bihar, AIR 1983 SC 339.

Virender Gaun vs. State of Raj AIR 2004 Raj. 176.

12. Stereotyping and Gender Dynamics: Portrayal of Women in the Bollywood Films and Crimes of Stalking and Sexual Harassment

Dr. Vrushti Patel
Assistant Professor, School of Law, AURO University, Surat
Email: Vrushti.patel@aurouniversity.edu.in

ABSTRACT: The representation of women in films has been a topic of debate for several decades. While films have the power to shape our perceptions and attitudes towards various social issues, the representation of women in films has often been problematic. Many times the depiction of women in the films leads to the objectification of women and the perpetuation of harmful stereotypes, which in turn can lead to offences of stalking and sexual harassment due to indecent representation in the Films.

Films often portray women as sexual objects or sex symbols, rather than as complex and multifaceted individuals with their agency and aspirations. This portrayal reinforces harmful gender roles and can lead to the normalisation of sexual harassment and violence against women.

Additionally, the representation of women in films like *Kabir Singh*, *Dabang*, *Darrar*, *Tere Naam*, etc. as passive and submissive has led to the perpetuation of harmful gender norms and stereotypes. This has contributed to a culture of misogyny and gender-based violence, where women are seen as inferior and are subjected to harassment and violence. Furthermore, the glorification and romanticisation of stalking and other forms of harassment in films like *Rehna Hai Tere Dil Me*, *Badrinath ki Dulhaniya*, *Ae Dil Hai Mushkil*, *Wanted*, *Rowdy Rathore*, *Ranjhana*, *Tanu Weds Manu Returns*, *Toilet – Ek Prem Katha*, etc. aids in normalising such behaviour, leading to an increase in real-life instances of stalking and harassment. Many Bollywood films glorify teasing, harassing and stalking a girl as an act of love, if you intend to marry. In the end, the woman will fall in love with the perpetrator or he will die as a martyr in love. This has created a dangerous and threatening environment for women, where they are unable to feel safe or secure in public spaces.

Chapter 12 DOI- 10.4324/9781003428213-12

It is important to recognise the impact that the representation of women in films can have on our attitudes and behaviour towards women and have a stringent law to stop the indecent representation of women and glorification of sexual harassment and stalking in films. Hence, through this paper, the authors attempt to find the relationship between the instances of sexual harassment and stalking and the influence of films on them.

KEYWORDS: Stalking, sexual harassment, gender stereotypes

1. INTRODUCTION

The representation of women in films has been a topic of debate for several decades. While films have the power to shape our perceptions and attitudes towards various social issues, the representation of women in films has often been problematic. Many times, the depiction of women in the films leads to the objectification of women and the perpetuation of harmful stereotypes, which in turn can lead to offences of stalking and sexual harassment due to the ill representation in the Films.

Films often portray women as sexual objects or sex symbols, rather than as complex and multifaceted individuals with their agency and aspirations, this projection reinforces harmful gender roles and has led to the normalisation of sexual harassment and violence against women.

Additionally, the representation of women in films like *Kabir Singh, Dabang, Darrar, Tere Naam*, etc. as passive and submissive beings has led to the perpetuation of harmful gender norms and stereotypes. This has contributed to a culture of misogyny and gender-based violence, where women are seen as inferior and are subjected to harassment and violence. Furthermore, the glorification and romanticisation of stalking and other forms of harassment in films like *Rehna hai Tere Dil me, Badrinath ki Dulhaniya, Ae Dil Hai Mushkil, Wanted, Rowdy Rathore, Ranjhana, Tanu weds Manu returns, Toilet – Ek Prem Katha*, etc. aids in normalising such behaviour, leading to an increase in real-life instances of stalking and harassment. Many Bollywood films glorify teasing, harassing and stalking a girl as an act of love, if you intend to marry. They justify the act as an act of wooing the girl and in the end, the girl will fall in love with the perpetrator or he will die as a martyr in love. In both situations, the act is depicted as an act of love, pride and honour. This has created a dangerous and threatening environment for women, where they are unable to feel safe or secure in public spaces. Society due to such influences of films has also normalised these acts of sexual harassment quoting '*Men will be Men*'.

To have a healthy and safe environment in society, it is important to recognise the impact of the representation of women in films. Through this paper, the author attempts to find the relationship between the representation of women in the films and the instances of sexual harassment and stalking and examines how the society too romanticised these films unknowingly and subconsciously which led to normalising such behaviour. The author of this paper also attempts to examine the role of the censor board in the same.

2. REVIEW OF LITERATURE

2.1. Misogyny in Bollywood

Cinema plays a very important role in forming public relations and there is a correlation between cinema and rapes. The item numbers in the films create a general perception, which further defines women in India. Though the offences used to happen in the past, however, rising of these cases has prompted a re-examination of the public portrayal of women (Burhan, 2013, pp. 42–43).

2.2. Prioritising Stalking as Popular Culture in Regional Films – A Threat to Woman Status in Resurgent India

This paper addresses the toxic demonstration of harassment in movies and further analyses the portrayal of women in these films. The paper further analyses its relation with the incidents of stalking and sexual harassment (Smith, 2017).

2.3. Women's Issues in India: Role and Importance of Media

The media serves as a reflection of society, with its reports reflecting the occurrences within it. Its influence on the masses is substantial; particularly in the context of the communication and IT revolution, that has magnified its significance. Regrettably, in recent times, the media seems to be deviating from its intended role by presenting biased information, thereby hindering societal progress. A crucial matter that has been neglected by the Indian media is the portrayal of women as equals in society. Sensitising the Indian media to gender issues is of utmost importance, and it must now prioritise addressing women's concerns in a resolute manner, as their empowerment is critical for the progress of women in India. Considering these aspects, this paper aims to shed light on women's issues in contemporary Indian society and the role of media in effectively tackling these challenges (Ojha, 2011, pp. 87–102).

3. RESEARCH METHODOLOGY

The author has adopted a doctrinal and exploratory method of data collection. Since both methods can complement each other in providing a comprehensive analysis of the interrelationship between gender stereotyping and gender dynamics, which further leads to the offences of stalking and sexual harassment.

4. WHAT IS STALKING AND SEXUAL HARASSMENT?

The offence of stalking is a serious crime that is characterised by a pattern of unwanted and obsessive behaviour towards another person. Stalking can take many different forms, including following someone, making unwanted phone calls or sending unwanted messages, and even physically assaulting someone. It is characterised by intrusive acts that create a sense of control in the victim, which might lead the victim to believe that he/she is living in an unsafe environment. (Maran and D'Argenio, 2019) The victim in this situation is in a constant state of threat even when the behaviour of the perpetrator is not marked by an explicit threat or by physical violence. (Maran and D'Argenio, 2019) In stalking, the person and his movements are monitored by the perpetrator, which raises a sense of fear in the mind of the victim.

Stalking tactics are the specific behaviours that stalkers direct towards their victims, a number of which have been observed. Spitzberg and Cupach (2003) identified five clusters of stalking tactics. These were labelled as – **hyper-intimacy tactics** – *including sending letters, emails and text messages, making telephone calls to the victim;* **pursuit or proximity tactics** – *including following the victim and hanging around the victim's home or workplace;* **invasion tactics** – *including breaking into or otherwise gaining access to the victim's property;* **intimidation tactics** – *including making threats against the victim;* and **violent tactics** – *including assault of the victim'* (Heckels and Roberts, 2010).

Similarly, eve-teasing, making sexual advances towards women, singing derogatory songs to make the women uncomfortable, making sexual jokes, making sexually coloured remarks, and requesting or demanding sexual favours amounts to sexual harassment.

In the past, the cases would go unregistered and unreported due to a lack of proper legal framework to protect them. After years of struggle, finally, stalking (**Section 354D**) and sexual harassment (**Section 354A**) were introduced as an offence through the Criminal Law (Amendment) Act of 2013, on the suggestion of Justice Verma Committee. According to the inserted provisions, physical contact or advances involving unwelcome and explicit sexual overtures, demanding sexual favours, making sexually coloured remarks, and showing pornography will amount to sexual harassment and following, trying to make contact and monitoring the movement of a woman through any means amounts to stalking. The committee observed that Stalking and sexual harassment can be considered the precursor to many other crimes and if it is stopped at the preliminary level, grievous offences can be prevented. For instance, the case of Santosh Kumar Singh v. State through CBI (2007 CriLJ 964), is a classic example of the same. Priyadarshini, a student of the Campus Law College, Delhi, was sexually harassed and stalked before she was raped and murdered in her own house. Santosh Kumar Singh, son of a former IPS officer, was her senior of Priyadarshini at Campus Law College, Delhi. She had filed multiple complaints against Santosh Kumar for Sexual harassment, indecent advancements and stalking. However, due to lack of explicit provisions for sexual harassment and stalking, an FIR was only filed under Section 354 of the Indian Penal Code. Each time the perpetrator was arrested, he was released on bail bonds. Looking to the severity of the offence security was provided to her, but finding her alone on 23 January 1996, Santosh entered her home, raped and murdered her. If the instances had been stopped at the very beginning, the gruesome offence could have been prevented. However, due to the lack of proper mechanisms to stop the act of stalking and sexual harassment, the perpetrator committed an even more gruesome offence.

5. PSYCHOLOGY OF PERPETRATOR – WHAT INFLUENCES THEM? AND WHY IS IT AN AREA OF CONCERN?

The Cultivation theory as promoted by George Gerbnes is a sociological and communications framework that suggests that people who are regularly exposed to media for long periods of time are more likely to perceive the world's social realities as they are presented by media they consume. This in turn affects their attributes and behaviour influenced by the messages from the world of television. The influence goes to such an extent that their views and perceptions start reflecting what they repeatedly see and hear. Hence, the soon sub-consciously start replicating the things they see and hear for long times.

There is a complex and multifaceted relationship between the portrayal of women in films and the occurrence of stalking and sexual harassment crimes. Studies have found that exposure to sexually objectifying media content can lead to greater acceptance of sexual harassment and violence against women. This is because such content has a capacity to reinforce harmful gender stereotypes and normalise the idea that women exist solely for the sexual gratification of men. Additionally, some research has found that certain portrayals of women in films, such as hyper-sexualisation or victimisation, may contribute to an increased risk of stalking and sexual harassment. This may occur because these depictions can create a sense of entitlement in perpetrators who feel that their actions are justified by the media they consume. Of course, media depictions of women are just one piece of a larger puzzle, factors such as cultural norms, individual attitudes and social structures play a role in shaping these behaviours. Social learning reiterates the same; it states that people learn by observing and imitating others whom they consider a hero/role model. They learn new behaviours, attitudes, attributes and values through their interactions with others, whether real or fictional. This theory is relevant to the offence of sexual harassment and stalking portrayed in films because films can be a powerful medium for shaping our understanding of how people behave in different situations.

One such example is a case that happened in Australia. Sandesh Baliga, a working security guard was accused of stalking two women in Australia. The defence raised on his behalf is that he was inspired by the Bollywood movies; he believed that the patient pursuit of a woman would make her fall in love with him, because that is what he has grown up watching in the Bollywood movies. He further added that he was inspired from the character of Shahrukh Khan from the movie *Darr* and had learnt the art of stalking from the movie. His lawyer, Greg Barns, told the court it was 'quite normal behaviour' for Indian men to pursue women similarly, which is why he did not realise that his actions could be criminal (ABC NEWS, 2015). This shows how much impact movies make and have in the lives of people living not only in Indian society but also in other countries. *Darr* is just an example, there are many movies glorify stalking and sexual harassment that were titled as the most romantic movies of all the times, to name a few: *Rehna Hai Tere Dil Me, Wanted, Tere Naam, Ae Dil hai Mushkil, Raanjhanaa, Toilet – Ek Prem Katha, Tanu Weds Manu returns*, etc. each of them portrayed the act of stalking and harassment as romantic that leads the women fall in love with him. The songs that every teenager has grown up singing: *Kab tak ruthegi, cheekhegi, chill aayegi? Dil kehta hai ek din haseena maan jayegi* – **Haseena Maan Jayegi** , *Tu ha kar ya na kar, Tu hai meri Kiran* – **Darr,** *Chal pyar karegi? Naji Naji, Mere Sath Chalegi? Naji Naji. Hum tujh ko utha kar lejayenge, doli me bitha kar le jayenge* – **Jab Pyar KisiSe Hota Hai** , *Raja beta banke maine jab sharafat dikhayi, Tune bola 'hatt mawaali' bhaav nahi diya re, Thandi aahein bhar li bohot, Acchi baatein kar li bohot, Ab karunga tere saath... Gandi baat...* – **R Rajkumar** , *Yeh uska style hoinga, hontho pe na dil me han hoinga, Aaj nahee toh kal bolegee, ai tu tension kai ko leta hai re* – **Josh** , *Tera peechha na main chodunga soniye.* – **Jugnu,** etc. has only portrayed moderate sexual harassment and stalking accepted as romantic and entertaining. For generations, young boys and men are influenced by such interactions, which shapes and defines their understanding of interactions with girls/women. These interactions have now so interwoven in the socio-cultural mechanism that it forms the social norms and functions that normalises eve-teasing and sexual abuse against the women.

6. ROLE OF THE CENSOR BOARD

Sivashankari vs. The Superintendent of Police is one of the many disturbing cases, which raises questions on the role of, censor boards. The girl hardly of 17 years old was stalked, harassed and woed into getting married to her stalker. When presented before the court, she stated that she was highly influenced by a Tamil film where school-going girls in school uniform were shown being stalked by heros under the guise of falling in love and taking them to various amusement places and also marrying them against the wishes of their respective parents. She further added that following suit, like the heroines in the said films, she went with her stalker and married him. Though the movie did not belong to the Bollywood banner, shows the influence of movies in general on young children and how it builds the perception. Cinema is indeed a very powerful medium, which can reach out to a large number of people at a lightning speed and has a potency to influence minds of the people at a tender age. Hence, it is necessary to ensure that cinema suitable for public exhibition should only be permitted to be exhibited.

The Censor Board has always been vigilant about the issues relating to religion and communal harmony and have censored the material that may result in communal disharmony. The recent censorship on OMG-2 also shows intolerance towards sex education, where the Movie got A certificate because it was thought that it may affect the young minds in the wrong manner. However, when it comes to portrayal of women, it has been quite liberal in granting U certificates or UA certificates without any cuts.

7. CONCLUSION

The aspects of art and cinema play a pivotal role in shaping the perception of the society. Bollywood has manifested abuse and violence as a romantic act since ages. These romantic demonstrations of stalking and harassment in the movies have a potential to translate into malicious criminal acts. The acts, which seem adorable and heroic on screen results in conscious or unconscious involvement in the offences of stalking and sexual harassment. The cases mentioned in this paper are just a brief outline of the larger damage it has caused to society. Hence, the author feels that Censor boards should be critical and vigilant about the portrayal of women in the Cinema. Amendments should be made to the Cinematograph Act, 1952 to promote conscious and responsible filmmaking in order to avoid the offences of Stalking and Sexual harassment, which can lead to reduction of grave offences against the women.

REFERENCES

Heckels, Victoria, and Karl Roberts (2010). *Stalking and Aarassment*. Palgrave.

Maran, Daniela A., Barbara Loera, and Alberto D'Argenio (2019). "Health care professionals' knowledge of stalking perpetrators, victims, behaviors, and coping strategies: a preliminary study among Italian hospitals," *Scientific World Journal* doi: 10.1155/2019/9190431.

Ojha, Purnima (2011). "Women's issues in India: role and importance of media," *The Indian Journal of Political Science* 72(1): 87–102. http://www.jstor.org/stable/42761809.

ABC NEWS (2015). "Bollywood excuse helps Hobart stalker avoid conviction," https://www.abc.net.au/news/2015-01-29/bollywood-helps-stalker-avoid-conviction/6053790.

Smith, Samandha (2017). "Prioritizing stalking as popular culture in regional films: a threat to woman status in resurgent India," *Research Gate*.

13. Gender Stereotyping in Media: Creating a Hurdle in the Socio-Legal Framework for Gender Mainstreaming

Dr. Ankita Kumar Gupta

Assistant Professor, Vivekananda School of Law and Legal Studies, Vivekananda Institute of Professional Studies, Affiliated to Guru Govind Singh Indraprastha University, New Delhi, India

Email: ankita.gupta@vips.edu

ABSTRACT: Gender stereotyping has been the roots on which the Indian Society has developed since ages. With the advancement of time, these roots have grown even deeper. It is an established fact that media can play a pivotal role in undoing the Gender stereotyping and can help in the socio-legal task of gender mainstreaming. But media in the modern times can be taken as a kind of weapon which can be used both ways; to create positive impact or negative impact on the society at large. Sadly, Media with all its new form like social media, OTT platforms are acting like a tool for engraving gender stereotyping in the mindset of the people. The paper intends to undertake an empirical study to find out the perception of the adolescents who are the key consumers of the modern-day media about their take-away on the portrayal of women in Media. A sample of 86 adolescents is taken by using a purposive sampling technique. The data are collected through survey method in which each sample has marked their response in a questionnaire. The data are further analysed which helped to come to a conclusion that the stereotypical depiction of women in media is reinforcing the patriarchal mindset.

KEYWORDS: Gender stereotyping, gender mainstreaming, women, media, portrayal

1. INTRODUCTION

Gender stereotyping means 'a generalized view or preconception about attributes or characteristics, or the roles that are or ought to be possessed by, or performed by, women and men'.('gender stereotyping' n.d.) People of a particular community are gendered according the stereotypical norms of that society. They are tuned to these stereotypical norms as soon as they are born. Infants are nurtured in a way that they abide by and stringently follow all the gender stereotypical norms.

Chapter 13 DOI- 10.4324/9781003428213-13

They are made to learn their gender roles initially by their family members, then by the media, social circle, toys, dress, colours etc.

The children are made to learn that there are two parallel gender lines on which they are obliged to walk which are demarcated for them by their biological sex. Any deviation from these pre-set gendered lines is a taboo. Every now and then these deviations are checked by 'Gender Accountability' (Hollander, 2013). The difference in the gender roles can be identified at a very early stage. As soon as a child is born in the family, the sex of the child would determine the road ahead. If a male child is born, the child is warmly welcomed in the family through celebrations. The gendered norms are showcased through the types of toys that are bought for him such as avengers, guns, cars, outdoor games depicting power and strength. The little boy is told to not to cry as it portrays him weak. He should learn the masculine traits and showcase the same like power, strength, dominance etc at the same time he is discouraged from showcasing any feminine traits like care, sensitivity, dependency etc.

On the other hand, the birth of a girl child not celebrated much. She is always thought to be someone else's wealth. From the very beginning, the girl child is made to learn the feminine straits such as being caring, motherly, loving and sensitive. All her life she is encouraged to be dependent, sensitive, submissive to orders, sacrificing etc at the same time she is also discouraged to have any outgoing traits. The whole family honour is shouldered on the girls and any deviation from the pre-set gendered roles would dishonour the community as a whole.

The theory of 'Social Construction' (Greco, 2013) explains that gender is an outcome of the social norms that and individual follows since his birth. Society teaches gender silently to all the participants and this teaching is a continuous process involving everyday practices. Here society comprises of different contributors like members of the family or community, external factors like colours, toys, dresses, profession. etc., one of the most dominating factors is Media which effectively affirms the norms created by the other contributors.

Judith Butler in her famous work *Gender Trouble: Feminism and the Subversion of Identity* mentions about the concept of '*Gender Performativity*' in the first chapter. According to her 'Gender is not just a process, but it is a particular type of process, a set of repeated acts within a highly rigid regulatory frame. Gender is not something one is, it is something one does, an act, or more precisely, a sequence of acts, a verb rather than a noun, a "doing" rather than a "being".' (Butler, 1999) This notion of gender performativity is supported by the present Media by re-establishing the very notion of Gender altogether.

Since ages gender stereotyping has been the cause of many social evils such as the fall in the child sex ratio, social, economic and educational inequalities. Patriarchal form of society has in itself deep-rooted notions of Gender. This has negatively affected the whole society where sons are taught the wrong notions of being a true man and on the other hand, daughters are taught the wrong notions of being a girl on whose shoulders lies the honour of the whole society. Evidently gender stereotyping has been the root cause of gender inequality in India.

2. GENDER MAINSTREAMING

Today, gender mainstreaming has become a global agenda and the fact is that it can only be achieved when there would be gender inclusivity and gender equality. Economic independence of women and their equal contribution at the work front can work towards sustainable development. This would need the society to be liberated from the gender stereotypes, which are deeply imbedded. Providing safe working environment free from sexual harassment for women is also essential. The challenge is massive and demands mission-mode effort on all fronts for Sustainable Development Goal 5 with a deadline of 2030 (Rajneesh, 2021).

The gender mainstreaming strategy is unique and aims to institutionalize equality by incorporating gender-sensitive norms and practices into the framework, procedures, and environment of public policy. Media can play a vital role in this but sadly it seems to be working in the opposite direction. The empirical study undertaken would showcase the same.

Feminist groups have often questioned how participation, equality, and inclusion will be incorporated into a society that was built on egregious exclusions and injustices. Among other issues two crucial issues in India are ending violence against women and empowering women economically. It also provides suggestions for how these commitments could be better realized in the execution of the SDGs, particularly SDG Goal 5 (Dhar, 2018).

3. GENDER STEREOTYPING IN THE INDIAN MEDIA

The media has a significant impact on how society's ideals are reflected and shaped. Media consumers, especially those who watch audio-visual media, incorporate its content into their daily lives. It is crucial that media content is properly regulated in light of the media's growing influence over people's lives, especially when it comes to how women are portrayed. The issue of indecent and obscene portrayals of women in media is addressed by laws like The Indecent Representation of Women (Prohibition) Act, 1986 and The Information Technology Act 2002. The travesty of the Indian legal system is that, despite the fact that we have a multiplicity of legislation to address the aforementioned issue, there are no sanctions for stereotypical and demeaning portrayals of women in the media.

Women are frequently sexually commodified in advertisements, soap operas and movies, or they are portrayed as the helpless dependent sex that submits to patriarchal norms, authorities and traditions. It is also impolite to judge a woman solely by her appealing physique or features. Constantly portraying a woman beneath a man is against both her sense of dignity and the idea of gender equality. This type of obscenity ought to be condemned as well.

Though international law has addressed gender stereotypes directly or indirectly, Indian law has mostly lagged behind on this front. Stereotyping has been deemed to be a violation of women's rights to equality & dignity and a catalyst for gender-based violence in the Fourth World Conference on Women Beijing Declaration ('Fourth World Conference on Women, Beijing 1995' n.d.).

The sexual objectification of women and the gender stereotyping of women are the two main aspects of the objectification of women on screen. Sexual objectification emphasizes on woman's body rather than her as a whole person. Many advertising for feminine products features this kind of portrayal. Treating a woman like a thing and emphasizing on her bodily parts in order to promote a commodity is degrading. These advertising spread the false notion that women are only acceptable when they resemble the ideal of beauty, which includes youth, thinness, fairness, careful grooming, and a polished manner. Any departure from that standard is treated with a great deal of scorn and hatred.

4. EMPIRICAL STUDY

The present study on 'Gender Stereotyping in Media: Creating a Hurdle in The Socio Legal Framework for Gender Mainstreaming' intends to highlight the patriarchal portrayal of women in media. Thus, an empirical study has been undertaken to find out the perception of the adolescents who are the key consumers of the modern-day media about their take-away on the portrayal of women in Media.

4.1. Sampling

A sample of 86 participants is taken by using purposive sampling technique. The sample was of 86 adolescents all belonging to the age group of 20–25. Out of 86 participants 43 where males and 43 were females.

4.2. Data Collection

The data are collected through survey method in which each sample has marked their response in a questionnaire. The responses of the participants were recorded with the help of a 'Google Form' questionnaire comprising 14 questions.

4.3. Data Analysis

The first two questions of the questionnaire inquired about the Gender Identity and age of the participants. The data collected indicated that the sample of 86 participants consisted equal number of males (50%) and females (50%) from the age group of 20–25 years. The next two questions inquired about the preferred mode of media entertainment among the participants (Figure 1) and about the most preferred OTT platform (Figure 2). Among television, OTT and others modes of Media entertainment OTT was the most preferred one with 87.2 % of the participants preferring it. And among Hotstar, Amazon Prime and Netflix;

Netflix was the most preferred OTT platform with 75.6% of the participants preferring it.

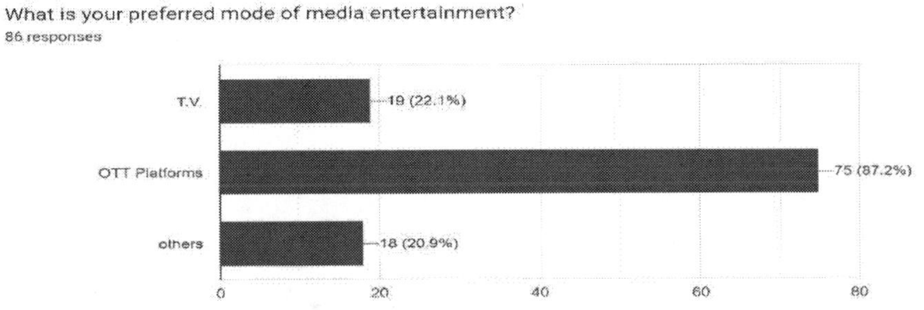

Figure 1. Preferred Mode of Media.
Source: Author's compilation.

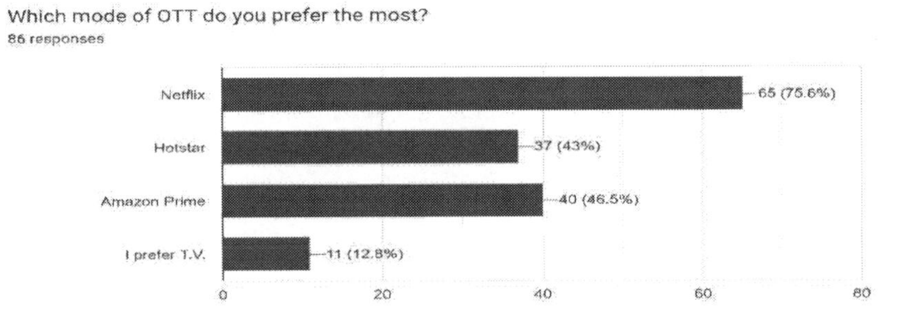

Figure 2. Preferred Mode of OTT.
Source: Author's compilation.

The next two questions inquired about the most important element of a movie for the younger generation and that why do they prefer OTT platforms as compared to the other traditional modes of Media. Almost 95.3% participants preferred that the movie should have a strong storyline alongside other elements like cast and crew (38.4%), dialogues (41.9%), comedy (31.4%) and finally songs (12.8%). Nearly 90.7% of the participants preferred OTT platform because it has better content, storyline & plot, while 18.6% preferred it because of explicit scenes, only 10.5% preferred traditional sitcoms as it caters to family audience and only 3.5% participants did not prefer OTT due to explicit scenes and language.

The next two questions recorded the outlook of the participants over the depiction of women (Figure 3) and men (Figure 4) in media including traditional and OTT platforms. The data so collected shows that there is still a long way to go for correcting the gender stereotypes in media. While 57% participants believed that the depiction of women has only partially improved rest believed that there is no improvement as the audience itself wants to see males in strong roles and females as just trophies which can be won over by men. As far as the depiction of males in media is concerned the participants pointed out and improvement in that where 64% of them believed that male actors are choosing relevant and meaning full roles. The reasons why only male actors are offered such roles has its answer in the pre-set stereotyped male dominating media industry.

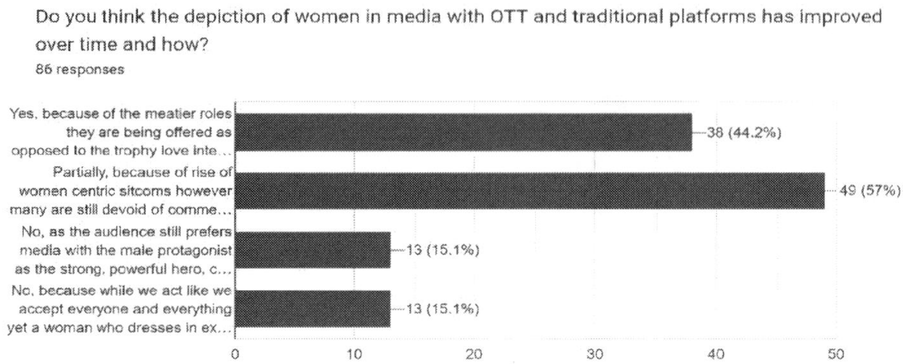

Figure 3. Depiction of Women in Media.
Source: Author's compilation.

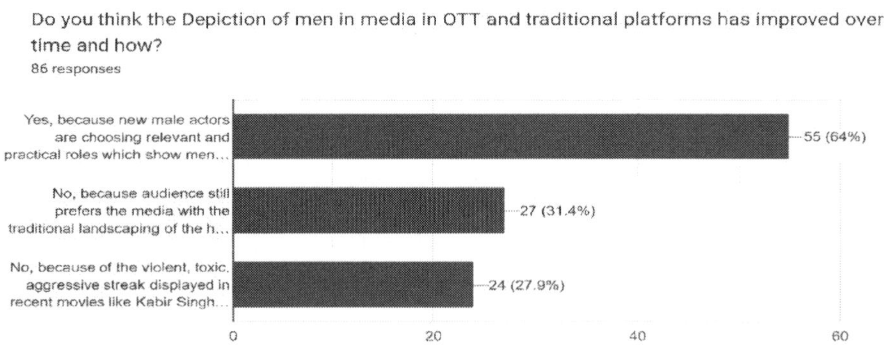

Figure 4. Depiction of Men in Media.
Source: Author's compilation.

The next question inquired about whether there is any improvement in the depiction of other genders including LGBTQIA+ community in OTT platforms or other traditional media platforms. Responses to the question the showed that the stereotypical gendering is not only limited to women but it also negatively effects and hampers other genders struggling with social acceptability. Further, 47.7% participants believed the improvement in depiction can only be said partial and

29.1% said that there is no improvement as the roles of people belonging to other gender are still enacted by straight actors and also that characters are shown to till have those age-old stereotypical characteristics like being loud etc. The next question inquired from the participants about the portrayal of women as mere 'eye candies' in Bollywood movies (Figure 5). 58.1% participants believed that female roles are casted only to glorify the male lead roles.

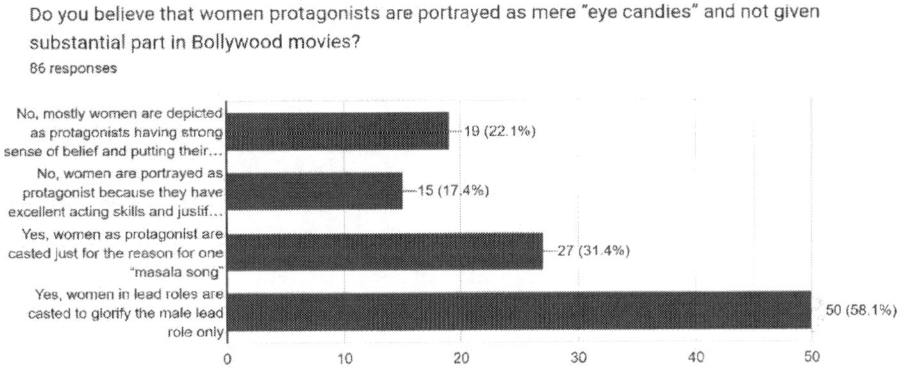

Figure 5. *Women portrayed as 'eye candies'.*

Source: Author's compilation.

The next question took inputs from the participants on movies or advertisements that promote gender stereotyping. Many of them pointed out the movie *Kabir Singh* (2019), *Mard* (1985), *Imperial Blue has an advertisement titled Men Will Be Men* (2020), *Pyar Ka Punchnama* (2011) and *Fair & Lovely* and other cosmetics advertisements that promote stereotypical beauty. The participant pointed out that even though media has a capacity to make a lot of positive difference in undoing the pre-existing stereotypes, it does not seem to be doing so.

The last part of the survey dealt with the impact of social media on the participants. The first question of this part inquired about the social media platform, which was used by the participants the most or which influenced them the most. The results show that 81.4% participants preferred and were influenced by 'Instagram' while among other social media platforms were Facebook 5.8%, Snapchat 14%, Telegram 10.5% and Twitter 22.5%. The data recorded also showed that 88.4% participants accessed social media on everyday basis. Furthermore, that 74.4% participants believed that social media memes have negative impact on their thinking.

5. SOCIO-LEGAL FRAMEWORK

The law relating to '*indecent representation*' of women in India is dealt by The Indian Penal Code, 1860; The Indecent Representation of women Act (Prohibition)

Act, 1986; The Information Technology Act, 2002 and The Cinematograph Act 1952. Section 2(c) of the Indecent Representation of Women Act defines the term '*indecent representation of women*' as '*the depiction in any manner of the figure of a woman, her form or body or any part thereof in such a way as to have the effect of being indecent, or derogatory to or denigrating women, or is likely to deprave, corrupt or injure the public morality or morals*'. The definition brings under its ambit two aspects; '*derogatory depiction of figure of a woman*' and '*such depiction injures the morals of the society*'.

The travesty of the Indian legal framework is that all the laws dealing with '*indecent representation of women*'; whether Section 292 which talk about Sale, etc., of obscene books, etc., 293 which talk about Sale, etc., of obscene objects to young person, 294 which talk about obscene acts and songs; of the Indian Penal Code, 1860 or Section 67 which talk about Punishment for publishing or transmitting obscene material in electronic form; of the Information Technology Act, or Indecent Representation of Women Act, 1986 or the guidelines issued under the Cinematograph Act 1952, all of them state that the presented content may not be profane, sexually explicit, or otherwise offensive to society's morals and values. However, a careful examination of these regulations reveals their inadequate nature and the fact that they are all restricted to solely physically offensive depictions of women. Particularly, the definition of 'indecent' in these regulations is limited and implies the word's limited pejorative meaning in Indian context. Obscenity and indecency, as defined by these regulations, are based on the Victorian idea that a man has a responsibility to safeguard a woman's sexuality. The protective legislation on the subject emphasizes the necessity to shield women based on their sexuality rather than the criteria of shielding their social status. The pervasive gender stereotyping of women in advertisements, movies, series in OTT platforms is being silently disregarded by legislature.

OTT platforms have grown in significance during the past ten years. The expansion of the OTT platform is facilitated by the growth of digital gadgets. OTT platforms are available around the clock, seven days a week, and may be accessed from any location. Depending on regional preferences, the OTT platform in India delivers material in 20 different languages. The Government of India amended the '*Government of India (Allocation of Business) Rules, 1961*' on 28 July 2023 and added two new categories 22A and 22C under Ministry of Information and Broadcasting. Category 22A included 'Films and Audio-Visual programmes/content made available by online content providers/publishers'. Category 22C included 'Online advertisements' while the already existing category 22B includes 'News and current affairs content on online platforms'. ('A Much Needed Move: Amendment in Allocation of Business Rule' n.d.) Also, the government of India unveiled '*the Information Technology (Intermediary Guidelines and Digital Media Ethics Code) Rules*' (*The Hindu* 2021) on 25 February 2021 for regulating OTT platforms in India, which were previously unregulated by the government.

6. CONCLUSION

Superfluous beauty is valued by women from a young age, and they invest a lot of time, money, and effort into striving to achieve this ideal. Then they fail in achieving the same and feel ashamed and guilty. But since the ideal media surrounds us with are built on absolute perfection, failure is unavoidable. On the other side, gender stereotypes claim that women are better suited to be housewives, are subordinate to their male counterparts, and are not allowed to act in their own best interests. They are shown to be dependent on and subject to the patriarchal rules, authorities, and traditions established by their male counterparts.

Issues such as woman facing a glass ceiling, the risks of sexual harassment at work, or her struggle to manage her time between work and family rarely make up the premise of any Indian series. Postpartum depression and homemakers' economic contributions to a nation are two highly pertinent yet underappreciated topics that don't offer material attractive enough for the attention-grabbing serials or movies. Even when portrayed as independent decision-makers in advertisements, they typically represent goods connected to food and drink, health and hygiene, and cosmetics. They hardly ever advertise high-end goods like real estate, shares, or cars.

Gender stereotyping has a lengthy and complicated history. Instilling the traditional values and beliefs in children is a responsibility shared by parents and society as a whole. Media can play a pivotal role in bringing about a positive change. The data collected by the empirical research shows that Media is working in the wrong direction. Though there are little positive steps that the Media has started to take through the medium of some movies or series or advertisements but still there is a long way to go to finally curb the gender stereotypes that has been or is still being created by the portrayal of women in such mediums.

The Education system also has a significant influence in influencing the attitudes and behaviours of society. The lives of men and women can be significantly impacted by education. Gender equality can be accepted as a fundamental social value by changing attitudes about gender stereotypes. Starting at home and continuing through higher education via the formal educational system can do wonders in creating awareness regarding gender stereotypes at a young age.

Further the legal system should also do its job to the best. India, since its independence has made a number of efforts to address the problems of gender inequality and stereotypes. The Indian government has worked to alleviate gender inequality through policies and legislative changes. For instance, the Indian Constitution has a provision ensuring the '*freedom from discrimination based on sex*' under Article 15 Sub-clause (1). Also, India ratified The Convention for the Elimination of All Forms of Discrimination Against Women (CEDAW) in the year 1980 which makes it obligatory for India to take measures for gender equality. India also has enacted various laws for the protection of women from indecent portrayal in media as mentioned above in the socio-legal framework section. However, proper implementation of the policies and legal reforms as well as societal cooperation are both necessary for curbing the problem. It would be much simpler to tackle the issue of gender stereotyping related to values and ideas instilled in our families if every member of society was made aware of gender equality and its importance to individual and societal growth with the help of media. An inclusive society requires a purposeful effort on the part of the community to alter attitudes and to accept differences.

REFERENCES

"A much-needed move: amendment in allocation of business rule," n.d. Accessed October 23, 2023. https://www.khuranaandkhurana.com/2023/03/24/analysis-of-recent-amendments-made-in-allocation-of-business-rules-2020-with-respect-to-digital-media/.

Butler, Judith (1999). *Gender Trouble: Feminism and the Subversion of Identity*. New York: Routledge.

Dhar, Suneeta (2018). "Gender and sustainable development goals (SDGs)." *Indian Journal of Gender Studies* 25(1): 47–78. https://doi.org/10.1177/0971521517738451.

"Fourth World Conference on Women, Beijing 1995," n.d. Accessed August 8, 2023. https://www.un.org/womenwatch/daw/beijing/platform/index.html.

"Gender Stereotyping," n.d. OHCHR. Accessed August 8, 2023. https://www.ohchr.org/en/women/gender-stereotyping.

Greco, Julianna (2013). "Gender: a social construction," *Sociological Imagination: Western's Undergraduate Sociology Student Journal* 2(2). https://ir.lib.uwo.ca/si/vol2/iss2/8.

Hollander, Jocelyn A. (2013). "'I DEMAND MORE OF PEOPLE': accountability, interaction, and gender change," *Gender and Society* 27(1): 5–29.

Rajneesh, Shalini (2021). "Gender mainstreaming: issues and challenges," *Gender Mainstreaming in India: Perspective and Concerns*, 1–15. Government of Karnataka, Fiscal Policy Institute. https://fpibengaluru.karnataka.gov.in/storage/pdf-files/Technical%20Reports/FPI%20Gender%20Mainstreeming%20Version-2%2013-07-2021.pdf.

The Hindu (2021). "On centre's new guidelines for digital media, OTT platforms," March 9, 2021, sec. India. https://www.thehindu.com/news/national/digital-media-regulation/article56832356.ece.

14. The Accountability of Stakeholders in Combating Domestic Violence with Women in India

Manika Singh

Research Scholar, School of Law, Christ (Deemed to be) University, Delhi-NCR, India; Assistant Professor, University Institute of Legal Studies, Chandigarh University, Punjab, India

Email: manika.singh@res.christuniversity.in; adv.manikaphd6@gmail.com

Dr. Meera Mathew

Associate Professor, School of Law, Christ (Deemed to be) University, Delhi-NCR, India

Email: meera.mathew@christuniversity.in

ABSTRACT: As per the Hindu tradition, women are considered as 'ardhangini' and the western civilisation considers them as 'better half'. Since ancient times, women have been considered as the epitome of love, kindness, care and above all 'the mother of mankind'. But on the contrary, the most terrible and horrifying cruelties are imposed upon her. The predominant type of violence which is inflicted upon a woman is 'domestic violence' also known as 'intimate partner violence'. According to the World Health Organisation, almost one third, i.e., 27% of the women aged between 15 and 49 years, who have been in a relationship report that they have been subjected to some form of physical or sexual violence by their intimate partner. The issue of domestic violence has been addressed at both international and national levels, but still there exists a persistent gap in enforcing and implementing them. And this can be easily proved from the continuous rise in the cases of domestic violence worldwide, especially during the COVID times. The problem that needs to be addressed at hand is the role of several accountable stakeholders involved in the process of providing access to justice to the women affected by domestic violence. According to the Protection of Women from Domestic Violence Act (2005), in India, the several stakeholders include the protection officers, service providers, lawyers, police officers, shelter homes and judges. These are the people with whom the power to protect and help the women are vested, but instead the affected women fall a prey to this system due to various reasons like lack of resources, fewer power and many more which will be further discussed in the article.

Chapter 14 DOI- 10.4324/9781003428213-14

KEYWORDS: Domestic violence, stakeholders, access to justice, intimate partner violence, woman

1. INTRODUCTION

Domestic violence is also known as spousal violence or intimate partner violence. It is a serious and pervasive issue that affects women worldwide. It is a pattern of abusive behaviour in which one spouse repeatedly uses physical, emotional, psychological, or economic violence against the other to achieve control over them. While domestic violence can occur in any type of intimate relationship, it disproportionately affects women, with women being the majority of victims. Some factors that contribute to the prevalence of domestic violence against women include gender inequality, cultural norms, substance abuse, intergenerational transmission and socioeconomic factors. The resulting in far-reaching and severe consequences includes physical injuries, long-term mental health issues, social isolation, economic dependence and many more.

The Protection of Women from Domestic Violence Act (PWDVA) was enacted in India in 2005 to provide legal protection to women against domestic violence. The Act recognises the right of women to live free from violence and abuse in the home and provides legal remedies and protective measures to support victims of domestic violence. Ending domestic violence against women requires a collective effort to challenge societal norms, promote gender equality and create safe environments for all individuals. Thus, it is important that the legal functionaries, as expressly mentioned in the PWDV Act, 2005 help the aggrieved persons in providing access to justice. To understand how this can be done, it is important to study the role of these functionaries by analysing the powers provided to them by the Act.

2. RESEARCH METHODOLOGY

Each research study has its own specific purpose and the purpose of this research study is to find out those loopholes in the Domestic Violence Act, 2005 which are affecting the proper and timely delivery of justice to the women sufferer. To understand the system and the formal stakeholders involved in this system, this study is carried out by following Doctrinal Research Methodology, where the law along with the existing data will be analysed and then the appropriate measures will be suggested by the author after making a comparative analytical study.

3. ROLE OF STAKEHOLDERS

Legal functionaries/relevant stakeholders play a crucial role in providing justice to victims of domestic violence under the Protection of Women from Domestic Violence Act (PWDVA) 2005. The Act recognises the importance of various legal officials and institutions in ensuring that victims' rights are protected and that perpetrators are held accountable. The combined efforts of these legal functionaries create a comprehensive system to address domestic violence cases and provide justice to victims. An in-depth study is done to understand the roles that these legal functionaries play, as mentioned subsequently.

3.1. Protection Officers

Under *Section 4, Section 8,* and *Section 9* of the Domestic Violence Act, 2005, the protection officer (PO) plays a crucial role in assisting and supporting victims of domestic violence. Here are the key roles and functions of a protection officer under the PWDVA:

i. Assisting the victim: the protection officer is responsible for assisting the victim in understanding her rights under the PWDVA and the remedies available to her. They provide information about the legal procedures and the process for filing an application for protection against domestic violence.
ii. Filing the complaint: the protection officer can help the victim in filing a complaint or an application before the Magistrate seeking protection orders against the respondent (the perpetrator of domestic violence). They assist the victim in preparing the necessary documentation and evidence to support her case.
iii. Serving protection orders: after the Magistrate issues protection orders in favour of the victim, the protection officer ensures that these orders are served on the respondent. These orders may include restraining the respondent from committing acts of domestic violence, prohibiting him from contacting or approaching the victim and providing her with a safe place of residence.
iv. Coordinating with service providers: the protection officer collaborates with various service providers, such as shelter homes, counselling centres, medical facilities and legal aid organisations, to ensure the victim receives the necessary support and assistance. They facilitate access to these services for the victim.
v. Safety planning: protection officers may work with the victim to develop safety plans tailored to her specific situation. These plans are designed to help the victim take steps to protect herself and her children from further violence and abuse.
vi. Conducting home visits: the protection officer may conduct home visits to the victim's residence to assess her safety and well-being. During these visits, they can ascertain the presence of any potential risks and provide appropriate interventions.

It is important to note that the protection officer's role is crucial in empowering the victim and facilitating her access to justice and support services. Their work is aimed at creating a safe and supportive environment for victims of domestic violence, helping them break free from the cycle of abuse and reclaiming control over their lives.

The concept of a 'protection officer' specifically designated for domestic violence victims is not unique to India. Several other countries have similar roles or positions aimed at providing assistance and support to victims of domestic violence. Here are a few examples:

United Kingdom	In the United Kingdom, there are various support services for domestic violence victims, including Domestic Abuse Support Officers (DASOs), Domestic Violence Liaison Officers (DVLOs) and Independent Domestic Violence Advisors (IDVAs). These officers provide information, support and safety planning for victims.
United States	In the United States, there are domestic violence advocates and counsellors who play a role similar to that of protection officers in India. They work with victims to provide support, safety planning and access to resources.
Australia	Australia has Family Violence Liaison Officers and Domestic Violence Support Workers who work closely with police and community organisations to support victims of domestic violence.
Canada	Canada has various services and personnel, such as Victim Services Officers, who provide assistance and support to victims of domestic violence.
South Africa	South Africa has specialised Family Violence, Child Protection and Sexual Offences Units (FCS Units) that handle cases related to domestic violence, child abuse and sexual offenses.
Spain	Spain has specialised support services, such as the Violence Against Women Units, which provide assistance to victims of gender-based violence.

It is important to note that the roles and titles may differ based on the legal and administrative structures of each country. Nonetheless, the common goal is to provide victims of domestic violence with the necessary support, protection and access to justice.

3.2. Service Providers

Service providers refer to various institutions and organisations that offer specialised services to victims to help them cope with the consequences of domestic violence. *Section 5* and *Section 10* of the Act specifically define the roles and responsibilities of the Service Providers. The key roles of service providers under the PWDVA are as follows:

i. Shelter homes: service providers help in providing shelter homes or women's shelters, mentioned under *Section 6* of the Act, which is a temporary accommodation and a safe environment for women who are facing immediate danger or are at risk of domestic violence. These shelter homes provide a secure place for the victim and her children, offering protection from the abuser.
ii. Counselling centres: counselling centres provide emotional support and counselling services to victims of domestic violence. Trained counsellors help victims cope with trauma, build self-esteem and develop coping strategies to navigate through the challenges they may encounter.
iii. Medical facilities: service providers may include medical facilities and healthcare professionals who can provide medical assistance and documentation of injuries sustained due to domestic violence, mentioned under *Section 7* of the Act. They can also offer medical examination and treatment, if needed.
iv. Legal aid services: legal aid organisations and lawyers offer free or subsidised legal assistance to victims who may not have the financial means to hire private legal representation. They help victims understand their legal rights and assist them in filing applications and presenting their case in court.
v. Rehabilitation and skill development: some service providers focus on the rehabilitation and skill development of victims to help them become financially independent and self-reliant. They offer vocational training, education and employment opportunities to empower victims to rebuild their lives after leaving abusive situations.
vi. Crisis intervention: service providers engage in crisis intervention to address immediate needs of victims. This may include providing emergency assistance, such as food, clothing and transportation, to those who are displaced or facing acute financial distress due to domestic violence.
vii. Public awareness and education: service providers also contribute to public awareness and education campaigns about domestic violence. They help in spreading information about the PWDVA, women's rights and the available resources for victims.
viii. Coordination and referral: service providers work in coordination with each other, sharing information and resources to provide comprehensive support to victims. They may also refer victims to other relevant services based on their specific needs.

Overall, the role of service providers under the Domestic Violence Act is to create a supportive ecosystem for victims of domestic violence, ensuring that they receive the necessary assistance, protection and empowerment to break free from abusive relationships and lead a life free from violence.

3.3. Police Officers

Section 5 of the Act specifically talks about the duties of the police officers as their role is vital in responding to complaints of domestic violence, ensuring the safety of the victims and taking appropriate actions to prevent further abuse. The key roles of police officers under the PWDVA are as follows:

i. Registering complaints: when a victim approaches the police with a complaint of domestic violence, the police officers are responsible for registering the complaint promptly. They must treat domestic violence cases with seriousness and sensitivity, recognising the urgency of the situation.
ii. Immediate assistance: police officers are required to provide immediate assistance to the victim and take necessary steps to prevent any further violence or harm. This may include separating the victim from the abuser, ensuring her safety and offering medical aid if required.
iii. Conducting investigation: police officers are responsible for conducting a thorough and impartial investigation into the allegations of domestic violence. They gather evidence, interview witnesses and document injuries or damages caused by the abuse.
iv. Arresting the perpetrator: if the investigation reveals evidence of domestic violence, police officers have the authority to arrest the perpetrator based on the severity of the offense and the provisions of the PWDVA.
v. Seizing weapons: in situations where the respondent has used weapons or is likely to use them to cause harm, police officers can seize such weapons to prevent further violence.
vi. Ensuring compliance: after protection orders are issued by the Magistrate, police officers ensure that the respondent complies with the orders and does not violate the victim's rights further.

By fulfilling these roles, police officers contribute significantly to the prevention and reduction of domestic violence and ensure that victims receive the necessary protection and support to break free from abusive situations

3.4. Lawyers/Public Prosecutors and Legal Aid Counsels

Lawyers and Legal Aid Counsels play significant roles in providing legal representation and support to victims of domestic violence under the Domestic Violence Act, 2005 (PWDVA). Their roles are instrumental in ensuring that victims have access to justice, understand their legal rights and receive the necessary protection and remedies under the law. Here are the key roles of Lawyers and Legal Aid Counsels under the PWDVA:

i. Legal representation: Lawyers and Legal Aid Counsels represent the aggrieved women in court during the legal proceedings under the PWDVA.

They act as advocates for the victim, representing her case and arguments before the Magistrate.

ii. Assisting in filing applications: Lawyers and Legal Aid Counsels help the victim in preparing and filing the application or complaint before the Magistrate seeking protection orders against domestic violence. They assist in gathering the necessary evidence and documentation to support the victim's case.

iii. Legal advice: Lawyers and Legal Aid Counsels provide legal advice to the victim, explaining her rights under the PWDVA and other relevant laws. They help the victim understand the available legal remedies, such as protection orders, residence orders and monetary reliefs.

iv. Preparing the case: Lawyers and Legal Aid Counsels prepare the case on behalf of the victim, organising and presenting the evidence, identifying witnesses, cross-examining witnesses and presenting a strong argument before the Magistrate.

v. Negotiations and settlements: in some cases, lawyers and Legal Aid Counsels may engage in negotiations with the respondent (the perpetrator) or their legal representatives to explore the possibility of reaching an amicable settlement. However, settlements cannot compromise the victim's safety or her rights under the law.

vi. Enforcement of protection orders: after protection orders are issued by the Magistrate, lawyers and Legal Aid Counsels assist the victim in enforcing these orders. They may take legal action against the respondent in case of violations of protection orders.

vii. Explaining legal proceedings: Lawyers and Legal Aid Counsels help the victim understand the legal process, the various stages of the case and what to expect during court hearings.

viii. Providing legal aid: Legal Aid Counsels, specifically, are appointed by the government to provide free legal assistance to victims who may not have the financial means to hire private representation. They ensure that the victim's right to legal aid is upheld.

Overall, the combined efforts of Lawyers and Legal Aid Counsels are critical in ensuring that victims of domestic violence have access to justice and receive appropriate legal remedies and support.

3.5. Judges/Magistrates

Section 5 talks about the duties of a magistrate, while *Sections 12–26* state the powers vested in a Magistrate. As adjudicators, they preside over court proceedings, interpret the law and make decisions that safeguard the rights and well-being of aggrieved women (victims). Here are the key roles of judges under the PWDVA:

i. Adjudication of cases: judges in Magistrates' Courts are responsible for adjudicating cases filed by aggrieved women seeking protection orders against domestic violence. They listen to the evidence presented by the victim and the respondent (the perpetrator) during court hearings.

ii. Ensuring due process: judges ensure that the legal process is fair and follows due process. They provide both the victim and the respondent with an opportunity to present their case, cross-examine witnesses and respond to allegations.

iii. Issuing protection, residence, and custody orders: based on the evidence presented, judges have the authority to issue protection order under *Section 18,* residence orders under *Section 19,* and custody order under *Section 21* of the Act, to protect the victim from further acts of domestic violence and safe custody of their child. These orders may include restraining the respondent from committing violence, prohibiting contact with the victim and providing her with a safe place of residence, granting temporary custody of the child, etc.

iv. Interim orders: when there is an immediate threat to the victim's safety, judges may issue interim orders under *Section* 23 of the Act, before a full hearing is conducted. Interim orders offer immediate protection until the case is fully heard.

v. Awarding compensation: if the evidence supports it, judges may order the respondent to pay compensation to the victim for the injuries and damages suffered due to domestic violence under *Section 20 and Section 22* of the Act.

vi. Counselling and mediation: in some cases, Magistrates may refer the parties to counselling or mediation under *Section 14* of the Act, encouraging them to resolve their disputes amicably. However, mediation cannot be used in cases involving violence or sexual abuse.

Overall, the role of judges under the Domestic Violence Act is to uphold the rule of law, protect the rights of victims and provide them with the necessary remedies and legal safeguards to break free from abusive situations and lead lives free from violence.

7. CRITICAL ANALYSIS OF FUNCTIONING OF THE STAKEHOLDERS

While the Domestic Violence Act, 2005 (PWDVA) is a crucial legislation aimed at protecting victims of domestic violence, various challenges and issues are faced by the key stakeholders involved in its implementation. Some of the common issues faced by these legal functionaries are – *insufficient resources* – protection officers and service providers often face challenges due to limited resources, inadequate funding and lack of proper infrastructure. This can affect the quality and extent of services they can provide to victims; *overburdened caseloads* – due to the prevalence of domestic violence cases, protection officers, lawyers and service providers may have to handle a high number of cases, leading to heavy workloads and potential delays in providing assistance to victims; *lack of specialised training* – protection and police officers, service providers –including counsellors and medical professionals, may require specialised training to effectively address the unique needs of victims of domestic violence. The lack of such training can impact the quality of support provided to victims; *victim safety and security* – police officers and protection officers may face challenges in ensuring the safety and security of victims, especially in cases where the abuser poses a high risk. Providing adequate protection to victims can be complex and resource-intensive; *lengthy legal procedure* – the legal process under the Act can sometimes be time-consuming. Lengthy court procedures may delay the issuance of protection orders, leaving victims vulnerable during the interim period; *lack of coordination* – coordination and collaboration among different stakeholders, such as police, lawyers, protection officer and service providers, may sometimes be lacking, leading to gaps in the support system for victims.

Despite these challenges, the key stakeholders continue to play vital roles in providing support and protection to victims of domestic violence.

8. THE ROLE OF INDIAN GOVERNMENT

The government of India plays a crucial role in combating domestic violence against women and ensuring their safety and well-being. *Section 11* of the PWDV Act, 2005 specifically lays down the duties of the government. It states that, the Central Government and each State Government shall take all necessary steps to ensure that: the provisions of the Act are widely publicised through public media, including television, radio and print media on a regular basis. The government conducts research and collects data on the prevalence and patterns of domestic violence. This data forms policy decisions and helps in resource allocation. The government also provides free or subsidised legal aid and counselling services to assist victims in understanding their rights and seeking legal remedies. Through these efforts, the government aims to combat domestic violence effectively and foster a society that respects and upholds the rights of women.

The Indian government had implemented several policies and schemes to combat domestic violence in the country. Here are some of the key initiatives in place at that time:

One stop centres (OSC)	Popularly known as Sakhi Centres, set-up across the country to provide integrated support and assistance to women affected by violence. These centres offer medical, legal, psychological and counselling services to victims
Women helpline (181)	A dedicated national helpline number – 181 established, to provide immediate assistance and support to women facing violence – available 24/7 – accessible from all over India.

Mahila police volunteer scheme	This scheme involves recruiting trained female volunteers at the village level to act as a link between the police and the community. They help in reporting and preventing domestic violence.
Swadhar Greh scheme	A government program that offers institutional support for women in challenging situations, aiding their rehabilitation and pursuit of dignified lives.
Working women hostel	A scheme to support safe housing and environments for working women and give creche facilities for their kids.

The Government has come up with several schemes but their success only depends upon the effective implementation of these.

9. CONCLUSION

Addressing domestic violence against women requires a multifaceted approach, involving individuals, communities, governments and organisations. Public awareness is very pivotal in curbing the issue of domestic violence since half of the women in India do not consider domestic violence as a problem. India already has a legal framework for combating domestic violence with women. The need of the hour is to strengthen this law and enforce strict penalties for domestic violence which can act as a deterrent and provide protection to victims. Another important step which has to be taken is to engage men in discussions about gender equality and nonviolent behavior since it is essential for changing harmful attitudes and behaviors.

There are also several measures that India can learn from other countries to combat violence effectively. *First*, India can study the domestic violence laws of countries like the United States, the United Kingdom and Canada to strengthen its own legal framework. Ensuring comprehensive laws that provide adequate protection, remedies and support to victims is essential. *Second*, establishing specialised domestic violence courts, similar to the Family Justice Centers in the United States, can help expedite cases and provide integrated services to victims under one roof. *Third*, India can draw inspiration from countries like Australia and New Zealand in running public awareness campaigns on violence prevention. These campaigns can be effective in changing societal attitudes and promoting a culture of nonviolence. *Fourth*, learning from countries like Sweden and Denmark, India can work towards providing safe and confidential housing options for victims of violence, including dedicated shelters for women and children. *Fifth*, the United Kingdom and Australia offer training programs for police, judges and legal professionals to handle domestic violence cases effectively. India can adopt similar training initiatives to improve the handling of such cases. *Sixth*, India can look to countries like Spain and France, where they have established integrated support services that provide medical, legal and psychological assistance to victims under one umbrella. Learning from countries like the United States and the United Kingdom, India can expand its helplines and develop user-friendly online reporting mechanisms to encourage victims to seek help and report incidents. India can take inspiration from countries like Sweden and Norway, where collaboration between the government and NGOs has been successful in combating violence. Partnering with NGOs can enhance support services and reach a wider section of the population. *Lastly,* Canada and New Zealand have implemented rehabilitation programs for offenders of domestic violence. Implementing such programs in India can help break the cycle of violence.

By adopting and customising successful strategies and best practices from other countries, India can strengthen its efforts to combat violence, protect victims and promote a safer and more inclusive society for all.

REFERENCES

Agnes, Flavia (2005). "Women domestic violence act: a portal of hope," *Combat Law* 4(6).

Balaji, T. (2016). "Domestic Violence Act 2005 - a critical analysis," *International Journal of Scientific Research* 5(9).

Barooah, Dr. Jeuti (2003). *Women, Law and Justice Delivery System in Assam.* Eastern Region: LRI.

Bhatia, Manjeet (2012). "Domestic violence in India: cases under the protection of women from Domestic Violence Act, 2005," *South Asia Research, Sage Journals.*

Farooqui, M. Sumaiya (2012). "Consequence of domestic violence," *Gender Inequality and Domestic Violence Study*, pp. 147–158. Kanpur, Uttar Pradesh, India: Department of English, Chhatrapati Sahuji Maharaj University. http://hdl.handle.net/10603/269247.

Jaising, Indira (2009). "Staying alive: third monitoring and evaluation report 2009 on the PWDVA, 2005," *Lawyer's Collective. Lawyers Collective Women's Rights Initiative and International Center for Research on Women.* https://nlrd.org/wp-content/uploads/2012/06/Staying-Alive-Third-ME-Report-2009-final.pdf.

Kannabiran, Kalpana (2009). "The law, gender and women," *Review of Women's Studies, Economic & Political Weekly* 44(44).

Kaur, Ravneet, and Suneela Garg (2008). "Addressing domestic violence against women: an unfinished agenda," *Indian Journal of Community Medicine* 33(2): 73–76.

Mahjebeen, Joanna (2009). "Domestic violence: the problem under study," *Domestic Violence against Women: A Study in Kamrup District of Assam*, pp. 82–123. Gauhati, Assam, India: Department of Political Science, Gauhati University, India. http://hdl.handle.net/10603/66438.

Ministry of Home Affairs. National Crime Record Bureau (2018). "Crime in India 2018," https://data.gov.in/catalog/crime-india-2018.

Ministry of Women and Child Development. Ministry of Women and Child Development, Government of India (2021). "National Report on Domestic Violence against Women," https://wcd.nic.in/annual-report.

Mishra, Preeti (2007). *Domestic Violence Against Women: Legal Control and Judicial Response.* New Delhi, India: Deep & Deep Publications.

Robertson, Kirsten, and Tamar Murachver (2009). "Attitudes and attributions associated with female and male partner violence," *Journal of Applied Social Psychology* 39(7): 481–512.

Roy, Priya, and Malini Singh (2017). "Understanding the impact of domestic violence on mental health: a Study in Indian context," *Proceedings of the International Conference on Gender Studies and Social Issues*, Chicago: Academic Publishing, pp. 78–89.

Sharma, Ruchita (2019). "Domestic violence against women in India: a comprehensive review of its prevalence and risk factors," *Journal of Gender-Based Violence* 7(2): 123–142. https://doi.org/10.1080/13552605.2018.1563402.

The Protection of Women from Domestic Violence Act (2005).

UN Women (2012). *Handbook for Legislation on Violence Against Women*. New York: UN Women.

15. Advancing Women's Health and Dignity: A Comprehensive Analysis of Menstrual Health Management and Rights in India

Subarna Ghosh
Ph.D. Research Scholar, Faculty of Law, University of Delhi

ABSTRACT: This study offers a comprehensive analysis of the intricate challenges and human rights implications related to menstrual health management and rights in India. It underscores the urgency of effective menstrual health management, encompassing key components such as menstrual literacy, access to sanitary products and the provision of safe and hygienic facilities. Despite the significant number of menstruating individuals in India, a pervasive lack of knowledge about menstruation perpetuates the use of unhygienic alternatives.

The study also highlights the various human rights intertwined with menstruation, including the right to health, water, sanitation, education, non-discrimination, gender equity and a dignified life. It delves into the environmental and health concerns tied to the disposal of menstrual waste, emphasising the necessity of sustainable alternatives. Furthermore, it discusses the roles of diverse stakeholders, such as the Indian government, NGOs, the private sector and individuals, in addressing menstrual health issues and calls for the recognition of menstrual health as a fundamental human right, emphasising the importance of standardised waste disposal practices and the provision of safe and hygienic facilities.

KEYWORDS: Menstrual hygiene management, menstrual literacy.

1. INTRODUCTION

Feminist theorists have long argued that women face paradoxical stereotypes throughout their lives. On one hand, they are often perceived as less competent and inherently less valuable than men, while simultaneously being idealised and glorified as wives and mothers (Dunnavant and Robert 2013). In her seminal work, 'The Second Sex' (de Beauvoir 1989), Simone de Beauvoir extensively analyses how society creates and perpetuates the inferior position of women,

Chapter 15 DOI- 10.4324/9781003428213-15

often categorising them as the 'Other,' both culturally and historically. De Beauvoir, while discussing menstruation, points out that it is one of the reasons why women are looked down upon as the inferior sex and writes, 'Certainly, there is more to it than a mere reaction to blood in general, however sacred it may be. Menstrual blood is distinct; it symbolises the essence of femininity' (de Beauvoir 1989).

Managing menstruation in a hygienic manner is an integral aspect of basic hygiene, sanitation and reproductive rights, fundamental to women's dignity and overall well-being. However, menstruation remains a taboo subject shrouded in silence and shame in India, even in the 21st century, despite significant scientific and technological progress. This, combined with the pervasive social construct of patriarchy, has turned menstruation into a significant source of gender-based inequality and injustice against women. Stigmatising adolescent girls and women through misguided beliefs rooted in age-old cultural practices perpetuates gender inequity and undermines their basic rights.

2. MANAGING MENSTRUAL HEALTH AND HYGIENE

The UNICEF and WHO Joint Monitoring Programme has provided a definition for menstrual health management, which encompasses women and adolescent girls using clean menstrual management materials to absorb or collect blood that can be changed in private as needed throughout the menstrual period. They should also have access to soap and water for body hygiene and facilities for the proper disposal of used menstrual management materials. Therefore, the right to manage menstruation must incorporate the following aspects:

2.1. Menstrual Literacy

In 2018-19, a survey conducted by the Ministry of Women and Child Development under the Integrated Child Development Services (ICDS) reported that more than one-fourth of total girls enrolled in middle school discontinued their education upon attaining puberty. The only source of information on menstruation that is affordable and accessible are views, tales, myths based on personal practices of the female members of their immediate family and biased social constructs on menstruation which are far from reality. Such practices make it difficult for adolescents to follow healthy and safe menstrual health practices. Menstrual etiquettes in India continue to be enveloped in a sense of shame, stigma and fears and are therefore either discussed behind closed doors or not discussed at all. Statistics reveal that the country has over 280 million individuals who are of menstruating age. A significant number of individuals have negligible knowledge of the biological process of menstruation. The absence of knowledge and awareness leads to a lack of acknowledgement of menstruation as a natural phenomenon, often stigmatising it as 'unclean'. Consequently, the practices related to menstrual management vary widely. Alarmingly, 88% of menstruating individuals use homemade alternatives, including rags, hay or potent ash, which not only are uncomfortable and inconvenient but also lead to diseases and infections ('Urban Sanitation' 2015). Efforts should be made to initiate open discussions about menstruation, providing essential information to enable its safe and dignified management. The current imperative is to strategically design and implement awareness programmes for all.

2.2. Access to Sanitary Products Along with Safe and Hygienic Spaces to Use Them

It is essential to recognise and disavow practices and narratives that are detrimental to the well-being of menstruating individuals. It is also essential to practise a very high level of personal hygiene during menstruation. Menstruation can be effectively managed in a healthy and safe manner through a thorough understanding of the appropriate use of safe sanitary products and materials, along with the proper care during and after their use. This must be supplemented with a heightened sense of hygiene, having a balanced diet and access to psychological support, and knowledge of pain management during and after the menstrual cycle.

The effective management of menstrual health management is impossible without reviewing the existing WASH guidelines and critically assessing the practical support that it aspires to provide for all in public places, at work, in correctional facilities and health care facilities, households, etc. Such facilities for the safe management of menstruation are only effective and adequate if they also consider the particular requirements of those who also experience biological, social and culturally constructed differences. Thus, WASH facilities should include water, soap, access to sanitary products and hygienic places to use and dispose of them as well. Policymakers need to redesign policies with a humanitarian approach that is inclusive of the experiences of the third gender and persons with disabilities. The government has a vital role to play in offering clear, understandable and accurate information on the what, why and how of menstruation, as well as promoting awareness of the available options for its management. The intended beneficiaries should also have access to safe, affordable, acceptable products to be able to make an informed choice. In addition, research, innovation and development of sanitary products must be encouraged by the state.

2.3. Adoption of Safe Practices and Procedures for the Hygienic and Environment-Friendly Disposal of Menstrual Waste

The by-products or end-products of menstruation waste comprise reusable and disposable sanitary napkins, tampons, cotton wool, pieces of fabric, product wrapping and tissue paper and the uterine lining shed by the body. Disposal of menstrual waste depends on the product one is using and some social and cultural factors.

An individual woman is estimated to generate as much as 125 kilograms of non-biodegradable waste during her menstruating years, posing significant health and environmental risks (Bhatia and Kaushik 2019). The plastic used in regular sanitary napkins is not biodegradable. This has led to menstrual waste disposal becoming a serious and ever-increasing problem and causing health and environmental hazards. The existing regulatory framework has categorised certain menstrual and sexual health products like soiled napkins, diapers, condoms, tampons and blood-soaked cotton as household waste. Sanitary products are supposed to be disposed of after segregating them based on their biodegradability status. However, there is a notable absence of clear guidelines regarding the safe disposal of sanitary pads. Present regulations mandate the disposal of menstrual waste in large-scale common bio-medical waste incinerators nationwide ('The Solid Waste Management Rules' 2016). Yet, organised segregation, collection and transportation of menstrual and other sanitary waste on a large scale are necessary for this purpose. Regrettably, no viable models for such a system have been formulated or implemented thus far. The most common practice of disposal happens to be washing sanitary napkins and disposing of it with other waste is neither hygienic nor environmentally friendly.

With the growth in environmental awareness, two primary sustainable products, menstrual cups and cloth pads, have emerged as alternatives for managing menstruation in a healthy and hygienic manner. While cloth pads have a historical usage among women and are easy to adapt to, they necessitate thorough washing and drying. This can be challenging in a country where taboos surrounding menstrual blood are prevalent.

The government, its policymakers, menstruating individuals and community stakeholders remain largely silent while profit-driven corporations continue to produce and sell disposable sanitary napkins, often unaware of the existence of healthier alternatives. If there is an intention to influence the choices women make regarding sanitary products, it is imperative to provide complete and unbiased information about the full spectrum of available, safe and affordable menstrual materials. The life cycle cost (LCC) approach, which evaluates the total cost of an asset over its entire lifecycle, encompassing initial capital costs, maintenance costs, operating costs and the asset's residual value at the end of its life, reveals that menstrual cups are estimated to have less than 1.5% of the environmental impact of disposable pads at a mere 10% of the cost (Gairikpati 2020). These products hold great promise for women as they offer a significantly cheaper and more environmentally friendly alternative to disposable pads.

3. SAFEGUARDING MENSTRUAL RIGHTS

The United Nations Population Fund, Human Rights Watch and WASH United concur in their identification of a set of human rights that have a direct connection to menstruation and thus have been globally guaranteed to every individual to have dignified menarche. They are as follows:

Right to Health-The human right to health not only encompasses access to healthcare and medicine but also extends to education and information regarding health, particularly sexual and reproductive health. The Supreme Court of India has consistently reaffirmed that Article 21 of the Constitution of India, which stipulates that 'No person shall be deprived of his life or personal liberty except according to the procedure established by law', inherently includes the right to health. The absence of facilities or support for menstrual hygiene not only poses a threat to women's reproductive health but also constitutes a broader public health concern.

Right to Water and Sanitation-The right to life inherently includes the right to human dignity, privacy and access to fundamental necessities for a dignified existence. Consequently, the human right to water aims to ensure that all individuals have access to safe, sufficient, physically accessible and affordable water for personal and domestic use. It is the primary responsibility of the state to facilitate and ensure the realisation of menstrual health and hygiene in a dignified manner. The High Court of Rajasthan in L.K. Koolwal vs State of Rajasthan and Others held that 'Maintenance of health, preservation of sanitation and the environment falls within the purview of Article 21 of the Constitution as it adversely affects the life of the citizen and amounts to slow poisoning and reducing the life of the citizen because of the hazards created, if not checked'. The central tenet of the human right to sanitation is therefore to provide safe, affordable, secure, hygienic, socially and culturally acceptable sanitation that ensures both privacy and dignity. The Indian Constitution empowers the State Governments to frame laws related to sanitation but the responsibility of effective implementation rests with the local governments.

Right to Education-The human right to education ensures access to free and mandatory primary education, along with education that is generally accessible to all. The 86th Constitutional Amendment Act of 2002 introduced Article 21A, which guarantees the right to education for every child between the ages of six and fourteen years. Furthermore, the Right of Children to Free and Compulsory Education Act was enacted and came into effect on 26 August 2009, aiming to provide free and compulsory education for children in the age group of six to fourteen years. The state is thus obligated under the Constitution of India to also address the various barriers to education that are particular to biological gender. In Court on its Own Motion Vs Government of India and Others, the High Court of Jammu and Kashmir observed that 'in order to achieve gender equality, it is crucial that girls are able to actualise their educational potential'.

Right to Work-The human right to work includes the right to freely choose and accept employment, with a crucial emphasis on the right to fair and favourable working conditions, particularly the right to safe and healthy working environments. The Supreme Court in Olga Tellis & Ors. Vs Bombay Municipal Corporation & Ors recognised the 'right to work' as an integral part of the fundamental right to life. Additionally, India happens to be a signatory to the provision of The Universal Declaration of Human Rights and the International Covenant on Economic, Social, and Cultural Rights which provides for the 'right to work'.

Right to Non-Discrimination and Gender Equity-For the complete realisation of human rights, it is important to identify and cater to existing inequalities and ensure that the rights which are fundamental to the growth and well-being of an individual are enjoyed by all. Where cultures, customs, practices, beliefs and even the legal system formally distinguish between genders and treat them differently, the need to view and frame menstrual health and hygiene concerns and policies in light of human rights is both crucial and decisive. The Convention on the Elimination of All Forms of Discrimination Against Women ('CEDAW' 1979) states that the non-identical treatment of women and men will be required to address the biological, social and culturally constructed differences between them. In India, the societal restrictions cast upon menstruating girls and women are plenty. From keeping women and/or girls in isolation to pickles turning sour, practices detrimental to their right to health, dignity, equality and privacy are still carried out in plenty during menstruation. The fundamental human right to non-discrimination and gender equity ensures that all individuals, regardless of their gender or any other characteristic, receive equal and fair treatment. This right assumes even greater significance in the context of menstrual health management, as discrimination and inequality in this sphere can result in severe consequences for women and girls.

Right to a Dignified Life-Decency and dignity have been acknowledged as non-negotiable aspects of human rights in the case of Municipal Council, Ratlam vs. Shri Vardhichand & Ors. In a significant legal decision, the Supreme Court recognised reproductive rights as an essential component of the Right to Life and Personal Liberty in the case of Suchita Srivastava & Anr vs. Chandigarh Administration. It also inferred women's right to make reproductive choices from a 'woman's right to privacy, dignity and bodily integrity' in the case of Justice K.S. Puttaswamy (Retd) vs. Union of India, 2018. In addressing the taboos and stigma associated with menstruation, the Supreme Court, in the case of Indian Young Lawyers Association and Others vs. State of Kerala and Others, emphasised that 'women have a constitutional entitlement to have their biological processes free from social and religious practices that enforce segregation and exclusion. These practices result in humiliation and violate human dignity'.

The sustainable development goals may not directly recognise menstrual health management; however, these goals can only be realised by effectively addressing the MHM needs of girls and women: ensuring healthy lives and promotion of the well-being for all across ages (Goal 3), inclusivity and equitable quality education and promotion of lifelong learning opportunities for all (Goal 4), elimination of gender disparities in education and ensuring equal access to all levels of education and vocational training for the vulnerable, including persons with disabilities, indigenous peoples and children in vulnerable situations by 2030 (Goal 4.5), achieving gender equality and empowering all women and girls, ending all forms of discrimination against all women and girls everywhere, ending all forms of discrimination against all women and girls everywhere (Goal 5), ensuring access to water and sanitation for all, achieving access to adequate and equitable sanitation and hygiene for all, paying special attention to the needs of women and girls and those in vulnerable situations (Goal 6), promotion of sustained, inclusive and sustainable economic growth, full and productive employment and decent work for all (Goal 8), and ensuring sustainable consumption and production patterns, substantially reduce waste generation through prevention, reduction, recycling and reuse by 2030 (Goal 12) ('THE 17 GOALS | Sustainable Development' 2015).

The Government of India, through the National Health Mission under the Ministry of Health and Family Welfare, initiated a scheme in 2011 to ensure the well-being of adolescent girls aged 10 to 19 years in rural areas, as part of the Adolescent Reproductive Sexual Health (ARSH) programme. This scheme also encompasses menstrual hygiene management and aligns with the Swachh Bharat Mission guidelines, issued by the Ministry of Drinking Water and Sanitation, to support adolescent girls and women. These guidelines aim to promote effective menstrual hygiene management while upholding the dignity of adolescent girls and women.

In 107 selected districts across 17 states, rural adolescent girls were provided with a package of six sanitary napkins at a nominal cost. Starting in 2014, funds have been allocated to states and union territories for the decentralised procurement of sanitary napkin packs. The primary responsibility for this procurement lies with the Accredited Social Health Activist (ASHA). This initiative is part of the Menstrual Hygiene Scheme (MHS) introduced in 2011.

4. ROLE OF DIFFERENT STAKEHOLDERS IN THE EFFECTIVE AND SUSTAINABLE MANAGEMENT OF MENSTRUAL RIGHTS IN INDIA

Sustainably managing menstruation in India is a monumental and vital task that requires immediate attention and comprehensive treatment. This task should not be undertaken in isolation but rather through collaborative efforts involving various stakeholders, including:

(a) The Government of India, particularly the Ministry of Health and Family Welfare, the Ministry of Education, the Ministry of Drinking Water and Sanitation, the Ministry of Women and Child Development, the Ministry of Social Justice and Empowerment, and the Ministry of Environment and Forest.

(b) Non-Governmental Organisations (NGOs) throughout the country and the private sector have a pivotal role to play in implementing the menstrual health policies of the government.

(c) Individuals also bear the responsibility of ensuring that they make informed choices and utilise the information available for free, both personally and within their immediate surroundings, to adopt safe and sustainable menstrual health practices.

The current national guidelines that focus on adolescent and school-going girls confer the responsibility of generating awareness on menstruation, making safe sanitary products accessible and available, ensuring adequate provisions for water and other sanitary facilities, capacity building of ground-level staff on the executive machinery of the state, district and local authorities. This overburdens the public officials leading to a failure in collaborating with the diverse stakeholder involved in the effective management of menstrual health and hygiene. These guidelines are also inadequate as it silent on the needs of the disabled, those who don't conform to the recognised gender.

Lastly, all the frontline personnel engaged in advocacy on menstrual and reproductive rights must have an awareness of the cultural norms and practices, social, economic and demographic contexts and particulars related to menstruation in their respective areas of work to be able to customise outreach programmes in a sensitive manner to address the discrimination that menstruating individuals have to face. Awareness programmes should be aimed towards empowering the beneficiaries with adequate knowledge and awareness on menstruation, exposing them to sustainable alternatives and scientific narratives of menstruation.

5. CONCLUSION

Modern democratic institutions have begun to acknowledge the importance of addressing the underlying social, economic and systemic factors that lead to inequality and discrimination. Unfortunately, menstruation and the existing inadequate and practically ineffective policies continue to negatively affect the human rights of menstruating individuals. The statement of objects and reasons of the Women's Sexual, Reproductive and Menstrual Rights Bill, 2018 highlights the failure to admit menstruation as a biological process which ensures the subsistence of the human species as a whole and calls for guaranteeing menstrual equity for all women by the state. The preamble of the Bill talks about the need to make amendments in legislation to emphasise the agency of a woman in her sexual and reproductive rights and to guarantee menstrual equity for all women by the state. In the same year, India took a step towards making menstrual health and hygiene an accessible reality by scrapping a 12% tax on sanitary products.

An effective and sustainable management of menstruation must essentially take into account the following key aspects-acknowledgement and acceptance of menstrual health rights as a human right; creating a general understanding and awareness of waste generation, segregation and treatment for all; setting standards to establish a uniformity in the manner menstrual waste leaves households and enforcing adherence to these state determined standards through appropriate punitive measures; re-designing public spaces to be equipped with safe and hygienic waste collection units; and launching of government schemes encouraging and supporting research and studies of management, handling and treatment of wastes.

These steps are fundamental and crucial in empowering women, the biological equal half in the procreation of the human species with knowledge and awareness of their basic rights to health and sanitation.

REFERENCES

Bhatia, S. and T. Kaushik, 2019. "Sustainable Menstruation: Bleed with Honor and Responsibility." Accessed October 15, 2023. https://unvoicedmedia.in/sustainable-menstruation.

Central Pollution Control Board, Ministry of Environment, Forest and Climate Change. 2016. "The Solid Waste Management Rules." Accessed October 15, 2023. https://cpcb.nic.in/uploads/MSW/SWM_2016.pdf.

Court on its Own Motion vs Government of India & Others 2020 WP PIL No. 36/2020.

Dasra. 2015. "Spot On!: Improving Menstrual Management in India." Accessed October 16, 2023. https://www.dasra.org/resource/improving-menstrual-health-and-hygiene.

de Beauvoir, S. 1989. *The Second Sex*. London, England: Vintage Classics.

Department of Economic and Social Affairs, Sustainable Development, United Nations. 2015. "The 17 Goals | Sustainable Development." Accessed October 15, 2023. https://sdgs.un.org/goals.

Dunnavant, N. C. and T.-A. Robert. 2013. "Restriction and renewal, pollution and power, constraint and community: the paradoxes of religious women's experiences of menstruation." *Sex Roles*, 68 (1): 121–131.

Gairikpati, S. 2020. "Tampon and Pad Shortages in Lockdown Means Now is the Time for Sustainable Period Products." Accessed October 16, 2023. https://www.independent.co.uk/news/long_reads/period-poverty-tampons-pads-lockdown-sustainable-cup-a9593946.html.

Indian Young Lawyers Association vs The State of Kerala on 28 September, 2018 WP(Civil) No. 373 of 2006.

Justice K.S. Puttaswamy & Anr. vs. Union of India 2017 10 SCC 1.

L.K. Koolwal vs State of Rajasthan & Ors. AIR 1988 Raj 2, 1987 (1) WLN 134.

Ministry of Health and Family Welfare, Government of India. 2011. "Menstrual Hygiene Scheme (MHS)." Accessed October 15, 2023. https://nhm.gov.in/index1.php?lang=1&level=3&sublinkid=1021&lid=391.

Municipal Council, Ratlam vs Shri Vardhichand & Ors 1980 AIR 1622, 1981 SCR (1) 97.

Olga Tellis & Ors vs Bombay Municipal Corporation & Ors, AIR 180, 1985 SCR Supl. (2)51.

Suchita Srivastava & Anr vs Chandigarh Administration Civil Appeal No. 5845 of 2009.

Tharoor, S. 2018. "The Women's Sexual, Reproductive and Menstrual Rights Bill." Accessed October 15, 2023. http://164.100.47.4/billstexts/lsbilltexts/asintroduced/2271as.pdf.

United Nations. 1979. "Convention on the Elimination of all Forms of Discrimination Against Women." Accessed October 15, 2023. https://www.un.org/womenwatch/daw/cedaw/.

WHO/UNICEF. 2012. "Consultation on Draft Long List of Goal, Target and Indicator Options for Future Global Monitoring of Water, Sanitation and Hygiene." Accessed October 15, 2023. https://washdata.org/sites/default/files/documents/reports/2017-06/JMP-2012-post2015-consultation.pdf.

16. Breaking Barriers: The Power of Cyber Feminism in Combating Revenge Porn

Dr. Swapnil Bangali

Advocate and Director, Centre for Information Communication Technology Law, Maharashtra National Law University Mumbai, Mumbai, India

Email: swapnilbangali@gmail.com

Ms. Aastha Tiwari

Ph.D. Scholar, Maharashtra National Law University Mumbai, Mumbai, India

Email: aastha.tiwari@mnlumumbai.edu.in

ABSTRACT: The digital landscape has witnessed a surge in privacy infringements, with sexual privacy being a prominent target. Among the most perilous cybercrimes is revenge porn, which not only traumatizes the victim but also leads to otheroffences such as stalking, doxing, sextortion, defamation, harassment, voyeurism and other similar victim-humiliating crimes. This research article aims to comprehensively examine revenge porn through the lens of privacy, shedding light on its socio-legal repercussions. Additionally, it aims to carve out the concept of 'sexual privacy' from the broader realm of privacy, exploring its significance in the present context. The permanent scar that revenge porn leaves on a victim's psyche is undeniable (Bates, 2017), and thus the article delves into the triggers of mental agony while exploring the potential of the 'right to be forgotten' as a means for victims to overcome trauma. In the ever-evolving society, individuals, especially women, are becoming increasingly vocal about their sexuality, freedom and empowerment and they use cyberfeminism as both a sword and shield in the process. Authors attempt to decode this intersection of feminism and technology, which is a tool to raise awareness, advocate for legal protection and provide support and resources for survivors of revenge porn. Lastly, this article aims to address the existing gaps in law, the culture of shame surrounding women and the insensitivity of enforcement agencies. Furthermore, it presents a comparative study of the jurisprudence present in the United Kingdom and suggests a model framework that contributes to a comprehensive approach to combating revenge porn.

KEYWORDS: Privacy, cybercrime, revenge porn, cyberfeminism, society

Chapter 16 DOI- 10.4324/9781003428213-16

1. INTRODUCTION

As the development of communication technologies continues, cyberspace has evolved at a rapid pace of change and so are cybercrimes. Its invisibility and disregard for geographical boundaries are further increasing the difficulty in the investigation in leaps and bounds. It is considered to be the most dangerous of all crimes because of the magnitude of the loss it is capable of causing today. Revenge porn is one such sexual offence where the victim is distraught, backstabbed and permanently scarred. The bodily pain becomes only a reminder of how much of their interiority is outraged. Revenge porn, as would be subsequently discussed in detail, is a kind of non-consensual pornography where nude or semi-nude pictures/video of a person is uploaded online without their consent (Bates, 2017, p. 1). The word 'kind' suggests that defining revenge porn as a mere nonconsensual act of pornography will not be appropriate. Such kind of abuse has grave consequences as once the sexually explicit image or obscene content gets viral on the internet, it may travel across the globe in seconds, making it more difficult for the victim to fight it. Another distinguishing characteristic of revenge porn is that it is an inchoate offence to the extent and in the context that it cannot be committed unless it is accompanied by other acts of similar nature. For instance, revenge porn invariably leads to voyeuristic spectatorship which ultimately leads to offences like defamation, stalking, extortion, etc. Individuals in romantic relationships are more likely to get involved in sexting and therefore chances of sextortion become higher in such cases (Patchin and Hinduja, 2020). Sexual privacy as a concept and a phenomenon has never been discussed much in detail previously. Especially, in a country like India, where attacks on a person's sexual modesty are often stigmatized, it becomes a matter to be brushed under the carpet. Having said that, it is also important to note that in today's progressive society where the Internet of Things has become more real than life itself, many people especially women feel more empowered as individuals and feel free to share their feelings, and thoughts without any hesitation. The internet serves as a forum for the development of fresh ideas as well as a feminist counterpart that challenges the rhetoric of the prevailing patriarchal mindset. Feminists have revived the conversation about equality, modernized methods and succeeded in getting the mainstream media to pay attention to their demands (Valente and Neris, 2018, p. 2). Despite having jurisdictional and regulatory constraints, especially in cases of hate speech, obscenity, revenge porn, etc., the internet bestows upon individuals the power of mass dissemination of their stories (Bailey and Telford, 2007, p. 2). In an interesting case, a New York-based website ('HollaBackNYC') empowered women to take a stand against everyday harassment by men who exposed themselves on New York's streets and subways. The creators of the website use a tagline '*if you can't slap them snap them*' indicating that if confronting the harasser physically is not possible, take a photo of them instead. By utilizing the power of technology through internet-enabled cell phones, women were able to capture these offenders and share their experiences on the site. This innovative approach represents a prime example of 'cyberfeminism' (Daniels, 2009). Amidst the disconcerting reality that within this digital landscape, individuals exploit technology as a means to exact vengeance upon their partners, with women being disproportionately targeted-violating personal privacy, there lies a transformative potential of cyberfeminism as a formidable tool for combating these egregious offences. By harnessing the power of technology and feminist principles, cyberfeminism empowers victims, raises awareness and challenges the societal norms that enable gender-based violence in the digital realm. The intricate interplay between technology and gender, with a particular focus on the instrumental role that cyberfeminism can play in fostering a safer and more equitable cyberspace for all individuals, especially the women and children, who are potential victims of revenge porn can be a separate area of research. However, in this article, the scope of cyberfeminism is limited to only being a tool for combating online crimes, especially revenge porn.

2. LITERATURE REVIEW

The term 'revenge porn' has been in discussion for a long time. Feminists and academicians suggest that the term is victim-blaming, inappropriate and capable of creating ambiguity in the minds of the public. G. S. Bajpai's work 'The Emergent Paradigm of Victim Justice' (2022) is an important literature to chart a way to redefine the term from a victim-centric justice mindset. It talks about having a paradigm shift from an accused-tilted approach to a victim-centric approach in the criminal justice system. The term 'revenge porn' is problematic also because revenge porn is not always committed in rage or vengeance. Sometimes it may be for purely monetary purposes. This is the reason why Dickson (2016) suggests that instead of calling it revenge porn or non-consensual pornography, labelling it as 'image-based sexual abuse' would give it a more comprehensive meaning. It is also to be noted that 'revenge porn' and 'voyeurism' are quite overlapping and the only distinguishing factor between the two is the relationship of trust between the victim and the perpetrator in revenge porn. Discussing revenge porn is incomplete without understanding 'sexual privacy'. It is significant to know how revenge porn violates the sexual privacy of the victim. An article by Pozen (2016) discusses the importance of sexual privacy and places it above many other dimensions of privacy. Citron (2019) goes a step further and expands the definition of sexual privacy by including not only intimate activities such as sexual intercourse but also personal information about sex, sexuality and gender. Sexual privacy, as we all know it today, was narrowly interpreted in ancient times as its significance was only limited to procreation. In this regard, Richards's work on 'Sexual Autonomy and the Constitutional Right to Privacy: A Case Study in Human Rights and the Unwritten Constitution' (2017) is relevant as it helps to understand the evolution of the word from St. Augustine's era.

Furthermore, to understand revenge porn in its entirety, it is important to understand the sociological factors that imply such crimes. Ways to combat such crimes can only be fathomed by understanding the plight of the stakeholders including women, children and transgender persons. One of the biggest problems with such offences is that victims who are mostly women do not report these cases out of fear and stigma attached to it. Thus, one of the ways to fight crime is to understand it from the victim-centric approach. Understanding the socio-psychological impact of abuse on women before diving into the nature of abuse (revenge porn in this article) is essential and therefore Leonard I. Pearlin and Carmi Schooler's (1978) work is particularly relevant as it examines a linkage between the social characteristics of people and their coping mechanisms. It discusses how an individual responds to a particular traumatic event in his/her life and leads to another research work by Bates (2017) where the author discusses how women victims get into excessive drinking of alcohol, loss of control, low esteem, etc. whenever their modesty is outraged. However, whether this coping mechanism is the same with respect to cybercrime victims is yet to be investigated; what needs to be further investigated is whether the same kind of mechanism is found in male and transgender victims as well. In this regard, research by Walter S. DeKeseredy (2021) covers the current status of online sexual violence and suggests new directions in this field. It is particularly more relevant because it sheds some light on how image-based sexual offence is inextricably connected to other types of sexual assault like stalking, defamation, harassment, rape, etc., and how most of such offences are committed by men on women. However, it misses out considering transgender women who are one of the biggest victims of cybercrime. Thus, the need of the hour is to have a complete law that takes sociological and psychological factors into consideration.

The bigger problem as discussed above and pointed out by Deb and Chowdhury (2018) is that despite having legal provisions under the Indian Penal Code (IPC), Information Technology (IT) Act, etc., the problem at hand is not sufficiently addressed, as these laws are inadequate things like the responsibility of intermediaries, uniformity of punishment, explaining sexual privacy, etc. There are many other challenges faced in prosecuting the perpetrators of revenge porn because of the sheer anonymity of the perpetrator and the online platforms. Another problem is that there is no law as yet that confers the 'right to be forgotten' upon every citizen as a statutory right. Consequently, once the sexual content gets uploaded on the internet, it only gets amplified. As suggested by Bailey and Telford (2007), to mitigate this growing problem collaboration between regulatory bodies and social media conglomerations is crucial. Another way by which revenge porn can be combatted is by using the internet as a means to practice and propagate feminism. As pointed out by Offen (1988), there are many dimensions to feminism. With the advent of technology, cyberspace has become one of the biggest platforms to cater the political, legal and sociological discussions. It is time, feminism is not a constraint in the limits of the physical world only, and like Rosser (2005) points out if used productively, it is capable of ending male superiority and breaking the glass ceilings constructed by a patriarchal mindset. What needs to be further investigated is how campaigns like the #Metoo can be effective in fighting cyber sexual offences like revenge porn. In this regard, Jessie Daniels' work on 'Rethinking Cyberfeminism(s): Race, Gender, and Embodiment' (2007) helps in providing for different perceptions of many cyber feminists across the globe. It offers an overview of cyberfeminist theories and practices.

3. METHODOLOGY

Given its subject matter and scope, the article is based on doctrinal methodology and exploratory research with limited yet vital aspects of comparative legal research work, accounting for the practical aspects finding their expression in terms of law application. The research began with the collection and analysis of the existing Indian and United Kingdom legal framework, legal reference works as well as, depending on their existence, court rulings concerning the subject matter of the field. The basic method was text analysis encompassing the principles of logic and legal argumentation. To obtain a complete picture, the author offered an assessment of the socio-legal implications of legislation in practice.

4. UNDERSTANDING SEXUAL PRIVACY

Due to its crucial role in supporting sexual agency, intimacy and equality, sexual privacy occupies a position of the utmost relevance among the numerous dimensions of privacy (Pozen, 2016). The situations, contexts and expectations in which borders are established determine whether privacy is justified. The human body, intimate activities, such as sexual relationships, personal information related to sex, sexuality, or gender as well as individual decisions regarding the body and intimate information, may all be present in those settings, contexts and expectations (Citron, 2019, p. 57). The great jurist Saint Augustine believed that since having sex involves losing control, it is a natural source of shame. As a result, Augustine believed that the only acceptable form of sex is that which is performed with the controlled intention of having children; having sex otherwise is, in Augustine's view, inherently degrading (Richards, 2017). Thus, if Augustine were to judge the cases of revenge porn today, both the victim and the perpetrator would have been the wrongdoers, as many times the image/video taken by the perpetrator or the image/video shared by the victim to the perpetrator is for pleasure. For a very long time, societal norms have dictated that women should remain silent about their sexual desires and keep their bodies covered and this is probably why whenever a woman or any other person is faced with an image-based sexual offence, it wounds them not only physically but also mentally. Technological advancements have made it possible for people to be seen and exposed while they are in their private spaces, engaging in intimate acts. Home surveillance equipment is used to monitor current and former partners. Without their knowledge or consent, hidden cameras are being installed in bathrooms, bedrooms and even up people's skirts. People are being intimidated and forced into releasing compromising photos and sex tapes under penalty of exposure to the public. As if that weren't enough, technology has improved to the point where people's faces can be added to pornography in incredibly realistic 'deep fake' sex films without their knowledge or agreement. It's a serious violation of their sexual privacy and can cause significant emotional distress for those affected by such deep fake pornography (Citron, 2019). In Indian jurisprudence, sexual privacy has not been explicitly defined but the Hon'ble Supreme Court has contoured its scope indirectly on multiple occasions. Recently, the Supreme Court in Navtej Singh Johar & Ors. v. Union of India thr. Secretary Ministry of Law and Justice, W. P. (Crl.) No. 76 of 2016 SC stated that it is imperative to widen the scope of the right to privacy to incorporate a right to sexual privacy and while analyzing sexual privacy, the court took inspiration from the K. S. Puttaswamy and Anr. vs. Union of India ((2017) 10 SCC 1) wherein Justice A. M. Sapre held that the right to privacy, being an intrinsic aspect of dignity, autonomy and liberty, is essentially a natural right that is innate in every individual and therefore an inextricable part of the right to life under Article 21 of the Constitution of India. There have been many other indirect references in the past; for instance, in State of U.P. v. Naushad (2013) 16 SCC 651 while adjudicating upon a sexual harassment matter, Justice V. Gopala Gowda said, 'A woman's body is not a man's plaything and he cannot take advantage of it to satisfy his lust and desires by fooling a woman'. In Pushpanjali Sahu v. State of Orissa (2012) 9 SCC 705 Justice H. L. Dattu and Justice C. K. Prasad acknowledged the fact women's sexuality is her honour and sexual violence offends her self-esteem and dignity and that it leaves a permanent scar on the most cherished possession of a woman, her dignity, honour, reputation and not the least her chastity. However, it is to be noted that the concept of 'sexual privacy' has always been associated with women, a shield to their chastity and therefore it has been a clandestine affair. There are no judicial precedents that acknowledge the sexual privacy of a man or a transgender.

5. DEFINING REVENGE PORN

The term 'revenge porn' is colloquially used but seldom explained and defined. In fact, Merriam-Webster added this word to its dictionary only in 2016 as '*sexually explicit images of a person posted online without that person's consent, especially as a form of revenge or harassment*'. Sometimes it is also defined as a nonconsensual distribution of private, sexual images by a malicious ex-partner (McGlynn *et al.*, 2017). The creation of images without consent includes the conversion of filming, recording, or photography of another person. Along with that, threats to distribute nude, sexual or sexually explicit images, are also included in 'revenge pornography', which is frequently understood exclusively in terms of the distribution of intimate images (Dickson, 2016). As has already been pointed out, the word 'revenge porn' seems misleading for more reasons than one. First, the word 'revenge' suggests that an act was first initiated by the victim, in retaliation for which the perpetrator committed the crime. It's time we as a civilization take a leap from the theoretical concept of victimology to the practical implications of victim justice. To make the conventional accused-titled criminal justice system turn into a victim-oriented system, it is imperative that the terminologies of the offences are revised (Bajpai, 2022). Second, in certain cases, the motivation of the perpetrator could be purely monetary without any element of revenge being in it (Salter, 2013). Interestingly, contrary to popular belief, in some cases, the victims of revenge porn are men (Dickson, 2016), therefore to define it as an act done by a male partner to a female partner would be appropriate. Moreover, revenge porn is similar to voyeurism, except for the fact that in revenge porn, the relationship is essentially trust-based, as by virtue of Section 354C of the IPC, voyeurism mainly has two components: (a) watching or capturing a woman's private moments without her consent or (b) despite her consent of capturing the image, its nonconsensual dissemination. Clearly, the second part of voyeurism gives a glimpse of revenge porn and therefore, defining revenge porn without voyeurism will give a half-baked definition. Thus, ideally, revenge porn must be defined as a voyeuristic act committed by a person who was in a trusted relationship with the person whose image/video has been disseminated online without consent.

6. EXISTING LEGAL FRAMEWORK ON REVENGE PORN

6.1. India

The continued absence of legal recognition for revenge pornography in India perpetuates an alarming situation where the true extent of the problem remains obscured. As per the NCRB Report, with a distressing 104% increase in the dissemination of obscene content online between 2012 and 2014, it is evident that urgent action is needed. The underreporting of cases, with only 35% of affected women coming forward, coupled with a staggering 18.3% unaware of their abuse, highlights the urgent need for comprehensive legal measures. There are no separate provisions for revenge porn under IPC, IT Act, or any other law for that matter. The IPC provides some provisions relevant to perpetrators and victims of revenge porn, including Section 354C which criminalizes voyeurism and Section 509 which deals with words or gestures intended to insult the modesty of woman. Also, certain other indirect references can be found in Sections 292 and 293 of the IPC which punishes a person who publicly gets involved in an 'obscene' act. Furthermore, Section 354A–354D provides for the penalties for several forms of sexual crimes like sexual harassment, stalking, etc. Section 384 of the IPC penalizes extortion. Thus, in case of extortion committed in cyberspace, this section can come into the picture. In certain cases of revenge porn, Section 406 of IPC can also come into play which provides criminal breach of trust. Along with the other provisions, there are Sections 499 and 500 which enable individuals to file a case for criminal defamation. In certain cases, it could also lead to criminal intimidation which is punishable under Section 506 of the IPC. Section 66E of the IT Act addresses penalties for privacy violations and is equivalent to voyeurism defined under IPC. It is more generic in character, though. Section 67 of the IT Act addresses the electronic publication and transmission of pornographic and lewd material. Section 72 outlines privacy and confidentiality violations are prohibited by this statute. The publication, mailing, sale, rental, or circulation of any paper, slide, film, writing, drawing, painting, or photograph that contains obscene depictions of women is prohibited by Section 4 of the Indecent Representation of Women (Prohibition) Act, 1986. Section 6 penalizes violations of Section 4, and the offender also faces a period of jail.

6.2. United Kingdom

Even though there is no specific legislation in the United Kingdom for revenge porn, there are certain provisions under specific legislation which endorse the protection of victims of revenge porn. The Protection from Harassment Act, 1997 prohibits a course of conduct that requires that the harassment took place on one or more occasions. Under Section 1 of the Malicious Communications Act, 1988, the communications which are by letters, electronic communication, or articles of any description that are grossly indecent or offensive, obscene, or convey a false threat, provided there is an intention to cause distress or anxiety to the victim, are outlawed. Similarly, under Section 127 of the Communications Act, 2003, the communications that are sent by means of public electronic communications networks, which include messages that are indecent or grossly offensive, obscene, or menacing or, false for the purpose of causing annoyance or causing needless inconvenience to another, are prohibited. Unfortunately, in India, after the decision of the Supreme Court in India in the case of *Shreya Singhal v. Union of India, AIR 2015 SC 1523*, the words, insult, injury, grossly offensive, inconvenience, annoyance were interpreted as 'too loose' and the provision of Section 66 of the IT Act, 2000 was held to be unconstitutional in the light of freedom of speech and expression under Article 19 of the Constitution.

7. SOCIO-LEGAL IMPLICATION OF REVENGE PORN

Durkheim's theory on suicide argues that suicide can be a result not only of psychological or emotional distress but of social factors also. As per the reports, cybercrime inflicts severe emotional distress on its victims, often leading to a state of emotional bankruptcy. The devastating impact can be so overwhelming that some individuals tragically resort to suicide upon realizing the extent of their losses at the hands of scammers. Consequently, it is not uncommon for victims of cybercrime to experience a significant decline in their mental well-being or even lose their lives shortly after being duped. Shock has been identified as a mechanism that aids individuals in regulating their emotional response to such a traumatic event (Pearlin and Schooler, 1978). Recent research shows that image-based sexual abuse (revenge porn) is committed mainly by men against women and it often co-occurs with offline forms of male-to-female assaults like rape, stalking and beatings (DeKeseredy, 2021). This leads to a cascading effect on the victim which makes her even more vulnerable. In some cases, women victims use negative coping mechanisms such as excessive drinking of alcohol and over victimization of their own selves, making them farther away from reality (Bates, 2017). Victims also experience anxiety, depression, loss of control, low esteem and post-traumatic stress disorder. Thus, events like revenge porn make victims socially and mentally handicapped. Furthermore, despite having laws under IPC, IT Act and other Indian legislations to punish revenge porn, more often than not, the availability of victims' image-based sexual assault on the internet haunts them for life as there is no clear law on the right to be forgotten. Furthermore, even though the Information Technology (Intermediaries Guidelines) Rules, 2011, framed by the Central Government in the exercise of the powers conferred by Section 87(2)(zg) read with Section 79(2) of the IT Act provides for the due diligence requirements to be fulfilled by the intermediaries, the IT Act is silent on the responsibility of the intermediaries that hosts or shares such videos (Deb and Chowdhury, 2018). A court order to remove content is frequently not a virtual assurance that it would be permanently removed from the internet because it would already have been distributed on other platforms. In addition, the middlemen are protected by Section 79 of the IT Act, therefore no blame may be placed on them.

8. CHALLENGES FACED IN PROSECUTING PERPETRATORS OF REVENGE PORN

Prosecutions for such criminal offences often lead to unsatisfactory outcomes due to legal gaps and ambiguities that make conviction seemingly impossible. Another challenge is posed by anonymous platforms as it makes it difficult to identify offenders on these platforms, given that users are allowed to conceal their identity. The use of technology has been proposed as a potential solution for tracing and establishing the identity of perpetrators; however, this approach also presents its own set of complexities. Furthermore, it becomes difficult for the investigating agencies to prevent the content from getting spread and help the victims as the image keeps floating on different websites. In a romantic relationship, the image is often shared by the victim only which may get leaked due to hacking of the recipient's device. In other cases, the recipient himself, due to vengeance, circulates the image and becomes the perpetrator. There is also no responsibility of intermediaries who provide a platform for such dissemination. However, recently online dating apps like Bumble and short video platform TikTok joined Facebook and Instagram as industry partners of StopNCII.org, a platform that helps users tackle revenge porn. A person who is being threatened with sexual image abuse can create a unique identifier of their images (also known as hashes or digital fingerprints) and share them with StopNCII.org. As and when the hashed image is uploaded, the concerned digital platform can remove and block the image from further sharing. However, success has been limited so far primarily due to resistance from tech giants who continue to place priority on user anonymity over security concerns. In India, victim cooperation has been identified as a significant factor in the successful prosecution of crimes. However, there are several socio-cultural factors that affect victim cooperation such as fear of retaliation and societal pressure to remain silent about the crime. One of the major challenges in addressing revenge porn is its prevalence across various online platforms, which makes it difficult to monitor and remove such content. Additionally, collaborations between regulatory bodies (e.g., cybercrime units) and social media conglomerates are still crucial to mitigate this growing problem effectively (Bailey and Telford, 2007).

9. PAST, PRESENT, FUTURE AND POTENTIAL OF CYBERFEMINISM IN COMBATING REVENGE PORN

In earlier days, understanding feminism was rather simplistic. Prior to 1970, feminism was perceived by its literal definition given in the American dictionary which defined it as 'a theory and/or movement concerned with advancing the position of women through such means as concerned with advancing the position of women through such means as achievement of political, legal, or economic rights equal to those granted to men'. Despite it being is a multifaceted movement that encompasses political, theoretical and social dimensions, the legality of 'equal rights' has been derived from the male adulthood norm (Offen, 1988, p. 123). The question as to what feminism really is, despite having it raised by scholars, academicians, politicians and sociologists on a daily basis, remains unanswered. To some the word 'feminism' could be empowering, to some it could be a polarizing tool. For Americans, it meant to be treated at par with men whereas for Europeans it meant accepting and celebrating women's sexuality along with its differences (Honeycutt, 1979). The first three waves of feminism focused on the political fight for women's suffrage, sexual and financial freedom, diversity and the individualism of women. Now with the advent of technology, the internet and other kinds of digital media offer potential as spaces for engagement, discussions, debates and activism. Unfortunately, it is also becoming a means to harass, abuse and troll women. Platforms like Twitter and Instagram, which are ideally meant for advocacy, political campaigning and free speech, are spaces where women are sometimes excluded and shut from public participation (Barker and Jurasz, 2019). Having said that, it is also important to note that with the changing socio-legal landscape, there is a new dimension to feminism that has emerged which is known as 'cyberfeminism' also known to be a part of the fourth wave of feminism. Cyberfeminism, a word coined in 1883, explored the role of technology as a means to liberate human experience (Bailey and Telford, 2007). It is a method by which women can make use of technology to talk about their grievances. Simply put, it is a process where feminists use technology as a tool to raise their voices. Individuals who defined cyberfeminism saw the potential of technology to act as a level playing field for women in the absence of sexism, racism and other oppression. It is seen as a woman-centric perspective that advocates women's use of technology for empowerment. Some cyber feminists believe that these technologies as inherently capable of ending male superiority because women are uniquely suited to life in digital space (Rosser, 2005). Clearly, the ambit of cyberfeminism is much wider than it appears.

10. CYBERFEMINISM: A TOOL TO COMBAT REVENGE PORN

The major challenge today is who will keep the watch on those who are watching the content which might fall within the category of revenge porn or for that matter any illegal or objectionable content in any manner. The modern digital world needs to have compact and more aggressive and stringent rules for the content monitoring and hoisting of the content. The content that objectifies the women victims must be understood from the victim's perspective and hence there must be a body of women or sensitive administrators monitoring the content which should be observed as a part and parcel of the general internet education initiative. The general internet education initiative is necessary not just from the point of view of alerting the victims but also to make the entire society aware of objectionable content and its legal outcome. The role of cyberfeminism shall not be restricted to the victim's protection and support, but it should encompass the cleansing of the social psychology towards such content-related offences and making the people aware of sensitive issues such as effects of the online defamation, continuous mental agony, demeaning of the character of the victim in eyes of others and other psychological barriers which the victims face after such incidences. The #MeToo campaign raised eyebrows and created an environment where victims could speak in front of society about the incidences the victims faced and also created a kind of platform where the accused is also exposed online. The idea of the #MeToo campaign was to expose the accused more than the inability of the victim to take legal recourse immediately after the incident. With the evolution of modern cyberfeminism in the era of exponential experimentation with information communication technology, the #MeToo campaign stands as a symbol of exposing the accused on social media for the offences that the accused have committed in the past. The social exposure of the victim was the major psychological barrier for the victim. This was used in the #MeToo campaign in the reverse manner to expose the accused. The effectiveness of #MeToo may be judged from the point of view of impact analysis and finding the truth behind any past event can be seen as an experiment of cyberfeminism in modern times.

11. CONCLUSION

Combating online sexual offences like revenge porn is an uphill battle for victims. One of the biggest challenges in India is that, unlike the United Kingdom where there is Sexual Offenders Act, there is no specific legislation to deal with sexual offences let alone revenge porn, because of which certain dimensions of revenge porn like deep fake and voyeurism often get ignored. Thus, the need of the hour is to enact specific gender-neutral legislation to address revenge porn as a distinct offence. Furthermore, it is often seen that one of the biggest victims of cybercrimes in India are transgender women, and therefore redefining 'victim' of cybercrimes becomes absolutely necessary. It is also seen that more often than not due to the lack of comprehensive legislation on revenge porn, its cognizance can be taken under multiple legislations, where there are different punishments given, which ultimately gives rise to more ambiguity. A range of studies shows that women are one of the most vulnerable groups to cyber violence. Thus, comprehensive remedies in the form of serious punishment through the provisions of a special statute like the proposed Digital India Bill, 2022 with a specific objective to protect women, children and transgender persons from digital violence and harassment are much awaited in countries like India. Some of the judicial interpretations and principles created for tackling the uncontrolled data or information on the internet are also fueling cyberfeminism in its own way. Honorable Justice S. K. Panigrahi in the case of *Subhranshu Rout @ Gugul v. State of Orrisa*, while dealing with the case of revenge porn committed by an ex-boyfriend of a girl, has observed that, allowing objectionable photos and videos to remain on a social media platform, without the consent of a woman, is a direct affront on a woman's modesty and, more importantly, her right to privacy. In such cases, either the victim herself or the prosecution, may if so advised, seek appropriate orders to protect the victim's fundamental right to privacy, by having such offensive content erased from the public platform. If such a right to be forgotten is not recognized in matters like these, any accused will surreptitiously outrage the modesty of the woman and misuse the same in cyberspace unhindered. Victims of cybercrime, especially image-based sexual offences like revenge porn are scared to speak out and face the humiliation, therefore apart from having an adequate law, it is important that law enforcement agencies are sensitized and trained with the victim-centric approach to handle such matters so that the social stigma attached to such offences does not prevent the victim to report such cases. Thus, along with drafting a law, increasing awareness about revenge porn and its consequences becomes of utmost importance. Educating people about online safety, consent and responsible use of technology will aid in the process of sensitizing the public about it. Another important intervention is demanding accountability from social media giants for law enforcement. Last but not least, cyberfeminism can play a crucial role in combating revenge porn by employing a combination of technological, legal, educational and societal approaches.

REFERENCES

Bailey, Jane, and Adrienne Telford (2007). "What's so 'cyber' about it?: Reflections on cyberfeminism's contribution to legal studies," *Canadian Journal of Women and the Law* 19(2): 243–271. https://muse.jhu.edu/article/240043.

Bajpai, G. S. (2022). "The emergent paradigm of victim justice," *Global Advances in Victimology and Psychological Studies* 1(1): 3–6. https://doi.org/10.54945/gavps.v1i1.4.

Barker, Kim, and Olga Jurasz (2019). "Online misogyny: a challenge for digital feminism?" *Journal of International Affairs* 72(2) (Spring/ Summer): 95–114. https://www.jstor.org/stable/26760834.

Bates, Samantha (2017). "Revenge porn and mental health: a qualitative analysis of the mental health effects of revenge porn on female survivors," *Feminist Criminology* 12(1): 22–42. https://doi.org/10.1177/1557085116654565.

Citron, Danielle K. (2019). "Why sexual privacy matters for trust," *Washington University Law Review* 96(6): 1189–1218. https://scholarship.law.bu.edu/faculty_scholarship/641.

Daniels, Jessie (2009). "Rethinking cyberfeminism(s): race, gender, and embodiment," *Women's Studies Quarterly* 37(1/2) (Spring-Summer): 101–124. https://www.jstor.org/stable/27655141

Deb, Aishwarya, and Prithwish Roy Chowdhury (2018). "A critical analysis of the Information Technology Act, 2000 Vis-à-Vis mitigation of child pornography," *Christ University Law Journal* 7(2): 1–22. https://doi.org/10.12728/culj.13.1.

DeKeseredy, Walter S. "Image-Based Sexual Abuse: Social and Legal Implications," *Current Addiction Reports* 8(2) (2021): 330–335. https://doi.org/10.1007/s40429-021-00363-x.

Dickson, Alyse (2016). "'Revenge porn': a victim focused response," *UniSA Student Law Review* 2: 42–69. https://doi.org/10.21913/USLRunisaslr.v2i0.1357.

Honeycutt, Karen (1979). "Socialism and feminism in imperial Germany," *Signs: Journal of Women in Culture and Society* 5(1) (Autumn): 30–41. https://doi.org/10.1086/493681.

McGlynn, Clare, Erika Rackley, and Ruth Houghton (2017). "Beyond 'revenge porn': the continuum of image-based sexual abuse," *Feminist Legal Studies* 25(1): 25–46. https://doi.org/10.1007/s10691-017-9343-2.

Offen, Karen (1988). "Defining feminism: a comparative historical approach," *Signs: Journal of Women in Culture and Society* 14(1) (Autumn): 119–157. https://www.jstor.org/stable/3174664.

Patchin, Justin W., and Sameer Hinduja (2020). "Sextortion among adolescents: results from a national survey of U.S. youth," *Sexual Abuse* 32(1): 30–54. https://doi.org/10.1177/1079063218800469.

Pearlin, Leonard I., and Carmi Schooler. "The structure of coping," *Journal of Health and Social Behavior* 19(1): 2–21. https://doi.org/10.2307/2136319.

Pozen, David E. (2016). "Privacy-privacy tradeoffs," *The University of Chicago Law Review* 83(1) (Winter): 221–247. https://www.jstor.org/stable/43741598.

Richards, David A.J. (1979). "Sexual Autonomy and the Constitutional Right to Privacy: A Case Study in Human Rights and the Unwritten Constitution," *Hastings Law Journal* 30(4): 957–1018. https://repository.uclawsf.edu/cgi/viewcontent.cgi?article=2600&context=hastings_law_journal.

Rosser, Sue Vilhauer (2005). "Through the lenses of feminist theory: focus on women and information technology," *Frontiers: A Journal of Women Studies* 26(1): 1–23. https://www.jstor.org/stable/4137430.

Salter, Michael (2013). "Justice and revenge in online counter-publics: emerging responses to sexual violence in the age of social media," *Crime, Media, Culture: An International Journal* 9(3): 225–242. https://doi.org/10.1177/1741659013493918.

Valente, Mariana, and Natalia Neris (2018). "Are we going to feminise the internet?" *International Journal on Human Rights* 15(27): 101–116. https://www.alexandria.unisg.ch/server/api/core/bitstreams/2f072a2f-7604-4ebf-8807-009f0f720bc6/content.

17. Facial Recognition? An Analysis of Facial Recognition and Criminal Justice in India

Bodhisattwa Som
Assistant Professor, School of Legal Studies, REVA University, Bengaluru, India
Email: bodhisattwa.som@reva.edu.in, sombodhisattwa@gmail.com
Delhi Chandana
Assistant Professor, School of Legal Studies, REVA University, Bengaluru, India
Email: delhichandana@hotmail.com

ABSTRACT: The turn of the decade has seen the application of artificial intelligence (AI) in all walks of life. Such rapid growth in the emergence of AI has prompted the application of facial recognition software in the criminal justice systems of countries around the world. In India, the criminal justice system has historically discriminated against Dalits and Muslims, the implications of using AI in the criminal justice system may be disastrous. These data when fed to the facial recognition system could possibly magnify systemic oppression, even if accuracy is discounted. As the AI would also predict future misdemeanours, this would in fact lead to state-sponsored predictive policing or surveillance. This system would, therefore, eventually make these biases inherent even in future use disabling the vulnerable sections from breaking these shackles. Thus, this article seeks to explore the impact that the use of facial recognition in the criminal justice system would have in India, especially when the data available are already skewed against the SCs, STs, OBCs and religious minorities.

KEYWORDS: Facial recognition, criminal justice, minorities, artificial intelligence

1. INTRODUCTION

The modern world is ruled by technology that affects nearly all facets of human activity. Today's complex modern problems cannot be solved by us alone, and thus this fuels the race to utilise technology and particularly artificial intelligence (AI)

Chapter 17 DOI- 10.4324/9781003428213-17

(Chesterman, 2022). In lucid terms, AI refers to software utilised by computers to demonstrate the aspects of cognitive intelligence, specifically used to perform various tasks across industries (Maheshwari, 2023). The concern of this article shall be the application of AI in the sphere of criminal law, particularly the use of facial recognition technology in criminal law. Facial recognition technologies (FRTs) are being used by the law enforcement agencies of India in the public sphere, simultaneously impacting the lives of millions of citizens.

Facial recognition is done by different facial recognition algorithms and all of them work in a different manner, regarding the extraction of the facial features and matching it. FRT basically extracts the facial characteristics from the probe image (the image that is required to be matched), identifies the corresponding face through mapping facial features, then converts it into a format that is compatible with the ones stored in the database (Vedavalli *et al.*, 2021). It then compares the probe image on top of all the images stored in the database obtained, for instance, through CCTV footage (Purhouse and Campbell, 2022). If the facial features of the subject show the possibility of some sort of resemblance with someone already on the database, it becomes easier to identify the suspect (Vedavalli *et al.*, 2021). Another use of FRT could be to link it with past demeanours with the help of a predictive AI tool (for instance, COMPAS – an AI to compute potential recidivism risk used in the United States) to get a viable probable percentage of the threat the person poses to society (Manheim and Kaplan, 2019).

There are also numerous concerns that have been raised about its usage, technically since AI systems are inherently opaque, which implies that it becomes difficult to explain the mechanism with which they arrive at a conclusion after it has been fed data, a phenomenon termed as the black box problem (Manheim and Kaplan, 2019). This is specifically true more so in the United States, specifically regarding it disproportionately targeting races more than others (Lee and Chin, 2022). Such concerns also continue to be raised in India where the widescale application by the law enforcement agencies could potentially target members of vulnerable and policed communities such as Dalits and members of minority communities such as Muslims (Singh, 2018). Furthermore, there are concerns in other areas as well such as AFRT being antithetical to the notion of the right to privacy, considered as an intrinsic part of the right to life under Article 21 of the Constitution. Also, it is important to note the usage of such technology to identify protestors at an Anti CAA protest exemplifies the chilling effect on free speech under Article 19(1)(a) of the Constitution (Hickock *et al.*, 2021).

Considering all these challenges to the usage of AI in the criminal justice system, the article shall focus on two aspects regarding implementation of FRT in the Indian criminal justice system, discrimination and privacy. Thus, in the first part of the article, we shall demonstrate the problem of accuracy which leads to discrimination with regards to the use of FRT in India. This has largely been based on the experience of countries such as the United States where the use of FRT has amplified racial discrimination. We draw similar parallels of such discrimination present in India. In the second part of the article, we discuss the implication of the usage of FRT by the police on fundamental rights such as the right to privacy under Article 21 of the Constitution.

2. REVIEW OF LITERATURE

2.1. Perils of Using FRT in Criminal Justice System

Scholars who have written about this particularly issue the opinions that are divided with most cautioning the incorporation of such technologies without oversight mechanisms to be perilous (Chesterman, 2022; Hill *et al.*, 2022; Tanna and Dunning, 2022). Most authors highlight the concerns of opacity with the usage of AI, also known as the *blackbox* problem (Bathaee, 2018). This means that it is easy to understand the decision that an AI may come out with, but it becomes very difficult to determine how it had reached the particular result (Chesterman, 2022). Many authors have also highlighted biased decision making by the AI against certain socially marginalised demographics due to bias in the historical data itself, both in the United States against African Americans and in India against Dalits and Muslims (Perkowitz, 2021). Other authors have focussed on the implications of using FRT, due to it causing violation of individual privacy, a protected fundamental right in India, by not following the principle of proportionality (Hickock *et al.*, 2021).

FRT cannot, at its present state, be utilised in the criminal justice system.

2.2. Advantages of Using FRT in the Criminal Justice System

However, there have been some scholars who have advocated the use of FRT by law enforcement agencies. They argue that as per their studies, that by using machine learning techniques they were able to predict and identify, with the help of facial recognition, some key identifying features of the likelihood of persons being a convicted criminal, with 90% accuracy (Wu and Zhang, 2016). This was done through feeding the AI random pictures of Uber drivers (Hickock *et al.*, 2021). Others have concluded that FRT with deep neural networks could be utilised *inter alia* to determine the criminal inclinations of persons using only their facial images (Kosinski, 2021). Facial recognition in the United States has also been proven to be useful in certain cases to identify suspects for crimes where it was nearly impossible to identify the subject (Bosman and Kovaleski, 2019).

FRT *can be utilised, in some specific areas, in the criminal justice system.*

3. RESEARCH METHODOLOGY

The research methodology undertaken for this study is doctrinal methodology to accurately deduce whether technologies such as FRT can be utilised in the sphere of criminal law. The study will undertake an analysis of case laws, law journal articles, research articles in other related disciplines and newspaper articles, to analyse the usage of AI through technologies like FRT in the criminal justice system in India.

4. ANALYSIS

FRT is a type of technology that is used to compare the facial features of two individuals through their images and determine their degree of similarity. It has recently been applied into the field of criminal law, since it helps in the identification of those suspects in certain cold cases, for instance, the Hyderabad police has used FRT in cordon and search operations, profiling suspects for the possession of narcotics and even phone searching activities (Ghosh, 2022). It was the National Crime Records Bureau (NCRB), which had initially floated a proposal on July 2019 (later recalled and revised in 2020), for developing a National Automated Facial Recognition System (Hickock *et al.*, 2021). The usage of such technologies directly affects individual human rights and the fundamental rights guaranteed by the Indian Constitution, such as the right to privacy, right to life and personal liberty, right to equality and the right to freedom of speech under Articles 21, 14 and 19 (Hickock *et al.*, 2021).

When such technology is hastily brought to the forefront without there being proper data protection laws; in a country where the criminal law is too archaic to accommodate it; no parliamentary oversight body; no understanding of the potential of such technology directly affecting the lives of marginalised communities; no debate or discussions as to the this type of technology affecting the human rights and fundamental rights of other individuals or, it being used beyond its stated purpose in order to identify protestors, human lives get affected (Hickock *et al.*, 2021). Therefore, it would perhaps be necessary right now to investigate some of the major concerns regarding the use of FRT in criminal law within the Indian legal system.

4.1. The Cost of Inaccuracy in FRT: Discrimination

Liberal democracies such as the United States and United Kingdom have also been hasty to adopt technologies such as FRT within their criminal law systems but have slowly started retracting the use of such technologies having experienced their preponderance toward causing racial discrimination and their potential to violate human rights (Purhouse and Campbell, 2022; Tanna and Dunning, 2022). Quite recently, an African American man in Detroit was wrongfully arrested due to an inaccuracy or bias or both by the facial recognition system (Kashmir, 2020). In another instance, people of colour were inaccurately identified as gorillas by a facial recognition system (Hern, 2018). However, a study expressly proved that this AI was biased against the Blacks and ended up profiling them as flight risks leading to very few bails granted (Stevenson, 2018). Additionally, the American Civil Liberties Union conducted a test on Amazon's Rekognition wherein it misidentified 28 members of Congress with mugshots of people who have been arrested for a crime, further, they observed that most of these misidentifications were either people of colour or women or both (Snow, 2018).

All these instances mentioned above demonstrate that FRT is not exactly accurate and has found support from a range of scholars and academics, with some stating it to be even less accurate than that of available biometric methods such as fingerprints (Garvie *et al.*, 2016). Since FRT systems are not that accurate they do have the tendency to target specific populations more than others, for instance, African Americans and Latinos in America and Dalits and Muslims in India. The reasoning for this discrimination is since FRT is dependent on the data that are fed into it (Chesterman, 2022). It is based on these historical data that the algorithm tries to recognise faces to implicate in a crime and in a sense reify existing discrepancies (Chesterman, 2022; Manheim and Kaplan, 2019). Now, historically if these data have been skewed against certain marginalised and overpoliced section of the society, there lies a possibility that they would be increasingly recognised, falsely implicated, and thus discriminated on, a phenomenon known as 'Bias Introduced by Data' (Tanna and Dunning, 2022). For instance, the Report titled 'Criminal Justice in the Shadow of Caste', looks at discrimination and police excesses when dealing with the Dalit and Adivasi communities (Singh, 2018). It highlights the main reason for such disproportionate over representation was identified as 'deeply entrenched prejudices' (Singh, 2018). The Dalits and Adivasis basically form an easy target for the State to incarcerate them. Other scholars also drive the point of marginalised sectors being overpoliced (Bokil and Sonavene, 2020; Sonavane and Bokil, 2020).

Turning our focus back on the present, the recent 2019 NCRB report on Prison Statistics has only buttressed the fact of the unbalanced rate of targeted policing incarceration faced by SCs, STs and OBCs in India, them constituting 65.90% of the prison inmate population (Mint, 2021; National Crime Records Bureau, 2019). A comprehensive analysis of the NCRB figures demonstrates that of the total 1,62,800 prisoners (34.01%) belonged to the OBC category, 99,273 (20.74%) to the SC category and 53,336 (11.14%) to the ST category (Mint, 2021; National Crime Records Bureau, 2019). The same report also stated that Muslims constituted 16.7% of convicts, 18.7% of undertrials and 35.8% detainees, although their population as per the census shows them to constitute 14.2% of the Indian population (Firstpost, 2020; National Crime Records Bureau, 2019).

In a research project that was carried out by Common Cause and the Centre for Developing Societies on the state of policing in India, published that ~38% of the persons covered by the study thought that the police wrongly incriminate Dalits in petty crimes such as theft and robbery (Common Cause and Centre for the Study of Developing Societies, 2018). Even the more recent Prison Statistics of India published in 2021 by the NCRB shows that marginalised communities constitute 66% of undertrial prisoners, unsurprisingly showing an increase in percentage of incarceration by 48% over the past five years (National Crime Records Bureau, 2021; Roy, 2022). It may also be observed that this trend of overrepresentation has been prevalent for the last 5 years (Roy, 2022).

Thus, through such great numbers of undertrial and convicted prisoners, that certain sections of the Indian population are thus policed more than others and are targeted by law enforcement and criminal justice agencies (Hickock *et al.*, 2021). Due to the bias present in the historical data against certain marginalised sections of the population (Dalits, Scheduled Tribes and Muslims), they would be targeted by from the very inception of the usage of FRT.

4.2. Privacy Concerns

The Supreme Court of India in the year 2017 in K.S. Puttaswamy (Retd. V. Union of India) held that the right to privacy as a fundamental right under the Constitution of India to be considered a part of Article 21, which stipulates the right to life and personal liberty. It is known that any fundamental right cannot be absolute and thus the right to privacy too has reasonable restrictions. However, Justice Chandrachud emphasised that these reasonable restrictions also must fulfil a threefold requirement; (i) the existence of a law, (ii) a legitimate state aim and (iii) proportionality. Therefore, the use of FRT must also be legally analysed with respect to the criteria enumerated by the Supreme Court.

Considering the first requirement of a legislation, India does not at present have any legislative sanction to utilise FRT either by the State or by other private enterprise. The Internet Freedom Foundation on July 2019 sought a response from the NCRB seeking a ban on the use of FRT due to the absence of any legislative sanction to incorporate such as system (Hickock *et al.*, 2021). The NCRB in its reply stated that a 2009 cabinet note *inter alia* had initiated the creation of an Automatic Facial Recognition System (Hickock *et al.*, 2021). Their argument thus was that this cabinet note signified the approval of the cabinet and therefore there was no further requirement of any legislative or executive order sanctioning the use of FRT (Hickock *et al.*, 2021). However, logically, a cabinet note cannot be equated with a law enacted by the Legislature or the Executive. It cannot be equated to a statutory enactment. Even the Supreme Court of India in the Puttaswamy case in 2019 had noted that an executive notification cannot be equated with the requirement of legislation passed by the Parliament enumerated in the earlier Puttaswamy case of 2017. More recently, the NITI Aayog in its draft discussion paper, Responsible AI #AIForAll has advocated for specific data protection norms for FRT in India, which highlights the urgent need to have comprehensive data protection norms within the country (NITI Aayog, 2022). Thus, in our opinion the requirement of specific legislation is not met.

The second requirement that the Supreme Court enumerated in the Puttaswamy case was that of a legitimate state aim so that the nature or the content of the law which would enumerate a restriction to the right to privacy is reasonable, a mandatory requirement under Article 14 of the Constitution. Now since there is no proper legal basis on the bedrock of which FRT is being applied, which would spell out the objectives and rationale of using FRT, it becomes unclear ascertaining if a legitimate or proportionate objective is indeed being satisfied (Hickock *et al.*, 2021). Now considering the multifarious purposes for which FRT is being utilised in it becomes clear that the agencies of the State are being given a free hand to deploy FRT in any situation where it could be useful, with no single, specific purpose where it can be deployed (Hickock *et al.*, 2021). Thus, we feel that this requirement is also not met.

The third requirement which must be followed is 'proportionality', which implies that the means that are espoused by the Legislature should be proportional to the object and requirement of the law. The concept of proportionality can be understood through certain standards: (a) that the measure which curtails a right must have a legitimate purpose; (b) that it must be an appropriate mean of advancing that purpose; (c) there must not be any less restrictive, but equally effective alternative; and (d) the measure must not unduly effect the holder of the right (Barak, 2012). The utilisation of FRT over many sectors by the State covering a large segment of the Indian population can be disproportionate to the advancement of a particular purpose sought to be realised. Regarding the usage of FRT for all these purposes, the State must consider whether it can utilise an alternative, less intrusive mechanism (Hickock *et al.*, 2021). Thus, we find that this requirement is also not fully satisfied as the state has not considered such other options in place of the usage of FRT. Therefore, we find that the use of facial recognition technology has severe implications regarding the violation of the conceptualisation of privacy envisaged and enumerated by the Indian Supreme Court.

5. CONCLUSION

Through this article, we have highlighted to primary concerns regarding the use of FRT in India. The first concern is about the fact that FRT relies on historical data within its algorithm to recognise faces. Historically, certain sections of the Indian society such as Scheduled Castes, Scheduled Tribes and Muslims have been subjected to increased policing, incarceration and discrimination by the State. The algorithm in the FRT system is thus more likely to wrongly identify persons from these communities as perpetrators of crimes and thus reify existing discriminatory practices. The second concern we have highlighted through this article has been the fact is that the widescale use of FRT by law enforcement agencies in India with no clearly defined purpose, in various situations, as per the convenience of the State, severely affects the privacy of individuals. Furthermore, the fact that FRT has been used by the Delhi Police to identify protestors for the Anti CAA protests highlights the fact that the continuous use of FRT may soon metamorphosize into mass surveillance of individuals who dissent on the government's policies. This would in turn have a chilling effect on the freedom of speech and expression.

Now, due to these chief concerns, we believe that FRT must not be deployed by the law enforcement agencies in India. FRT, like an unruly horse, cannot be given a free run as issues of systematic discrimination, violation of fundamental rights and mass surveillance would also have to be tackled with. This can be done when we do have a specific data protection norm regarding the use of FRT. From this argument, it is logically conclusive that we do not imply that we propose an absolute ban on the use of facial recognition technology permanently. FRT has a lot of areas where it can find use within criminal law such as in terms of its evidentiary value of recognising suspects from data, facilitating crime investigation and detecting criminals or missing children or unidentified persons (Vedavalli *et al.*, 2021). Better evidence gathered in this manner will reduce the burden on the police and would lead to the faster disposal of cases (Vedavalli *et al.*, 2021). Furthermore, it also illuminates a path that reduces third degree torture methods used by the police to nab a suspect (Vedavalli *et al.*, 2021). However, the costs of using such technology, highlighted in this article, in our opinion, outweigh the benefits and thus we would not endorse the use of FRT by the law enforcement agencies in India now in the absence of proper legislation, policy and norms concerning its use.

REFERENCES

Barak, Aharon (2012). "Proportionality (2)," *The Oxford Handbook of Comparative Constitutional Law*, ed. Michel Rosenfeld and András Sajó, Oxford: Oxford University Press, pp. 739–752.

Bathaee, Yavar (2018). "The artificial intelligence blackbox and the failure of intent and causation," *Harv. J. L. & Tech.* 31(2): 890–938.

Bokil, Ameya, and Nikita Sonavene (2020). *Indramal Bai's Death and How the Police Got Away.* 30 May. Accessed July 17, 2023. www.article-14.com/post/indramal-bai-s-death-and-how-the-police-got-away?fbclid=IwAR3jjUj4iyrIU5aoV4b3dmIpLHQPIfqyE_gg4r3d59xPGmrgj3gUsqv0Tk.

Bosman, Julie, and Serge F Kovaleski (2019). *Facial Recognition: Dawn of Dystopia, or Just the New Fingerprint?* May 18. Accessed July 14, 2023. https://www.nytimes.com/2019/05/18/us/facial-recognition-police.html.

Chesterman, Simon. (2022). *We the Robots? Regulating Artificial Intelligence and the Limits of the Law.* Padstow, Cornwall: Cambridge University Press.

Common Cause and Centre for the Study of Developing Societies (2018). "Status of Policing in India Report 2018, A Study of Performance and Perceptions," *TATA Trusts.* Accessed July 17, 2023. https://www.tatatrusts.org/upload/pdf/spir-2018-common-cause.pdf.

D'Cunha, Joanne (2019). *We Might be in the Market for a New Kind of Face Mask.* July 18. Accessed July 21, 2023. https://internetfreedom.in/maskon/.

Firstpost (2020). *NCRB Data Shows Muslims, Dalits, Tribal population in Prisons Disproportionate to their Numbers Outside.* September 2. Accessed July 17, 2023.

https://www.firstpost.com/india/ncrb-data-shows-muslims-dalits-tribal-population-in-prisons-disproportionate-to-their-numbers-outside-8775161.html.

Garvie, Clare, Alvora M. Bedoya, and Jonathan Frankle (2016). *The Perpetual Line Up, Unregulated Police Face Recognition in Amercia.* October 18. Accessed July 17, 2023. https://www.perpetuallineup.org/sites/default/files/2016-12/The%20Perpetual%20 LineUp%20%20Center%20on%20Privacy%20and%20Technology%20at%20 Georgetown%20Law%20-%20121616.pdf.

Ghosh, Agnee (2022). *Facial Recognition is out of Control in India.* June 13. Accessed July 15, 2023. https://www.vice.com/en/article/akew98/facial-recognition-is-out-of-control-in-india.

Hern, Alex (2018). *Google's Solution to Accidental Algorithmic Racism: Ban Gorillas.* January 12. Accessed July 15, 2023. https:// www.theguardian.com/technology/2018/jan/12/google-racism-ban-gorilla-black-people.

Hickock, Elonai, Pallavi Bedi, Aman Nair, and Amber Sinha (2021). "Facial Recognition Technology in India," *The Centre for Internet and Society.* August 31. Accessed July 7, 2023. https://cis-india.org/internet-governance/blog/hrbdt-and-cis-august-31-2021-facial-recognition-technology-in-india.

Hill, Dallas, Christopher D. O'Conner, and Andrea Slane (2022). "Police use of facial recognition technology: the potential for engaging the public through co-constructed policy making," *Int. J. Police Sci. Manag.* (SAGE Publications) 24(3): 325–335.

Kashmir, Hill (2020). *Wrongfully Accused by an Algorithm.* June 24. Accessed July 15, 2023. https://www.nytimes.com/2020/06/24/ technology/facial-recognition-arrest.html.

Kosinski, Michal (2021). "Facial recognition technology can expose political orientation from naturalistic facial images," *Nature.* January 11. Accessed July 14, 2023. https://www.nature.com/articles/s41598-020-79310-1#article-info.

Lee, Nicole Turner, and Caitlin Chin (2022). *Police Surveillance and Facial Recognition: Why Data Privacy is Imperative for Communities of Color.* April 12. Accessed July 8, 2023. https://www.brookings.edu/articles/police-surveillance-and-facial-recognition-why-data-privacy-is-an-imperative-for-communities-of-color/.

Maheshwari, Rashi (2023). *What Is Artificial Intelligence (AI) And How Does It Work?* April 3. Accessed July 7, 2023. https://www.forbes.com/advisor/in/business/software/what-is-ai/.

Manheim, Karl, and Lyric Kaplan (2019). "Artificial intelligence: risks to privacy and democracy," *Yale J.L. & Tech.* 21: 106–188.

Math Vault. n.d. *The Definitive Glossary of Higher Mathematical Jargon.* Accessed July 15, 2023. https://mathvault.ca/math-glossary/#algo.

Mint (2021). *65.90% Prison Inmates are from SC,ST and OBC Categories, NCRB Datasays.* February 10. Accessed July 17, 2023. https://www.livemint.com/news/india/6590-prison-inmates-are-from-sc-st-and-obc-categories-ncrb-data-says 11612951470742.html.

National Crime Records Bureau (2019). *Prison Statistics India 2019.* Accessed July 17, 2023. https://ncrb.gov.in/sites/default/files/PSI-2019-27-08-2020.pdf.

NITI Aayog (2022). "Responsible AI #AIForAll adopting the framework: a case approach on facial recognition technology," *NITI Aayog.* Novemeber. Accessed July 21, 2023. https://www.niti.gov.in/sites/default/files/202211/Ai_for_All_2022_0211 2022_0.pdf.

Perkowitz, Sidney (2021). *The Bias in the Machine: Facial Recognition Technology and Racial Disparities*. February 6. Accessed July 9, 2023. https://mit-serc.pubpub.org/pub/bias-in-machine/release/1.

Purhouse, Joe, and Liz Campbell (2022). "Automated facial recognition and policing: a bridge too far?" *Legal Studies* (Cambridge University Press) 42(2): 209–227.

Roy, Rohini (2022). *Undertrial Prisoners in India: Why Are 66% From Marginalised Castes?* December 24. Accessed July 17, 2023. https://www.thequint.com/news/law/indias-undertrial-prisoners-why-are-are-66-percent-from-marginalised-castes#read-more.

Singh, Rahul (2018). "Criminal justice in the shadow of caste, study on discrimination against Dalit and Adivasi prisoners and victims of police excesses," *Annihilatecaste*. Accessed July 9, 2023. http://www.annihilatecaste.in/uploads/downloads/data_190118030229_21000.pdf.

Snow, Jacob (2018). *Amazon's Face Recognition Falsely Matched 28 Members of Congress With Mugshots*. July 26. Accessed July 15, 2023. https://www.aclu.org/blog/privacy-technology/surveillance-technologies/amazons-face-recognition-falsely-matched-28.

Sonavane, Nikita, and Ameya Bokil (2020). *How Poverty-Struck Tribals Become 'Habitual Offenders'*. May 30. Accessed July 17, 2023. https://www.article-14.com/post/born-a-criminal-how-poverty-struck-tribals-become-habitual-offenders.

Stevenson, Megan (2018). "Assessing risk assessment in action," *The Minnesotta Law Review* 103: 321–333.

Tanna, Minesh, and William Dunning (2022). "Bias and discrimination," *Artificial Intelligence Law and Regulation*, ed. Charles Kerrigen, Cheltenham, Gloucestershire: Edward Elgar Publishing, pp. 438–440.

Vedavalli, Priya, Prakhar Misra, Tvesha Sippy, Avanti Durani, Neha Sinha, and Vikram Sinha (2021). "Facial recognition technology in law enforcement in India: concerns and solutions," *IDFC Institute*. April 22. Accessed July 15, 2023. https://www.idfcinstitute.org/knowledge/publications/working-and-briefing-papers/facial-recognition-technology-in-law-enforcement-in-india/.

Wu, Xiaolin, and Xi Zhang (2016). "Automated inference on criminality using face images," *Semantic Scholar*. November 13. Accessed July 14, 2023. https://www.semanticscholar.org/paper/Automated-Inference-on-Criminality-using-Face-Wu-Zhang/1cd357b675a659413e8abf2eafad2a463272a85f.

18. Artificial Intelligence: The Modern Panopticon

Ms. Vinati Kishor Tahilianey

Teaching & Research Associate (Law), Gujarat National Law University, Gandhinagar, India

Email: vinati.tahilianey@gmail.com

ABSTRACT: 'I would rather have a mind opened by wonder than one closed by belief'. It is not just a magic mantra when one is caught up in the midst of an argument (about something new) where he has nothing else to say, but it is a rather interesting mantra that can lead to innovations. Who would have thought that a social reformist and father of utilitarian theory could be an inevitable part of economic history as well? In this research, an attempt has been made to study and coincide with this wonderful interface.

KEYWORDS: Artificial intelligence, Bentham, human rights, implied consent, informed consent, panopticon, utilitarianism

1. INTRODUCTION

Panopticon has its roots in Greece. *The Free Dictionary* defines the word *panópt(ēs)* in Greek as *all-seeing*. The term panopticon also evolved from this word and as Jermey Bentham had in his mind, the panopticon is a circular architecture with a tower in the middle from where an eye can be kept on all the rooms in the circumference.

The 'panopticon' is a fascinating work by Bentham that is a part of the Utopias. According to its creator, the 'panopticon' was a 'mill for grinding rogues, honest, and idle men industrious' according to (Brissot, 2013). A concept created by his brother in Russia suggested that a sizable house be occupied by workers and set up in such a way that they could be constantly watched. Bentham was pursuing humanitarian reform along the tried-and-true lines. He had long been intrigued by the plans for jail reform that Howard's efforts had spurred (Backhaus, 2012).

Panopticon, i.e. Bentham's idea for a prison rose to popularity because of Michel Foucault, a well-known scholar of contemporary uses of power, who saw it as a paradigm for contemporary methods of internalising authority and discipline.

Chapter 18 DOI- 10.4324/9781003428213-18

Artificial intelligence, apparently invisible seem to be following the same line of thought. Where, instead of a human body, hardware in the apparent, central tower is keeping an eye over all the inmates of, the presumed, jail?

Does that mean, in a hypothetical sense, Bentham's prison reforms might be being applied to the human race at large without their knowledge? Without their consent? Should it be acceptable if there is *informed* or *implied* consent? For example, 'Smile. You are under CCTV Surveillance' or a simple warning like 'CCTV in operation' would suffice or be regarded as *informed* consent? And if people are still entering or using the premises, despite the warning, shall it be regarded as *implied* consent? Amidst the ever-increasing questions, even more than the once artificial intelligence has been able to answer, research on the inherited or probable problems becomes inevitable.

The **aim** of this research is to study *artificial intelligence as a panopticon,* thereby generating a genus.

The **objectives** of the current research are:

(a) To study the concept of *panopticon* in modern parlance;
(b) To understand *artificial intelligence* as a practical approach to the utilitarian theory.

The **research questions** for the present research are:

i. What is the meaning of *panopticon*?
ii. How can artificial intelligence be considered as a modern panopticon?

The **scope** of research is limited to Jeremy Bentham's utility theory and his concept of *the panopticon*. Moreover, an effort to recognize *artificial intelligence as modern-day panopticon* has been made.

The **methodology adopted** for research is a purely doctrinal method and the footnoting is done as per *The Chicago style*. Research being doctrinal, the data have been collected from libraries and from the internet.

The **hypothesis** for the current research is: 'Artificial intelligence puts utilitarian theory into practice'.

2. WHAT IS A PANOPTICON?

Every time this topic is discussed, the first question that comes to any and everybody's mind is 'What is a Panopticon, where did the word come from?' The answer seems to be rooted in Jeremy Bentham's utilitarian theory (which is discussed in the second part of this article) from where Michel Foucault came up with an interpretation of the panopticon 'as a model, or paradigm, for modern strategies for the internalization of discipline and authority'. As seen in Figure 1, panopticon is a ring - shaped building (Tahilianey, 2021, p. 25), i.e. a circular building on the outside but hollow on the inside. The perimeter (i.e. the outer circular building) contains the cells of the prisoners, with each 'cell block' i.e. the prison being fourteen inches by fourteen inches and by six feet (14″ * 14″ * 6 ft) tall. A pretty comfortable space for any criminal. Moreover, the internal hollow space is utilised by leaving a perimeter, an 'annular well' so to say, i.e. an empty space of fourteen inches (14″). This empty space works as 'a well' and does not let the outer circular building connect with the central tower in any way. The central tower (christened 'Watch Tower') is where the guard or the supervisor is supposed to be located. The central watch tower is lined with windows, through which, the guard or the supervisor can keep an eye on the prisoners or the inmates of the prison or cell blocks respectively. Basically, a lesser number of guards can keep an eye on more number of prisoners.

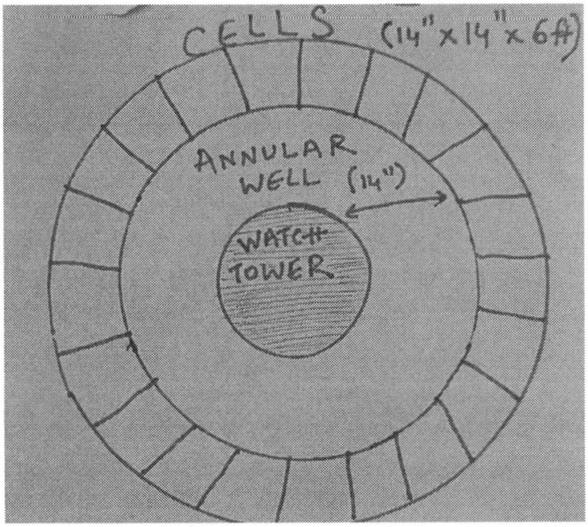

Figure 1. *The Panopticon. Source: Self-made, inspired from Pinterest.com*

Succinctly, a panopticon is an annular building with a tower at the centre.

The concept of the panopticon was considered a reformative approach to the prison system. It was considered one of the best prison reforms and a better form of punishment as compared to various other punishments, like beheading, amputating and others, prevalent at the time (Foucault, 1995). The aim was, essentially, to instil discipline in the prisoners.

The concept of panopticon falls on the lines of psychological disciplining:

1. where the prisoners are reformed with minimal time, money and effort invested on behalf of the authorities.
2. where the prisoners are conditioned psychologically,
    a. that they are being watched every moment;
    b. that their actions have consequences;
    c. that to live in peace with society, they need to be reformed.
3. where the prisoners, once reformed, are sent back to the society for peaceful coexistence.

3. WHAT IS CONSENT?

Consent: A term as old as time and yet, worthy of being a contemporary research theme (not even a topic but a theme). The word has evolved so much over time, encompassing concepts, imbibing judgements and yet growing. Consent comes from the Latin verb 'consentīre' which means 'to share or join in a sensation or feeling, be in unison or harmony'. The term 'Consentīre' itself is a compound of the Latin prefix con-, a variant of com- meaning 'together, with' and the Latin verb 'sentīre' which can mean 'to perceive by any of the senses, feel, be aware of, recognize, discern, hold an opinion, think, cast a vote, give a verdict'. Apart from Latin, the 'verb' use of the word consent was introduced in English in the 13th century, the 'noun' use was introduced in the 14th century.

In common parlance, the word means 'to give assent or approval' (*The Merriam Webster Dictionary)*. While in legal parlance it means 'that a person voluntarily and willfully agrees in response to another person's proposition. The person who consents must possess sufficient mental capacity. Consent also requires the absence of coercion, fraud or error. Consent is an essential constituent of a contract and a defence to a tort. However, consent is generally not a defence to criminal charges, with the possible exceptions of rape and sexual assault'. (Legal Information Institute, Cornell Law School, 2022) Over time, the legal parlance has effectively preceded the common parlance.

In India, the concept of consent has prevailed since time immemorial (Laik, 2021). As of today, the meaning of consent under different laws can be noted as under:

- Civil – 'Two or more persons are said to consent when they agree upon the same thing in the same sense without coercion, undue influence, fraud or misrepresentation'. (Section 13 of The Indian Contract Act, 1872)
- Criminal – 'A consent is not such a consent as is intended by any section of this Code if the consent is given by a person under fear of injury, or a misconception of fact, and if the person doing the act knows, or has reason to believe, that the consent was given in consequence of such fear or misconception; or
    - Consent of insane person – if the consent is given by a person who, from unsoundness of mind, or intoxication, is unable to understand the nature and consequence of that to which he gives his consent; or
    - Consent of child – unless the contrary appears from the context if the consent is given by a person who is under twelve years of age'. (Section 90 of Indian Penal Code, IPC)
- Medical – 'A process in which patients are given important information, including possible risks and benefits, about a medical procedure or treatment, genetic testing, or a clinical trial. This is to help them decide if they want to be treated, tested, or take part in the trial. Patients are also given any new information that might affect their decision to continue. Also called consent process'. (National Cancer Institute, An official website of the United States Government)

Simply put, when two parties willingly agree to the same thing at the same time, none has influenced the other, none has enticed the other, none has intimidated the other.

3.1. Types of Consent

Depending on the situations and circumstances, i.e. case to case basis the type of consent varies. Some types of consent are:

- Implied Consent
- Express Consent
- Informed Consent
- Proxy Consent (Singh and Bhushan, 2004)

3.2. What is Informed Consent?

Figure 2. *Smile Please. Source: Self-clicked.*

The meaning of consent can be construed as assent. An assent to 'to do', or 'not to do' something. However, the question arises, what is the meaning of informed consent? Is it different from consent? When consent is obtained from someone, it has to be clear free consent that is without coercion, undue influence, fraud or misrepresentation. The care is taken to see if the party is able to give consent or not, i.e. to say the party is sane, not under the influence of caffeine or Luna. That being said, obtaining consent means **the party has understood** the assignment and has knowingly agreed to 'to do' or 'not to do' something.

The element of **'understanding the information'** is of paramount importance. For example, if Figure 2 is hung outside an office, but the client does not know how to read it, will he/she be able to understand the image? The answer is **NO**. He/She will have to be explained whenever they see the image for the first time. Thereafter, one can assume the knowledge of the image but not at first sight.

When one party, consciously, informs another party about all the risks involved, all the benefits involved and others, it is considered as informed consent. It is usually prevalent in fields involving technical information or in contracts involving business jargon. The best example of a profession where informed consent is most prevalent is the Medical Profession. In the medical profession, the implied consent is informal, but informed consent, to be valid, has to pass the 7-pointer test. The test is designed as under:

1. Competency to give consent;
2. Free consent, without fear or force;
3. Sufficient information has been provided (including positive as well as negative outcomes);
4. A complete Plan of Action has been informed;
5. Ability to understand all of the above;
6. Consent for decision on treatment;
7. Authorization of treatment plan (jotform.com).

A question arises, if informed consent is relevant to our discussion of artificial intelligence as a modern panopticon. Let us take an example of social media sites. Where content is uploaded every day in bulk (Bernardmarr.com) and that content is freely available on the sites for almost everyone to view and use. For the media site, for its users, for the government, and even for the **hackers**. So, if social media accounts get a 'I agree' checked in, is it still considered as informed consent?

3.3. What is Implied Consent?

Or is it a form of implied consent? If one is willingly uploading any information on social media platforms, is he/she not implying that his/her data might be **used**? NO, absolutely – certainly not. However, all the permissions granted while downloading and installing apps or software are considered as CONSENT. One is willingly 'I agree'ing to share any and every kind of data. One might not, outright, upload it on social media, the data might just be in his/her phone or laptop or palmtop or other digital gadget; an app, if given permission, can not only read (or view) that data but can also share it with others.

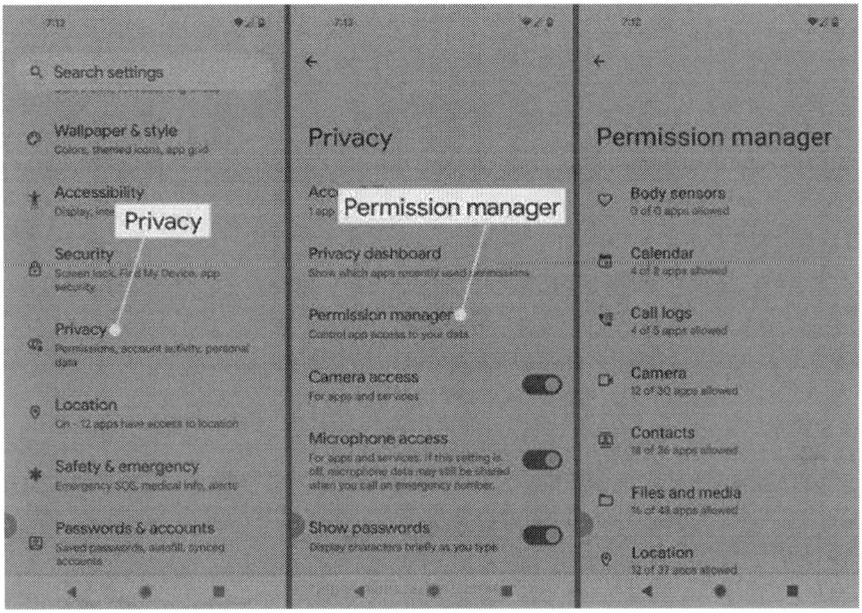

Figure 3. *The screenshots. Source: Mobile settings' screenshots.*

Meaning: The data are not safe, and one has wholeheartedly (even though subconsciously) given permission for that.

Implied consent means when someone does something which implies his willingness. That is to say 'actions speak louder than words'. When any person's action indicates or suggests that he/she agrees to 'to do' or 'not to do' something, then that is considered as implied consent, i.e. one which is not expressly given:

- maybe without saying 'I consent' or 'I agree';
- maybe without putting a signature on the piece of contract).

Both modes are absent in social media uploads and yet it cannot be said to have been implied that the party agrees for its data to be used by others. Similarly, when one puts a signature, even without reading a contract, will it be considered implied consent? Again, the answer is no. However, if the contracts are easily understood and non-ambiguous in any way, then the courts have interpreted, and decided the matters in favour of insurance companies rather than the party signing without reading (Sharbono v. Universal Underwriters Ins. Co., 139 Wash. App. 383, 394 (2007)).

3.4. Are Informed Consent and Implied Consent Different?

After discussing both concepts, let us now, try to understand the difference between the two:

Table 1: Difference between informed and implied consent.

Sr. No.	Point of Difference	Informed Consent	Implied Consent
1	Action speaks louder than Word	Just an act cannot be considered as consent	An act is considered consent (act = behaviour)
2	Formal Agreement	Required	Not required
3	Informal	Cannot be informal	Usually, it is informal
4	Duration	Before acting upon the contract	At any time, before or during the acting upon contract
5	Urgency (Medical)	If it is a matter of life and death, then informed consent may not be obtained	Not applicable
6	Information	Complete information needs to be provided, including risks involved (even if it might result in death)	Usually, given before complete information
7	Signature	Required	Not required
8	Standard Format Contract	Usually, a set format is made to obtain consent	Not applicable
9	Co operation	Active	Passive
10	Documentation	Required	need not be documented
11	Refusal	needs to be informed	cannot be implied
12	Example:	Signing a consent form for operation at a hospital	Extending your arm to a doctor, to be examined

Source: Self-made.

4. BENTHAM'S UTILITARIANISM

The proponent of utilitarian theory, Jeremy Bentham, has said that in some ways, utilitarianism is a reaction against the metaphysical and abstract nature of 18th century political and legal philosophy. Its creator, Bentham, devoted a large portion of his writing to ferocious assaults on the entire natural law theory. But even though utilitarianism is one of the periodic movements from the abstract to the concrete, from the idealistic to the materialistic, and from the a priori to the empirical, it also expresses goals that are distinctly 19th century in nature, even if he is impatient with the ambiguity and inconsistencies of the natural law theories (Friedmann, 2003).

The legal thought of Bentham is one of utilitarian individualism. His individualism served as the driving force behind his numerous and forceful legislative initiatives, all of which were aimed at freeing the individual from the numerous constitutional constraints and injustices that, at least in England, prevented the free play of forces that would allow for the full development of the individual. Legislation should be withdrawn, and the free play of forces would serve the general good best if these injustices (such as the 'rotten boroughs') were eliminated, and people had achieved equality of situation. The utilitarian philosophy of Bentham exhibits the same individualism (Friedmann, 2003). To sum up the essence of this philosophy in Bentham's own words:

> 'Nature has placed man under the empire of pleasure and pain. We owe to them all our ideas, we refer to them all our judgments, and all the determination of our life. He who pretends to withdraw himself from this subjection knows not what he says, His only object is to sock pleasure and to shun pain.... These eternal and irresistible sentiments ought to be the great study of the moralist and the legislator. The principle of utility subjects everything to these two motives'. (Bentham, 2015)

Pleasure and pain are Bentham's 'Law of Nature'. Utility he defines as expressing 'the property or tendency of a thing to prevent some evil or to procure some good'. **Now good is pleasure, evil is pain**:

> 'That which is conformable to the utility or the interest of an individual is what tends to augment the total sum of his happiness. That which is conformable to the utility or the interests of a community is what tends to augment the total sum of the happiness of the individuals that compose it'. (Bentham, 2015)

As a result, pleasure and pain are related to good and evil, and the purpose of the law is to promote good and prevent evil, or to promote utility. For Bentham, concepts like justice and injustice, morality or immorality and virtue or vice, are replaced by pleasure and pain. However, Bentham's examination of the various forms of pleasure and misery modifies this sensualistic assessment of existence in several ways. Bentham lists sense, wealth and power among the pleasures; other pleasures include friendship, a good name, kindness, knowledge and companionship. In general, pains are the antithesis of pleasures. The magnitude of either determines the degree of agony, and the individual's pain (hence a bad to be avoided) may be one brought on by his connection to or interest in the initial victim (Friedmann, 2003).

Bentham is an egalitarian and an individualist. He rejects the general will or the idea of an organic community. The goal of law is to create conditions that allow each individual to have the most freedom possible so that he can seek what is best for him. The individual is an end in himself; every man counts for one.

However, social and legal reformer Bentham is not an anarchist. He is aware that a community's entire population must benefit from the law. Friedmann (2003) views the greatest happiness for the largest number of people as the ultimate goal of legislation.

As Hobhouse has shown, Bentham's development of this principle was inescapably going to lead to the deference of individual rights to collective necessities. Bentham was adamantly opposed to any idea of unalienable natural rights, and this objection stems from his greatest happiness principle (Friedmann, 2003).

5. CONCLUSION

5.1. Artificial Intelligence puts Utilitarian Theory into Practice

Utilitarian theory has two pioneering flag bearers, pain and pleasure. If we recollect the example of geotag on photos from above, we shall understand that willingly posting something on social media gives us pleasure but if we have to, under pressure provide our data, results in pain. Thus, artificial intelligence does put utilitarian theory into practice.

5.2. Artificial Intelligence as a Modern Panopticon

Artificial intelligence, a persona of its own, a program capable of **thinking** for itself, a program capable of **evolving** itself, a program capable of **influencing** others, a program capable of **destroying** others; all on its own, or by being in the wrong hands at the wrong time.

Artificial intelligence has already become all pervasive. One cannot imagine life apart from artificial intelligence, be it 'Hey Alexa, play the music' in morning or 'Hey Siri, set the alarm' at night; be it 'Ok Google, find nearby places' in a new city or booking Uber for going to market bazaar, everybody is becoming, or already is dependent on artificial intelligence, in some form or another.

Someone somewhere is uploading photos from a beach, someone from a hill station, or someone from a stadium but would either of them prefer to add a geotag to their photos? The answer is no. Why? Privacy.

Someone from somewhere is posting his/her current location on social media, maybe a good restaurant, maybe a school, maybe anything, so are they implying that they can be kidnapped from that place? The answer is no. Why? Freedom.

Artificial intelligence, apparently invisible, i.e. applications through the means of hardware, is able to 'see' (collect, interpret and share the data) everyone. But we might not be aware. Or we might be giving our free consent, albeit subconsciously, to be viewed. For example, video surveillance paired with monitoring can identify (read analyse) people based on colour, dress code, sports shoes, a very specific type of bag, etc. An excellent friend for the police but what about the public at large? Not everyone happens to be a criminal. Amidst the questionable threat to rights and freedoms, such surveillance poses questions to a person's psychological well-being.

Does this situation seem similar to the panopticon? Where, instead of a human body, with a natural brain and its adaptive cognitive processes, hardware (maybe a laptop or a robot or a humanoid) in the apparent, central tower is keeping an eye over all the inmates of, the presumed, jail?

However, we came across the willingness of people to post on social media and share their data. Given the intonation, one can conclude that artificial intelligence might not be a jail (panopticon) for its users but may be a participatory panopticon in nature.

REFERENCES

Backhaus, Jurgen Georg (2012). *Handbook of the History of Economic Thought: Insights on the Founders of Modern Economics*. New York: Springer.

Bentham, Jeremy (2015). *Theory of Legislation*. Creative Media Partners, LLC.

Brissot, Jacques Pierre (2013). Who assumed the name of de Warville, was a leading member of the Girondist movement during the French Revolution. April 23, 2013.

Friedmann, W. (2003). *Legal Theory*. 5th ed. Universal Law Publishing Co. Pvt. Ltd.

Foucault, Michel (1995). *Discipline and Punish*. Vintage.

Laik, Kaushik (2021). *Consensus ad idem*. Thomson Reuters.

Legal Information Institute, Cornell Law School (2022).

Singh, Dr Jagdish, and Vishwa Bhushan (2004). *Medical Negligence and Compensation*, Bharat Law Publications.

Tahilianey, Vinati (2021). "Bentham's panopticon: an interface between economics & utilitarianism," Quest, no. XI (August): 25.

The Indian Contract Act (1872).

The Indian Penal Code.

Made in the USA
Monee, IL
14 September 2026

62978579R00111